Charles Williams:
A Celebration

Charles Williams:
A Celebration

Edited by Brian Horne

First Published in 1995
Gracewing
Fowler Wright Books
Southern Avenue, Leominster
Herefordshire HR6 0QF

Gracewing Books are distributed

In New Zealand by
Catholic Supplies Ltd
80 Adelaide Road
Wellington
New Zealand

In Australia by
Charles Paine Pty
8 Ferris Street
North Parramatta
NSW 2151 Australia

In U.S.A. by
Morehouse Publishing
P.O. Box 1321
Harrisburg
PA 17105
U.S.A.

In Canada by
Meakin & Associates
Unit 17, 81 Auriga Drive
Nepean, Ontario, KZE 7YS
Canada

Cover design by Gill Onions

Typesetting by Action Typesetting Limited, Gloucester
Printed by Cromwell Press, Trowbridge, Wiltshire.

ISBN 0 85244 3315

Contents

Introduction

Fifty years ago Charles Williams was buried in the graveyard next to the church of St Cross in Oxford. His tombstone bears the simple inscription: 'Charles Williams. Poet. Under the Mercy'. There is a poignant irony about this epitaph, for his poetry remains the least accessible part of his work; yet he had a profound belief in himself as a poet and throughout his life his love of poetry was a compulsive and definitive force. Everything he said and wrote was done under the pressure of the poetic imagination; and unless this fact is grasped the mysterious heart of Williams's work will never be reached by even the most diligent of readers.

Few poets live what, in the eyes of the world, would be considered 'exciting' lives. There are, of course, exceptions: Dante immersed in the complicated politics of thirteenth-century Italy and ending his days in exile from his beloved Florence; Villon roistering his way through fifteenth-century France narrowly excaping execution; Byron, profligate and charming, joining the Greek revolutionaries in the early 1820s; Walt Whitman caught up in the carnage of the American Civil War. But more usually poets have lived quiet, even sequestered lives, nurturing their interior vision away from the blare of public affairs. So it was with Charles Williams. A bald recitation of the facts would never lead one to suppose that out of this apparently uneventful existence there would emerge some of the most extraordinary poetry and profound theology that have been written in English in the last century. On 20 September 1886 he was born in an unassuming terrace house in a quiet street of north London. In 1894 the family moved to St Albans where a shop was opened which sold stationery and artists' materials.

The young Charles received a good education at St Albans School and later at University College, London. A job was found, first in the Methodist Bookroom and then, in June 1908, at the Oxford University Press. There he remained until his death thirty-seven years later. He married in 1917. and a son was born in 1922. He rarely travelled abroad and would not take holidays. His name was never in the headlines and there were no prizes for Literature. But he was a poet and, like all poets, if he was to change the lives of men and women it would be by the power of his words. He never tried, like Dante or Byron, to affect the course of history. He observed, he loved, he prayed, he laughed and talked, and, above all, he wrote: a stream of poems, plays, novels, biographies, reviews, essays; a body of work which still astonishes the reader with its variety and vitality. Moreover, nothing is quite what it seems: each piece evokes something other than itself; his imagination delighted in unexpected connections – and he found connections everywhere. A review of a detective novel for a newspaper will contain a sentence that opens on to a huge theological vista; an essay on literary criticism will lead one into a complex piece of psychological analysis; a footnote in a biography will encapsulate an entire historical era; a piece of theological speculation will reveal itself to be intimately concerned with the hidden pains of everyday loss and disappointment. Throughout the immense variety of genre the unique vision remains constant; the 'voice' of Williams is unmistakable.

It could not be otherwise, for he saw, more clearly than almost anyone else of his generation, and expressed more passionately than most, a belief that life was not only meaningful, but that this meaning could be articulated in a number of fundamental propositions. To say this is to give the impression that he was cold and intellectual: a philosopher trying to impose a set of speculative principles upon the rich untidiness of normal existence. Not at all, he knew as much about the untidiness of life as anyone else, but he also believed that there was an over-arching 'narrative' to life within which all, apparently disparate and bewildering events and actions, thoughts and emotions, could find their place and derive their meaning. For him the universe was held together by certain 'facts' — laws of existence — the affirmation of which would lead to enlightenment and joy and the denial of which would cause emptiness and despair. These 'facts' are the great central themes of his writing; themes which are played over and over again in innumerable variations and in a variety of styles. His was a comprehensive vision and in this he was no different from Dante or Tolstoy. Like them, there are times when the reader will be uncomfortably aware that the 'idea' has overmastered the 'art', occasions when enthusiasm for the intellectual content of the message has overthrown the artistic medium in which it has been presented; but the integrity of purpose never wavers.

For these reasons Williams will be disliked by those of our contemporaries who have surrendered to the fashion of 'post-modernism', who have accepted the proposition that the only truth we possess is that there is no truth, the only surety we have is that there is no surety. His work, from first to last, is a challenge to the current, prevailing philosophy of multi-valence and fragmentation; but, as will be seen from the essays in this book, it is precisely because he experienced, inwardly, the possibility of fragmentation and dissolution so acutely that he was able to expose the dangers of this 'reading' of life so cogently.

I shall not spell out the central themes that bind his work together: they will emerge as the reader passes through the essays assembled in this celebration of his work. Produced over a period of twenty years, they were all originally presented to the members of the Charles Williams society. Eric Mascall and Charles Hadfield recall the man and his 'setting': London, Oxford and the University Press. Erik Routley approaches him from what might seem to be an unlikely direction, the Puritan tradition, and enriches our understanding of both Williams and that tradition. Ralph Townsend sets him against the background of a way of thought and feeling that was in many ways opposed to Puritanism: the Caroline Anglicanism of Lancelot Andrewes. John Heath-Stubbs examines Williams's presentation of the Figure of Cressida in the context of the many presentations which preceded his in English literature. Charles Huttar's essay is an extended analysis of another central female figure in Williams's writings: that of Beatrice. Elisabeth

Brewer takes up the theme of femininity and the presentation of women with her reading of the Arthurian
Poems. The figures of the slaves in those same poems
are the subject of Brenda Boughton's contribution, while
Kerryl Lynn Henderson offers a discussion of something
that is rarely scrutinised: the early poetry. The connections
between the ideas of that group of friends and scholars
known as the 'Inklings' is the subject of Richard Sturch's
essay; and George Sayer, more specifically, compares the
literary criticism of Williams with that of his close friend
C. S. Lewis. It must be admitted that Charles Williams as
a personality remains unattractive to many people and his
work inaccessible to many others: Stephen Medcalf exposes
the many problems that lie in the way of appreciating the
work and the person of this peculiar genius. Glen Cavaliero
looks at the contribution that Charles Williams made to
the stage in the form of a drama which achieved great
popularity in the first part of this century, but which
has almost totally disappeared: modern verse-plays. Gwen
Watkins draws parallels between Charles Williams's novels
and those of R. H. Benson; James Brabazon, in completely
different vein, sees connections between Charles Williams
and Albert Schweitzer. The biographies that Williams wrote
are seldom read and rarely discussed, but those who have
read them invariably come away with the impression that
something extraordinary has been created by Williams's historical vision: Donald Nicholson, in his essay on *James I*,
attempts to describe and analyse their unique quality. There
is a short essay by George Every on the image of Byzantium;
and Huw Mordecai, in a reading of the novels, confronts
the most troubling aspect of Williams's life and work; his
interest in the occult.

Shortly after the beginning of the Second World War the
Oxford University Press decided to evacuate its offices in
Amen House in the City of London and move to Oxford.
Charles Williams, now fifty-three years old, was among
those who went with the Press; and his life entered a new
phase. Few realised how important — and how brief — this
phase was to be. There he was invited to join a group of
friends: dons and scholars, the Inklings, who met regularly
in C. S. Lewis's rooms to discuss, mainly, literary matters: J.

R. R. Tolkien, Owen Barfield, W. H. Lewis, Hugo Dyson, Gervase Mathew were frequent attenders at these convivial gatherings. Williams was also invited to lecture in the university and act as a tutor to a number of undergraduates. John Wain, the novelist, critic, and, later, Professor of Poetry in the University of Oxford, was an undergraduate during the Second World War, and had vivid recollections of Williams as a teacher. 'His lectures were crowded out. Even I, who chose to be very supercilious about lectures, seldom missed one.' He was in Oxford at the time of Williams's death and in his autobiography gave a touching account of his feelings on hearing the news: 'I was walking from Longwall Street, where I lodged, towards St John's, and had just reached the Clarendon Building when a girl I knew by sight came peddling round the corner from New College Lane. "John", she called out, "Charles Williams is dead." She had never spoken to me before, and normally would have avoided using my Christian name. But this was a general disaster, like an air-raid, and the touch of comradeliness was right. I asked her for details, but she knew nothing except that he was dead. In any case, she could not talk, she was only just not crying. I walked on towards St John's. The war with Germany was over. Charles Williams was dead. And suddenly Oxford was a different place. There was still so much to enjoy, much to love and hate, much to get used to; but the war-time Oxford of my undergraduate days had disappeared. Its pulse had stopped with the pulse of Williams.' (*Sprightly Running*, London, Macmillan, 1962.)

He died on Tuesday 15 May 1945 having been admitted to the Radcliffe Infirmary a few days earlier. C. S. Lewis went to the hospital that morning to visit his friend. He arrived to be told that he was dead. He wrote later: 'The world seemed to us at that moment primarily a *strange* one. . . . No event has so corroborated my faith in the next world as Williams did simply by dying. When the idea of death and the idea of Williams thus met in my mind, it was the idea of death that changed.' (*Essays Presented to Charles Williams*. Preface by C. S. Lewis. Oxford, O.U.P. 1947.)

Brian Horne
King's College, London

Notes on Contributors

Brenda Boughton

Teacher of English literature and language. Former pupil of Charles Williams at the University of Oxford.

James Brabazon

Writer and Broadcaster. Author of *Albert Schweitzer. A Biography*, 1976; *Dorothy L. Sayers, The Life of a Courageous Woman*, 1981.

Elisabeth Brewer

Writer. Author (with Beverley Taylor) of *The Return of King Arthur, British and American Arthurian Literature since 1900*, 1983; *Studying Chaucer*, 1987.

Glen Cavaliero

Poet and critic. Member of the English Faculty of the University Cambridge. Author of *John Cowper Powys*, 1973; *Charles Williams, Poet of Theology*, 1983.

George Every

Historian and theologian. Author of *The Byzantine Patriarchate 451–1204;* 1947. *Poetry and Responsibility*, 1949; *Understanding Eastern Christianity*, 1978.

Charles Hadfield

Writer and publisher. Colleague of Charles Williams at the Oxford University Press. Husband of the late Alice Mary Hadfield, biographer of Charles Williams. Author of several books on canals and waterways. *Afloat in America* (with Alice Mary Hadfield) 1987.

John Heath-Stubbs

Poet. Winner of the Queen's Medal for Poetry 1973. President of the Poetry Society 1993. Author of several volumes of poems. *Hindsights*. Autobiography, 1993,

Kerryl Lynn Henderson   Currently completing a doctorate in English literature at the University of Oxford. Her thesis includes a critical edition of Charles William's first four volumes of poetry. She hopes to publish a new edition of Williams's early poetry in the near future.

Brian Horne   Lecturer in Theology, King's College, University of London. Author of *A World to Gain*, 1983.

Charles Huttar   Professor of English at Hope College, Holland, Michigan. Editor of *Imagination and the Spirit*, 1971 and *Word and Story in C.S. Lewis*, 1991.

Eric Mascall   Late Professor of Theology at King's College, University of London. Theologian and writer. Author of *He Who Is*, 1943; *Christ, the Christian and the Church*, 1946; *Christian Theology Natural Science*, 1956; *The Openness of Being* 1971.

Stephen Medcalf   Reader in English, the University of Sussex. Editor *The Later Middle Ages*, 1981; *Poems for all Purposes, The Selected Poems of G.K. Chesterton* 1994.

Huw Mordecai   Chaplain of Warwick School.

Donald Nicholson   Historian. Canon of Edinburgh and Aberdeen cathedrals. Sometime vice-principal of Edinburgh Theological College.

Eric Routley   Musician and Theologian. Late Professor of Church Music at Westminster Choir College, Princeton. Author of *The Church and Music*, 1950; *English Religious Dissent*, 1961; *Twentieth Century Church Music*, 1964.

George Sayer   Writer. Close friend of C.S. Lewis. Author of *Jack, C.S. Lewis and his times*, 1988.

Richard Sturch   Theologian. Rector of Islip. Sometime lecturer in the University of Nigeria and the London Bible College. Author of

	The New Deism, 1991; *The Word and the Christ*, 1991.
Ralph Townsend	Theologian. Headmaster of Sydney Grammar School. Author of *Faith, prayer and devotion*, 1983.
Gwen Watkins	Writer and lecturer. Author of *Vernon Watkins. Poet of the Elegiac Muse*, 1973, *I that was born in Wales: A new selection from the poems of Vernon Watkins. Chosen and introduced by Gwen Watkins and Ruth Pryor,*1976; *Portrait of a Friend,* 1983.

Chapter One

Charles Williams as I Knew Him

E. L. Mascall

Charles Williams, novelist, poet, dramatist and brilliant lay theologian, who died, suddenly, at a comparatively early age in 1945, was one of the most invigorating and stimulating men that it has been my good fortune ever to encounter. We met on a number of occasions in the 1930s, usually at gatherings of the Christendom Group, that remarkable society of sociologically orientated Anglicans which included in various degrees of attachment such outstanding laypeople as Maurice Reckitt, T. S. Eliot, C. S. Lewis, Ruth Kenyon, Donald Mackinnon and Hugo Dyson. A conversation between Williams and Reckitt was as entertaining a display of spontaneous wit and wisdom as I have experienced.

Physically, Williams was not particularly impressive until one noticed the vivacity of his facial expression. He was rather below middle height and peered through rather thick glasses. It was in the excitability and volubility of his speech that his enormous interior energy and enthusiasm were manifested and became infectious. Though largely self-educated, he was a man of profound intellectual depth and, with this, of great spiritual integrity. With the emotional temperament of a Welshman and the accent and sense of humour of a cockney, the impression which an audience received from him on their first meeting could begin with a kind of stunned incredulity, which rapidly passed into wild enthusiasm. I vividly remember the effect which he produced on the students of Lincoln Theological College by reciting the opening lines of Milton's *Paradise Lost*:

> Of man's first disobedience an' the fruit.
> Of that forbidden tree, 'ose mortal tiste
> Brort death into the world and all our wow ...
> Sing, 'eavenly muse, that on the sicred top ...

— which was probably much more like Milton's own pronunciation than the etiolated accents of our modern academics.

Most readers of Williams easily recognise how deeply concerned he was to emphasise the goodness and authenticity of the physical, including the sexual, aspect of human existence and human nature, 'the holy and glorious flesh' as he sometimes described it. What they do not always understand is that, with all the exuberance with which he would extol the glories of romantic love, he was firmly and no less exuberantly committed to the great traditional Christian values of chastity, fidelity and monogamy. C. S. Lewis describes in one of his letters the impact made by a lecture of Williams's on Milton's *Comus*:

> We actually heard a lecture on *Comus* which put the importance where Milton put it. In fact the lecture was a panegyric of chastity. Just imagine the incredulity with which (at first) an audience of undergraduates listened to something so unheard of. But he beat them in the end.
>
> He is an ugly man with rather a cockney voice. But no one ever thinks of this for five minutes after he has begun speaking. His face becomes almost angelic. Both in public and in private he is of nearly all the men I have met, the one whose address most overflows with *love*. It is simply irresistible. These young men and women were lapping up what he said about Chastity before the end of the hour. It's a big thing to have done. (*Letters of C. S. Lewis*, p 196.)

Nevertheless, with all his enthusiasm for the romantic nature of married love, Williams made no pretence of glossing over the more banal aspects of domesticity. I remember him describing how he used to make early-morning tea for his wife. 'I usually really enjoy doing it. But there are times when there's nothing that I feel I want to do less. And then I say to myself, "Well, dash it all, I am married to the woman!" And then I get up and make it.'

It would be quite wrong to suppose that with his intense aesthetic sensibility Williams was inclined to underrate the importance of the rational and intellectual aspect of human experience. He once arrived rather late at a meeting at which I was speaking, I entirely forget about what topic. But in the discussion after my speech he mentioned that he had just come from Fleet Street, where everyone seemed to be living in a world of false values. 'I've just seen a poster saying "Tragic Death of a Peer". Just fancy that − what is there tragic about the death of a peer? And then, when I came into this room I heard Father Mascall saying "What is really important is to be careful how we define our terms." And my heart leapt up when I be'eld a rinebow in the sky!'

At the expense of being outrageously egoistic I will dare to illustrate this same point from a review which Williams wrote in 1943 of my first serious theological work *He Who Is* in the now defunct journal *Time and Tide*. He began by saying that in writing on philosophical theology I had confirmed the line in *Comus* where the Elder Brother says that philosophy is

a perpetual feast of nectar'd sweets
Where no crude surfeit reigns.

and then continued:

This is supposed to be a simile of intellectual satisfaction. So it is, but it is also a perfectly correct literal statement. There was a moment in *He Who Is* when I found myself savouring a particular doctrine with an almost physical delight; and, except from false fear, I do not know why I say almost. It was in my mouth 'sweet as honey'; it melted exquisitely into my corporeal organism and bestowed a richness. Perhaps the apocalyptic John also was talking more sense than we know when he spoke of 'eating a book'. It would be humbling if we discovered that the saints and prophets were physiologically as well as psychologically accurate. The physical effect of intellectual ideas has still to be examined by psycho-analysts and doctors. We shall yet perhaps see graphs showing the relative effects on a fifty-years-old one-legged west-country industrialist of the Platonic Ideas, the Cartesian dualism and the geo-politics of Houshofer.

No doubt it will come as a surprise to some that 'the particular doctrine in question was that of the self-sufficiency of God', even when he added that 'one's physical reactions have nothing to do — at least, calculably — with the truth of the doctrine, nor was the doctrine new', but I have quoted this passage in order to show how very organically in Williams's view of reality the intellectual and the aesthetic were mutually integrated. Indeed I think that one of the reasons for Williams's concern with the language of poetry was that it seemed to him that aesthetic images were often more successful than conceptual forms in expressing the depth and multiplicity of the real world. I once very daringly asked him whether the line, in one of the Taliessin poems, 'the feet of creation walk backward through the waters' was meant as a description of the effects of sin and the Fall. With characteristic humility he replied after a moment's thought, 'I have never thought of that before, but that is certainly one of the things that it means'. Paradoxical and even frivolous as this answer might seem to some, there could hardly be a clearer spontaneous avowal that the poet's function is not to give expression to the dredged-up precipitates of his own subconscious but to witness to his imperfect but nevertheless authentic perceptions of the manifold aspects of objective reality. But this is not the place for a discussion of Williams's theology, fascinating as that topic would be.

One last recollection; I cannot recall the context of this incident but it is entirely characteristic and I tell it as I remember it. Williams told us that he had been having his hair cut and the barber had told him that he (the barber) had just got engaged to be married. 'He said to me, "Yer know, sir, it just makes yer feel fine. I felt that if a bloke 'ad dotted me in the eye I'd 'ave stood 'im a pint." I leapt out of the chair and seized him by the hand and said, "My friend, do you know that's just what Dante said in the *Vita Nuova*: 'Such warmth of charity came upon me that most certainly in that moment if anyone had done me an injury I would have forgiven him.'"?' What effect this produced upon the other occupants of the barber's saloon Williams did not tell us; I imagine that to him his reaction seemed the most natural thing in the world. For if there was ever a Christian to whom it seemed obvious that grace does not destroy nature but perfects it, that Christian was Charles Williams.

In these days when for so many professional theologians the fundamental theological criterion appears to be that of drabness, it is comforting to remember the life and work of this inspired and inspiring layman.

Chapter Two

CW at Amen House

Charles Hadfield

Stand with your back to Ludgate Circus, and look up Ludgate Hill. Behind you is the line of the old Fleet River, now New Bridge Street and Farringdon Street. On your left is a pub, 'The Old King Lud' – which may introduce us to the myth of the City, for from 'Lud' the name London is hopefully said to be derived. Half of the pub is under the railway bridge built in 1865 by the London, Chatham & Dover Railway. Across from 'The Old King Lud', on your right and also under the bridge, the site of Sherriff's Wine Bar and Restaurant where CW went when he could afford. First came the long bar, where I remember sitting on high stools with Alice Mary and CW drinking hock and soda – a favourite of CW's in summertime. Behind was the restaurant where once – so CW's story went – a waiter had pleased him immensely by saying he had seen his beloved dropping light as she walked.

As we climb the hill, and just before St Martin's church on the left, we pass the site of Ludgate itself – it was pulled down in 1760 – and through the City Wall enter Roman London, capital of Britannia that was once a province of Byzantium, capital of the Eastern Roman Empire. Ahead is Wren's St Paul's, upon the site of old St Paul's, upon the site of a pottery works the Romans built on one of the two hills of Londinium – the other is Cornhill – upon the site of a British village. All our work in the Oxford Press was done to the striking of Paul's clock and, once a week, bell-ringing practice.

How thankful we were in those days that after the great fire of London, the town planning of the time had come to nothing, and higgledy-piggledy London had been rebuilt with its lanes and corners and courts. When I joined the Press in 1936, our bit of it was London's book-publishing centre, though new fangled firms like Faber and Cape had set up in the West End. On the left going up Ludgate Hill, for instance, was Cassells in Belle Sauvage Yard. Beyond, Ave Maria Lane turns off to the left. A little way down it, again on the left, is Stationer's Hall, and beyond it, a turning to the left, Amen Corner. The old corner building here before the war − it is gone now − was the older office of the Press, where CW came to work in 1908, and where he remained until Amen House opened in 1924. I myself remember Amen Corner, later on, as then the headquarters of the book wholesaling firm of Simpkin Marshall. Working as I did in a bookshop before joining O.U.P., I used to go there with my list of orders and a sack over my shoulder to collect the books we wanted from Simpkin's trade counter.

Opposite Amen Corner, to the right, was the beginning of Old Paternoster Row running through to Cheapside, narrow, huddled with publishers, bookshops and all manner of firms that depended upon print and paper for a living. No. 34 was the address, for instance, of the ramshackle kingdom over which presided the erratic Walter Hutchinson. He called his firm the 'biggest publishers in the world', but we in the Oxford University Press knew better. Ave Maria Lane now becomes Warwick Lane. Further along on the right was narrow White Hart Street leading into Old Paternoster Square, where was a pub, the 'Red Cross', where, when I could afford it, I stood Alice Mary a half pint of beer. Further still along Warwick Lane, on the left, was a sharp turning into Warwick Square. On the left, the offices of Hodder & Stoughton, the publishers; on the right a carpet warehouse, and in the centre usually a welter of vans loading or unloading carpets.

At the far end was eighteenth-century, brick-built Amen House, its windows a little out of true, to which the Press had moved in 1924, and which, except during the War, remained its London headquarters until 1965. It had been two adjacent houses, and still had two front doors, that on the left was the entrance, that on the right led to the music department. The site was historic, for half way down the basement stairs, visible behind glass, was a piece of Roman Wall. Behind Amen House, a modern seven-storey building had been put up adjoining the Old Bailey, part offices, part warehouse for the Press's stock of three-quarters of a million books. CW would have known its mysteries well, but by my time a great new warehouse had been opened miles away at Neasden, and the building's floors had become additional offices. When I became head of Juvenile Department in 1939, my room had an excellent view of prisoners being escorted into the Old Bailey in black marias – so had CW's below mine. To the left of the Amen House front door a passage ran to the trade counter where booksellers could go with their sacks and get the king of Oxford book that Simpkin Marshall did not stock.

Up the three front steps and through the double entrance doors. On the left are the brightly-polished handles of the showroom door. The showroom is presided over by Mr Jo Mash and Miss Poppy Cattell of the ever-golden hair. There customers can inspect Bibles large and small and medium in every kind of plain or fancy leather binding, prayer books ditto, or leather bound editions of the World's Classics or Oxford Standard Authors. An Oxford India paper Bible is kept hung from a clip by a single leaf, to show the strength of the paper. There also is a range of the rather incongruous juvenile books produced by a learned Press – Biggles, Dimsies, Annuals, Rewards and the rest. On the right of the hall, opposite the showroom doors, is a beautiful waiting room with fine furniture, a decorated plaster ceiling and Adam fireplace and, leading off it, the social – as differentiated from the administrative – centre of the Press, the Library.

Before we leave the Hall, however, we must meet two Press characters: 'Sergeant', elderly, scarred of face from the First World War, and dignified of demeanour, who receives visitors and, if necessary, transports them upwards in the small, hydraulically-powered lift which he works by pulling on a vertical cable running through roof and floor and Miss Winnie Cox in the telephone cubbly-hole next to the showroom, knitting interminable garments between calls.

Miss Cox – happily she is still alive – made an internal telephone system almost unnecessary. If one wanted to know anything, one talked to Miss Cox.

The Library, long, low, beautifully furnished, book-lined throughout except where its front windows look out over Warwick Square, is in theory maintained for the reference use of the staff and so that members of the public can look at and, if they wish, buy Press publications. Before my time it had been presided over by pretty, vivacious, fair-haired Phyllis Jones. She had, however, left to get married, and I discovered a tall girl with piled red hair who doubled the job of librarian with that of Editor of the *Oxford Dictionary of Familiar Quotations* then being assembled – Alice Mary Smyth. Round these two – and on the front stairs leading up from or down to the Library – used to gather, on any excuse or none, the personalities of the Press, and the sound of their voices would penetrate to my first little room hidden behind the lift.

In a high-backed chair, grey-suited, grey-haired, bright-eyed, remote, watchful, might be the Publisher himself – Sir Humphrey Milford, the head of the Press, whom we called H.S.M. Walking briskly up and down, quick words pouring out, arms waving, would be Charles Williams from Editorial – often the active centre of the group, but never dominating it – a man who drew people in and then drew them out. Gathered round, arguing, questioning, fencing, might be long-haired Hubert Foss, Head of Music Publishing, a real musician; Lynton Lamb, chief Art Editor; Gerry Hopkins, big and burly, nephew of the poet, head of Publicity; strict-looking Fred Page, also from Editorial, who shared CW's room, short with curly grey hair; Helen Peacock, head of Production, tall, plain, honest-looking, blunt of speech, with piled untidy greying hair pulled back in a bun, always dressed in blouse and skirt, the battleaxe of the Press. She was the Press's German expert as Gerry was its French. CW's assistant, Ralph Binfield, might come in with a message, or one of Miss Peacock's assistants, Peter Burney or Jo Harris (on loan from Printing Office) might arrive to fetch her back to her office. On the outskirts could be found those who, strangely, often needed to use the library shelves – the aspirants, one of whom was me. Any of these might suddenly be called into the group to give an opinion, answer a question, in an offered moment of intellectual equality. Listening to the talk, we shall soon realise that some of the names flying about are unlikely to be real: 'Dorinda' for Miss Peacock, 'Alexis' for Gerry Hopkins, 'Colin' for Fred Page, 'Phillida' for Phyllis Jones and above all, 'Caesar' for Sir Humphrey. They date from two Masques that were written by CW for acting by his colleagues of the Press, and which were concerned with their common life and work in Amen House. We shall return to them.

Before we leave the library, let us note some revealing bits of the Press's presentation of itself to the public. There was a working table for the Librarian, and a carved one used by no-one but Caesar and special visitors. On it were a visitor's book, a clean blotting pad, a copper ink tray, a cabinet for stationery, a pen (quill at one time), twin goblets, and the current *Times Literary Supplement, New Statesman, Nation and Athenaeum* and *Notes and Queries.* The circumambient bookshelves contained most of the books currently in print (except those held in the showroom) plus some special originals such as Clarendon's *History of the Rebellion*, upon the profits of which the Press had been founded. Beside the library, on the ground floor of the right-hand building, dwelt the Department presided over by Hubert Foss. In 1923 Foss had persuaded Sir Humphrey to start a Music Department. He did, and it flourished exceedingly. Foss did CW many good turns. Being a director of the printing firm of Henderson and Spalding, the Sylvan Press, he used his influence with them to print CW's *An Urbanity, Carol of Amen House* (for which Foss wrote the music), the two *Masques* that were acted, and also *Heroes and Kings*, which carries the Sylvan Press imprint.

Let us now walk up the broad, shallow staircase — or take the lift with Sergeant — to the first floor, that of authority. Over the library was a magnificent room with an Adam celing where dwelt the Publisher — Sir Humphrey Milford. I myself only entered it once — some two years after I had joined the firm. I had come in on the sales side, and had then gone onto dogsbody publicity work — until not long ago some of my jacket blurbs still survived on World's Classics volumes – but knew nothing of editorial of the processes of publishing. Sent for, I entered trembling, reviewing my past sins. H.S.M. waved me to a chair. 'Oh, Hadfield, yes', said he, putting his fingertips together. 'Do you know Mr L'Estrange'? – Mr L'Estrange was head of the large Juvenile Department, and with his friend Mr Ely, head of Educational, also wrote profitably and prolifically under the penname of Herbert Strang. 'No, sir', said I. 'Well', said he, 'He's retiring on 31 March, and you'll be taking his place. You'd better go along and meet him'. No question of whether I wanted the job or thought I could do it or of training for it or even mention of salary. Those were the days, and that was Sir Humphrey. In a room of his own sat H.S.M.'s male secretary, Mr Budgen, and across the way the staff manager, Mr Cannon. Both were Plymouth Brethren with close-cropped hair. Cannon – aptly named – was the man we battled with to get a rise, and a battle it was. He defended the Press's funds with a zeal that was just occasionally mistaken – I'm thinking of Tommy Sycamore from Miss Peacock's team who, asking Mr Cannon for a modest increase, was given one shilling and sixpence a week. He resigned, and went on in later years to become Managing Director of the Oxo combine.

On the first floor was Gerry Hopkins in Publicity, and also Dorinda – Miss Peacock – presiding over Production, the Department that received manuscripts from the Editors and got them estimated, designed and prepared for the printing office. In a corner Caesar's letters were press-copied. We lesser mortals used carbon-paper, but Caesar's were put into a press between sheets of a sort of flannel and so facsimile-copied in the way James Watt had invented about 1800. No need to modernise if you are Caesar. Charles Williams, coming up from the library, would have gone straight to the second floor. On coming out of the lift, he would have passed the binding office on his left, gone at high speed through a swing door, turned right along a corridor, and passed the printing office before reaching his own room, which was immediately above Gerry Hopkins, and looked out on the Old Bailey courtyard. He shared it with Fred Page. CW, in his swivelling and tippable chair, sat on the right, Page on the left. Beside CW was a hatstand upon which he would hang his coat and hat – he always wore a homburg – and slap his gloves, as soon as he entered. Page – the 'Colin' of the Masques, and cleverly named, because when young with a mop of hair he'd been known to contemporaries as 'Curly' – was the biographer of Coventry Patmore. He was a Roman Catholic, and also a great reader of Swedenborg. Between the two desks was a chair for visitors, and above that file copies of all the Oxford Poets, containing every reported correction, ready for the next reprint. A similar set of nearly 500 World's Classics were on the shelves behind Fred Page, together with his favourite books – Alice Meynell, Chesterton, Swedenborg. Behind CW was a miscellaneous collection, including Middleton Murrey, Malory and, later, T. S. Eliot. Along the south wall were all the Oxford Standard Authors, Oxford Books of Verse, and a portrait of Henry James; and down behind CW's chair was a litter of his own manuscripts in wooden boxes. There wasn't a spare inch anywhere – the overflow of books from the room was guarded by Ralph Binfield next door. Although Ralph was CW's assistant, his and Page's room had no space for a third, so Ralph was accommodated in two square yards of the printing office. Earlier, at Amen Corner, CW and Fred Page had themselves to work in a corner of the printing office – there's a reference in a poem in *Divorce* to 'Seven spiders each spinning its separate web in the same corner', the corner being Amen Corner.

Two people on this second floor played a special part in CW's life. Jo – Jocelyn – Harris was a typist in printing office. One day she asked CW for 'a book to read', and he disinterred the manuscript of *The Corpse* from his wooden box where it had lain since Jonathan Cape had rejected it. Jo liked it and rekindled CW's enthusiasm. So he sent it to Victor Gollancz, who sat up all night reading it. However, Gollancz thought the title too conventional, so CW, his mind full of *Paradise Lost*, changed it to *War in Heaven*. Thus began the publication of the novels.

The other was Norman Collins, who filled a tiny office – it had once been a broom cupboard – off a stone staircase near CW's room. Collins – the 'Menalcas' of *An Urbanity* – was a great friend of CW's when he left the Press – like

Tommy Sycamore later, after a difference of opinion with Mr Cannon about his salary – he went to join Robert Lynd on the old *News-Chronicle*'s literary page, whence he would send CW batches of detective novels to review. Later still he went to Gollancz while the firm were publishing CW's novels, and thence to a career as a novelist, to be a founder of commercial television, and to be awarded a knighthood.

So much for background. I'd like now to try to assess what working for O.U.P. did for CW, and what CW did for the Press, and then seek a synthesis. We've seen the help CW's literary work received from Hubert Foss, Jo Harris and Norman Collins. There was also Fred Page and of course Milford himself. Page it was who introduced CW to his friends Alice and Wilfred Meynell and gave them the manuscript to read of what was to become *The Silver Stair*. As we know, they agreed to finance that first of CW's published books. That was in 1912. Thereafter, Milford thought enough of his employee to publish his next four books. *Poems of Conformity, Divorce, Windows of Night* and *A Myth of Shakespeare*, between 1917 and 1929. Not until 1930, when CW was 44, did he first have a book published commercially – when, thanks to Jo Harris, Gollancz accepted *War in Heaven*. Thereafter, CW received the accolade of the learned Clarendon Press imprint (part, of course, of the same firm) for *Poetry at Present* (1930), *The English Poetic Mind* (1932), and *Reason and Beauty in the Poetic Mind* (1933), while Milford between 1931 and 1939 published four more of his works, and a last one as an epitaph, *Arthurian Torso*. Twelve altogether, therefore, bore Oxford imprints. CW is, of course, only one of many authors who would probably have got fewer books published had they not worked in a publisher's office. I can perhaps appreciate the help CW had from his position in the firm, for it was the same with me: three out of the five books I wrote while working for the Press were published by them, including the first. I can never be sufficiently grateful – though I fear Sir Humphrey never appreciated the genius he was rearing.

What, in turn, did CW contribute? Let us take his work first. He and Fred Page were what a publishing firm would now call Book Editors. On the executive side, they had to work through every manuscript to correct mistypings and wrong spellings, pick up inconsistencies and words used in their wrong meaning — like 'intriguing' for 'interesting' — and make sure it was house-styled — that is, words were spelled not only in a uniform way throughout the book, but in conformity with the standard for all Oxford books. When proofs came in — three lots sometimes in those expensive days — first unpaged galleys, then paged proofs, then final queries on any point on which the head printer's reader (who was also checking on his own account) was not satisfied — CW or Page read them too. Ralph Binfield says that before he joined the Press, CW and Page had between them proof-read the whole of Dickens, Scott and Thackeray. Later, with him, they added the whole of Trollope, Tolstoy, Constance Holme and Peacock's *English Verse* in five volumes. CW's job was also to advise on any manuscript sent to him from H.S.M.'s office — such titles as Flora Thompson's *Lark Rise* books and Mrs Hughes' *London Child of the Seventies* came to Oxford this way. When a manuscript was clearly one for a specialist, one was chosen, and the work sent on for a report. Were the manuscript accepted, CW then compiled the preliminaries or 'prelims' — the pages that come before the start of the text — wrote blurbs — publicity copy — for book jackets, and in early days compiled indexes, until later he shed that job on to Ralph Binfield. Indeed, CW's responsibility began with the manuscript or the previous edition of the book, and ended when the bound and jacketed copy was placed on his desk, and he waited apprehensively lest H.S.M. should find a misprint in it.

I myself sat for a time on two committees with CW — one for selecting new titles for the World's Classics — CW was more or less in charge of the series, including choosing authors to write the introductions — the other for deciding which of the many books coming in from the American University Presses were worthy of being published — as against merely distributed — over here. On the first, wet behind the ears as I was, still I knew enough to be astonished at the range of his reading. On the American committee he could pick up a fat book, concentrate upon it for sixty seconds, and give an opinion. Those of us who heard Dr Routley talk will remember his distinction between two methods of communication − pencil-passing and ball-tossing. I'm a pencil-passer and I know it, but CW was a ball-tosser − ideas, comments, warnings, hopes, would be tossed on to the table to be picked up − or not. A decision made, he accepted it good-humouredly, and on we went to the next item. He was a good committee man. Alice Mary remembers CW on the committee choosing entries for the first *Dictionary of Familiar Quotations*. She writes: 'CW generally tilted his chair back horribly dangerously, and smoked took off his glasses and rubbed his eyes ... and was always perfectly clear and accurate about every quotation. Sometimes he would exclaim: 'But the best bit has been left out', or 'Flared', not 'stared' − 'Good God in Heaven, "Flared forth in the dark" '. 'CW', she goes on, 'knew everything, particularly on Shakespeare (*all* of him), Milton and Wordsworth, Malory, Marlowe and the Elizabethans, Donne and the Metaphysicals, Pope, Keats, Tennyson, Bridges, Kipling, Chesterton − and, of course the Bible, Hymns, and the Book of Common Prayer'.

It would be tedious to list his contributions to Oxford publishing, but a few should be mentioned − his decisive support for the proposal to publish Kierkegaard in English, his suggestion of W. B. Yeats as Editor for the original *Oxford Book of Modern Verse*, his considerable contribution towards the creation of Harvey's *Companion to English Literature* − the first of the Oxford companions − and his supervision of the centenary edition of Tolstoy, the whole series being edited by the difficult Aylmer Maude, and each volume with a different, famous and often temperamental introducer. They included Bernard Shaw, H. G. Wells and Rebecca West.

But CW's contribution was not just through his work. There are men and women who are granted a special gift − that of being able to unite their fellows in the living of a common life and the doing of a common work. One finds them in commerce and industry, in the Civil Service, in voluntary organisations − but not nearly enough of them. They are the natural leaders. CW was one. He would not have wanted − and probably would not have been able to cope with − formal leadership, say as Head of a Publishing Department, still less in

Milford's place. Nevertheless, I think myself that in the late twenties and thirties the Press was fortunate to have two natural leaders – one Sir Humphrey, the other CW. The efficient cause, as the philosophers say, of CW's flowering was probably the move from Amen Corner to Amen House in 1924. The old building had not sparked him off – the new one did. Its architectural beauty, maybe the fragment of Roman Wall on the basement stairs, the library – there hadn't been one at Amen Corner – and the intellectual excitement that grew within it along with his feeling for Phyllis Jones the new librarian, the liveliness of the Press's publishing policy and its growing reputation under Milford's leadership – they must all have contributed.

So, in 1926, the dance began when *An Urbanity* was written, a lament by himself as 'Tityrus' to Phyllis as 'Phillida' upon the absence on holiday of five of their colleagues from 'The Court' – 'The Court' – the first projection of a world of the imagination permeating the world of publishing:

> The entrance hall is blank and bare;
> Unfriendly lies the central stair.
> The first floor – O the first floor – dead!
> There were but three, and all are fled!
> And in my little niche aloft
> Who enters, enters once too oft, ...

The first floor. Dorinda had gone from it, and Alexis, and Caesar:

> He has left the accustomed seat;
> If through the corridors we move
> That flickering sweet and dangerous love
> No more allures us; he puts by
> The crown that is the o'erarching sky
> Of all our lesser lives; he flies,
> And leaves us finally to sighs.

Dorinda, Alexis and Caesar – Helen Peacock, Gerry Hopkins, Sir Humphrey Milford. And on his own floor above, Colin – Fred Page – and Menalcas – whom CW calls 'the sudden comet of the Court' – Norman Collins, who if he had stayed with the Press would probably have been in the Masques and become one of the personalities. *An Urbanity* is a poem of much delight, which also shows that CW never for a moment confused within Amen House the Caesar of imagination with the real Sir Humphrey Milford in the days before redundancy payments and employment legislation. He is addressing Phillida:

> But on whose world should we intrude
> Since none at least could think *you* rude?
> Not Caesar's – naturally not;
> Not he whose word could bid us rot
> In slums and gutters, if he broke
> The use that binds us of his folk;
> My childhood knew too well the fate
> That hangs o'er servants, and the strait
> Wherethrough the large unneeded go,
> Ever thereafter not to know,
> Ever thereafter to forget
> Within all courtesy the threat
> Of the unused thunderbolt; 'tis there,
> For all that Caesar is so fair!
> For all the veiling of his throne,
> Know that our lord is God alone.

The key line here is 'The use that binds us of his folk' – pure feudalism and deep humanity – we served Caesar, and he, as CW goes on to say, 'Bears the private weight of public cares, Being the root of our affairs And their condition'. As in the feudal manor, as in the Victorian home, we knew our places, for there was always 'the threat of the unused thunderbolt'. On the other hand, neither Alice Mary nor I can in fact remember anyone actually being fired, and indeed the Press looked after its staff as well as it paid them badly. During the War my Fire Service pay was made up to my Press salary until, after three years, I got enough promotion to earn it for myself.

A stream of light verse followed *An Urbanity* – little of it, of course, printed. More importantly, there followed also,

on 27 April 1927, Sir Humphrey's birthday, and three years
after the move to Amen House, the production in the library
of *The Masque of the Manuscript.* In it *A Carol of Amen
House* was sung, to Herbert Foss' music:

> Over this house a star
> Shines in the heavens high,
> Beauty remote and afar,
> Beauty that shall not die;
> Beauty desired and dreamed,
> Followed in storm and sun,
> Beauty the gods have schemed
> And mortals at last have won.
> Beauty arose of old
> And dreamed of a perfect thing,
> Where none shall be angry or cold
> Or armed with an evil sting;
> Where the world shall be made anew,
> For the gods shall breathe its air,
> And Phoebus Apollo there-through
> Shall move on a golden stair.
> The star that all lives shall seek,
> That makers of books desire;
> All that in anywise speak
> Look to this silver fire:
> Shakespeare in utmost night
> Moved on no other quest
> Than waits him who reads aright
> Edition and Palimpsest.
> O'er the toil that is giv'n to do,
> O'er the search and the grinding pain
> Seen by the holy few,
> Perfection glimmers again.
> O dreamed in an eager youth,
> O known between friend and friend,
> Seen by the seekers of truth,
> Lo, peace and the perfect end!

The *Carol,* and the whole *Masque* of which it is a part,
powered by his feeling for Sir Humphrey, his colleagues, and
the work that bound them together, fuelled by his love for

Phillida, was perhaps CW's most confident assertion of the union of imagination and reality, of the Heavenly and the Earthly City, of Amen House in London and Byzantium.

As Alice Mary says in her book on Charles: 'The effect of the *Masque* on CW's position in the Press and with Sir Humphrey was incalculable. The atmosphere was changed from that of an office to a Court, with Caesar on the throne and CW among the Paladins. He was never afterwards one of the ... staff'. A second Masque, that of *Perusal*, was performed two years later, but no more, although a third was written. The efflorescence had subsided, but the life went on.

It ended in September 1939, when War came and the Press moved to Southfield House, Oxford. There CW began a new life, but lost the old one. He was never again to work in Amen House, or live in his beloved London, or hear Paul's bells at work. In H.S.M., and at Amen House, CW found his home. Dr Routley detected in CW the basic quality of the puritan — the ability to see through make-believe. In all he said and did, CW knew reality and followed it. Imagination — rich and burgeoning, imagination, yes, but never any confusion between worlds. The affinity between H.S.M. and CW was so strong because H.S.M. was like-minded, a man of unconfused imagination and reality. And both of them worked in a business that, above all, demanded of its workers two gifts: of extreme accuracy (Clarendon Press used then to offer a guinea to anyone who could find a misprint in an Oxford Bible) — of extreme accuracy and yet of imagination, the power to make living books out of dead words:

> Shakespeare in utmost night
> Moved on no other quest
> Than waits him who reads aright
> Edition and Palimpsest.

Let us sum it all up in a sentence from an obituary of CW written by Gerry Hopkins: 'The City of God in which he never ceased to dwell, contained Amen House as its noblest human monument, and all who lived and worked in it were citizens with him.'

Amen House is gone now; CW is gone, Alexis and

Dorinda and Colin. Only a few of us are still alive who
once served at Caesar's court. Yet, when the last of us is
gone, a Heavenly Amen House will live still, with Caesar
on the first floor and CW on the second, to strengthen
and encourage all those who try to live as they lived, in
imagination and reality without confusing the two, recognising fact, requiring accuracy, seeing through make-believe,
seeking always the truth ... and yet ... and yet ...

> When our translated cities
>   Are joyous and divine,
> And through the streets of London
>   The streets of Sarras shine,
> When what is hid in London
>   Doth then in Sarras show,
> And we in that new township
>   The ancient highways know,
> Through the bricks sing together
>   In those celestial walls,
> Shall we not long, o'er Ludgate,
>   To see the dome of Paul's?

Chapter Three

Charles Williams: A Comment from the Puritan Tradition

Dr Erik Routley

I have never in my life been invited to match wits with a major poet, and I have always managed to retain a place on the outer edges of theological debate. I know I have no business even to appear to be instructing people who have seen so much further than I in a direction in which I blame myself for not having seen more. But it's just possible that I am one of the few people who would claim to be a direct heir of the English puritan tradition. That may be saying too much, since I would actually argue with some passion that we're all heirs of that tradition, no matter how revolting we find the image of Cromwell, or how ignorant we are of the works of Thomas Goodwin. I have lived, however ineptly and unsteadily, in the tradition of John Milton and Isaac Watts, and I have one or two things to say about what I think of as the authentic puritan tradition that I don't hear other people saying. That could well be because I'm wrong: but that hasn't been proved. So let me say those things.

Puritans are a peculiarly English breed. They don't exist even in Scotland. Perhaps to some extent they exist in Holland. In America there's hardly a trace of them. The word 'puritan' was, I am told by people I pay to know these things, coined about 1564 by people who weren't puritans as a convenient label for other people of a certain moral and religious stamp who were considered a nuisance. That is, it was coined by those who didn't understand or approve of puritans. So it is like the word 'Christian': it is, I was told only the other day, like the word *baroque*, which is a word of French form invented by the French to describe a tendency in the arts of Italy and Germany of which they disapproved.

A puritan, anyhow, is a child of the renaissance who leans heavily on certain propositions about life in general and who almost ceases to exist when a majority of his neighbours agree with him. He's a minority interest almost by definition. He doesn't always realise that, and that is why he not only made himself a nuisance but was barking up an impossible tree when he tried to sell his ideas and life-style to the whole of England.

It's a delicate business being a puritan. If you are a professional minority-interest, then you can't logically say that you and only you are always right: you can't live without those other people who by sheer numbers force you to be a minority. You go sour if you attempt to live without them. This is what lies behind that epic description of the ideals of Erasmus in Huizinsa's biography of him, where the biographer attributes to him this definition of the good life: 'Good conversation between friends in a garden'. Good conversation means controversy: it requires a limited number of people and a definable area. You can't have it with five hundred people at once, and you can't have it between people who are on a moor half a mile from each other. Hence the proverbial protest against those who frustrate conversation: 'Kindly don't address me as if I were at a public meeting'.

Good conversation is of the intellect: that intellect must be neither lonely nor dogmatic. It must be correctable, flexible, yet never limply submissive. The puritan was basically a person who thought life ought to be like that. He even wanted to organise churches and parliament like that.

Of course he was a bit of an élitist. The characteristics of puritans don't include much patience with the lazy, the muddle-headed, or the shiftless, and their view of the poor was that they were probably poor by their own fault.

They never made good missionaries. (Dear me, no: something went very wrong when a puritan establishment got into its stride in South Africa.) It is evangelicals who make good missionaries and evangelicals are a very different cup of tea. Puritans aren't noisy preachers, and they used to call their churches meeting houses, not chapels.

The puritan mind loved to take hold of a mystery or a problem and worry at it until everything that couldn't be handled by argument had been shaken out, and what could be handled by intellect was ready to be processed. It's no accident that the longest, most detailed, and most ruthlessly logical of all treatises on the Holy Spirit — a subject which even the early Fathers were often shy of — were composed by the puritan divines John Owen and Thomas Goodwin.

Those of you who don't like puritans will say that they had no imagination and no poetry. If that's all you want to say you can go and say it somewhere else, because it's a half-truth of which you've got hold of the messy half. I'd like to stick those two halves together in what I am going to say.

I judge that the English puritan at his best — and he could be an anglican or a protestant or indeed both at once like Richard Baxter — was fanatical about very few things, but if there was something he was really obstinate about it is what we might call *make-believe*. That's a convenient word because you can take it in two senses, in both of which the puritan resented it. If it means somebody making you believe something and penalising you if you don't, he fought that: and if it means pretending, even innocently, to be what we aren't, he fought that too.

You can put that another way by saying that the puritan was rather specially conscious of people's need to grow up, and resisted any public attempts to frustrate people's maturity. I think the puritans may have been weak on child psychology — though I wouldn't argue that they were any weaker than most modern pontificators on that subject turn out to be. There was (I remember Stephen Neill saying this thirty-plus years ago) a tendency to think that being young was a kind of sin, certainly in the decadent puritanism of the 18th century. But although we can afford to smile at Watts's children's hymns, the vulnerability of the young to the bad example of their elders was only half the point.

The other half was, what fun it is to grow up. I think that a truly puritan interpretation of, for example, the Parable of the Prodigal, is to lay emphasis on the point that it isn't the prodigal's supposed penitence that does him credit. Indeed, I myself doubt whether he meant anything in his well-rehearsed speech (which his Father never gave him the chance to finish) about having sinned against heaven beyond making certain that when he got home he'd get a safe job in the kitchen. The punch-line, a puritan would certainly say, is the monstrous shock the young waster got when his father said, 'You will certainly not be a hired servant: you will wear the robe and the ring and you will like it.' A puritan particularly detested either a political or ecclesiastical system that kept people children, or a temperament that welcomed infantilism. It was this that made some of them harsh critics of public entertainments, especially the new-found and newly-secularised entertainment of the theatre. That's make-believe. So are Christmas carols with their legendary and extra-biblical associations. So, in the other sense of make-believe, are bishops. They do appear to have been difficult to please; but if they objected to make-believe, they surely followed a principle which, even if in detail we wouldn't put it quite the same way now, we in our time would be wise not to reject too hastily. It's not good enough to ban Shakespeare, but have we nothing to offer about the pop-culture? It's nice to have *In dulci jubilo* back in the repertory, to say nothing of *Pange lingua*, and to be allowed to observe Christmas and Good Friday, but what about Mother's Day and World Concern Sunday (or whatever you call it)? And we now look benevolently on bishops – in America, even on Methodist bishops – but then they don't do all that much about the forming of public opinion in the church, and I often feel I should welcome some good conversation in a garden with certain modern liturgists and certain other sanctified bureaucrats who are so very sure what's good for me as a minister, and even more sure, and with less adequate research on which to found their assurance, what people in the congregations want.

Well, what has any of this to do with Charles Williams? Why, this, I think: that although I don't at all know whether he'd have been horrified to be told so, he's the teacher of the 20th century who better than any other rehabilitates the puritan ideal of communication. Really? Is that a thing to say about the author or *Taliessin*? I don't see why not. Rather especially it's what we can say about the author of *He Came Down From Heaven* and *The Descent of the Dove*. I have no intention of giving a commentary on these works: it would be superfluous because they are written on two of the most obvious subjects in the world: the Christian Creed and the history of the Christian church. I am not concerned, then, with his main argument about which there's nothing to be said, but rather with the overtones which we hear in some of those flashing asides which make these books such stirring conversation. I well remember the two occasions when I heard Williams lecture. On both of these he seemed to start in the middle of a sentence, as if he was already talking to somebody and you were brought in, as it were, after the programme had started. It reminds me now of something written about the service of anglican Evensong by my revered friend Canon Joseph Poole, until recently Precentor of Coventry, where he says, 'Evensong is a conversation which began long before you were born, and will go on long after you are dead.' That's what he sounded like, exactly, and it's why he goes on long after he is dead.

I came on this, then, in the last chapter of *He Came Down*, which is headed 'The City' (a word he had a special way of pronouncing). Starting away out from the central point, he writes of Samuel Johnson's dictum that it is a man's duty to be happy; he then notices a tendency in Church speech and demeanour either to urge us to be miserable or to exhort us to be cheerful. Then he says this: 'It is some comfort to reflect that Messias was against our being bright as he was against our being gloomy. He was against our being anything at áll. He indicated continually that it was our wish to do or be something by ourselves, even to be saved by ourselves, that was the root of the trouble.' (pp. 135−6). That aphorism strikes me as being of cosmic importance. Out of it I want to extract three comments on what seem to be the most important things Williams says to us. 1. *BEING*. The first is about this verb 'to be'. I don't think anyone said before quite what Williams says in what I have quoted. 'He was against our being anything at all.'

But another very different writer about fifteen years later had much to say about this business of *being*: I mean, of course, Paul Tillich in *The Courage to Be*. Now Tillich was in some ways an old heathen (he was born, I think, in the same year as Williams), and he certainly never laughed in print. He wrote books which you congratulate yourself that you've read. But he wrestled fruitfully with this problem. Take him up in the opening words of his second chapter, headed 'Being, Non-Being and Anxiety'. He says: 'Courage is self-affirmation "in-spite-of": that is, in spite of that which tends to prevent the self from affirming itself.' He isolates in the early part of his argument three 'anxieties' which afflict, in turn or at once, any society: the anxieties of guilt, of meaninglessness, and of being. He opposes to being, which demands courage, non-being, which is a conspiracy to annihilate the self. ('I am that nothing which without God is holy' — that's the Skeleton in Williams's *Cranmer*). He goes on to say that being only becomes possible when it's 'being in participation': then he says, 'participation in what? Well, in God,' Then he says, 'but not the God of the churches and the definitions: I mean the God-above-God' (that's his expression). The book ends with this sentence — 'The courage to be is rooted in the God who appears when God has disappeared in the anxiety of doubt.' (p. 180). Hear Williams, then, on this: 'I sent you to reap that whereon ye bestowed no labour'. The harvest is of others, as the beginning was in others and the process is by others. This man's patience shall adorn that man, and that man's celerity this; and magnificence and thruft exchanged; and chastity and generosity; and tenderness and truth, and so on throughout the kingdom' (p. 132). The Psalmist spoke, we recall, of mercy and truth, righteousness and peace, embracing each other in the same kind of riotous counterpoint. Williams goes on: 'We shall be graced by one and all, only never by ourselves; the only thing that can be ours is the fiery blush of laughter of humility when the shame of Adam has become the shyness of the saints. The first and final maxim in the present earth is deny the self, but — there or here — when the need for denial has paused, it may be possible to be astonished at the self as at everything else. . . .'

Tillich is sombre and Teutonic, Williams vivid and so quintessentially English. I see in Williams what I saw when I first read John Owen's *Pneumatologia* – 500 close printed pages on the Holy Spirit, proving that the one thing nobody can afford is an unregenerate conscience: laborious stuff, but the best thing on Conscience I know. I hear the same note in the anonymous work, *The Marrow of Modern Divinity* (c. 1647): that after you've worked on being good, the only thing to hope for is to relax into goodness, into a kingdom where duty and delight are really the same.

Being, for Tillich, becomes, through courage, an active verb. But that becoming is a process involving a self-giving, a self-forgetting. The one thing Tillich doesn't know about is what Williams calls the City. He ends up with a groping mysticism, Williams ends up in the High Street. But what Williams says about Messias not wanting us to be any-thing (in the sense which is now obvious) judges, in one piercing phrase, all human attempts to work on the indi-vidual's 'image', or, worse, the church's 'image'. I can see what he means about an unaffected person, a person who's really there, not worrying for a moment about being, and I know the difference – it's one of the things a pastoral life makes one good at spotting – between a person who comes to meet you and one who always sends a representative. What about an unaffected church? Well, that's what the puritans wanted and dreamed of and never achieved. But good heavens, they did have the vision, and that's some-thing. A church without make-believe: one that without opening its mouth 'tells it the way it is'. Of one thing I am sure: that is that churches were never so far from even knowing about that ideal, let alone wanting it, than they are now. Posturing benevolence, public-relations activism, blue-jeans priests, throw-away music, vote-catching democ-ratization of speech and dress and manner: don't get me started on all that.

2. My second point is about belief and commitment, and I hang it on two texts from *He Came Down*: this, in chapter III: 'It (the idea that the pot shouldn't argue with the potter, as in Romans 9) has been used too often by the pious to encourage them to say, in love or in laziness, "Our little minds were never meant . . ." Fortunately there is the book

of Job to make it clear that our little minds were meant. A great curiosity ought to exist concerning divine things' (p 33). The quotation, by the way, is adapted from Isaac Watts who in one of his risible poems for children wrote:

> Our little hands were never meant
> to tear each other's eyes.

In the previous chapter he says this: 'The distinction between necessary belief and unnecessary credulity is as necessary as belief; it is the heightening and purifying of belief' (p 25). It is at this point that we can turn to *The Descent of the Dove*. In the chapter 'The Quality of Disbelief' he concerns himself not only with the Reformation but with that extraordinary collapse of organised faith that followed the Thirty Years War, and that produced German pietism, and through that, English Methodism and evangelicalism. Referring to the Thirty Years War, which is one of the best examples of the hideous truth that wars are always made by righteous men (and the more righteous, the more gruesome the suffering they generate), he remarks that: 'Contrition and the taking of faith seriously had meant untold suffering, had meant fierce and continual horrors, within nations and between nations' (p. 189). As a consequence of this, he goes on: 'Something general and very deep in man awoke to revolt, . . . It may have been mere exhaustion, or perhaps mere humanitarianism (which at such times is seen to have a beauty all its own) which gave it its opportunity. But it rose. It was a quality of spirit, . . . a manner, a temperament, a nature, which may be encouraged or discouraged; it is most particularly not irony, though irony may be an element in it. It is a qualitative mode of belief rather than a qualititative denial of dogma. It is a rare thing, and it may be called the quality of disbelief' (p. 189–90).

We will note that carefully because it introduces a penetrating description of what I've been accustomed to call 'orthodox Dissent'. After mentioning as an example Lorenzo Valla's defence of what were attributed to him as heretical comments on the Faith (the result of applying humanistic scholarship to its pronouncements: saying things such as that Cicero's Latin is better than that of the Vulgate), Williams goes on: 'The answer (Valla's answer) is an example of this quality of disbelief. It is entirely accurate; it comes straight from the Creed. It covers all the doctrines. It is entirely consistent with sanctity. Yet undoubtedly it also involves as much disbelief as possible; it allows for, encourages, the sense of agnosticism and the possibility of error.... Such a method has the same dangers as any other; that is, it is quite sound when a master uses it, cheapens as it becomes popular, and is unendurable when it becomes merely fashionable' (p. 191). Williams here attributes the rise of this to the Thirty Years' War; in a sense, though, it's precisely what the Renaissance and the Reformation were about. 'Look, we don't have to believe *all that*, surely.' Better: 'Do we have to believe *all that* in the same way in which we believe the basic things?' This, he says, isn't unbelief, but disbelief. What is here being described is the 'humanity's coming of age' syndrome: the kind of thing we overhear in Luther's Preface to the 1526 German Mass, where he says that a child needs the old Latin Mass, a growing person needs the new German one, and a fully mature Christian needs no liturgy at all: or in the famous epigram coined thirty years ago by Herbert Butterfield, 'Hold fast to Christ, and in all else be uncommitted.' Warren Bartley in his book '*The Retreat to Commitment*' (1964: a very 1964 book too) argues that commitment can be misdirected love. That is the sort of thing and we're all entirely familiar with it. It is certainly there in the later pages of Tillich's book that I mentioned earlier: belief is hardly possible at all unless we can find the 'God-above-God'. It is there in a way in that theology of the 'death of God' which was so fashionable fifteen years ago. It is there, much more eloquently expressed and wisely judged, in this passage from Daniel Jenkins's *Tradition and the Spirit* (1951): 'Before joining our testimony to that of the Creeds we must honestly face the possibility that they may be mistaken and find assurance of their truth for ourselves'. (This is expressed as an agreed position on the part of the reader he is conversing with.) 'If the hesitation of many ... to make Credal subscription a formal test of membership meant that alone, it would be fully justified, but it is a good illustration of the ambiguity of motives in theology that it has often been taken too readily as an excuse for evading the challenge of the Creeds to the Church. The Church does right, therefore, to maintain that the Creeds be treated with full seriousness as great landmarks in the articulation of tradition about which all succeeding generations must make up their minds, but her understanding of the nature of the act of 'traditioning' will prompt her to add the warning that they must not be used as false short cuts to the reality of faith' (p. 132–3).

Personally I think the path down which Williams invites us in assigning this 'spirit of disbelief' to the generations after 1648 is inviting, because what the Thirty Years' War gave birth to was not the Reformation (it was fought *about* the Reformation) but a Reformation new deal – evangelicalism. And not only Protestant evangelicalism either. Basically it was the substitution for federal or organised or institutionalized religion of solo religion. Why, look at the popular songs of the pietist faith – the hymns of Gerhargt, for example, or those of vintage Methodism. The texts are all in the first person singular and the music is scored always for solo singing, not corporate singing. Of no movement was it more true that it's fine in the hands of a master, pale when it becomes popular, and sour when it becomes fashionable.

Pietism, remember, is never a denomination: it was a network like the Iona Community or the Order of This and That which are designed to bind together Christians of any allegiance who are of a certain mind. The mind here required was one which left doctrine on one side, was impatient of what I am sure people about then started calling denominational barriers, and concentrated on personal testimony and experience and on the duty of the Christian to engage in works of mercy (a duty which fairly soon narrowed itself down to converting those suspected of not being Christians). The War had made institutional religion physically impossible by snapping normal communications; it had fostered private and solo religion by throwing people and small groups back on their own resources; and it had exposed the inability both of organised confessional Lutheranism and of Counter-Reformation Catholicism to arouse in individual people a faith that would stand up to the sufferings it brought on them. So – a new Reformation deal, a new twist in the course of orthodox disbelief or dissent. If we remember that pietism was the religious framework within which J. S. Bach wrote all his Cantatas and major sacred works, we can admit that it's all right in the hands of a master; if we recall how much organised benevolence and philanthropy which we now take for granted was brought into being by disciples of Wesley (anglican or dissenting) we can happily count Wesley a master. On the other hand if we read the scandalous story of the Count Nicolas von Zinzendorf, the tyrant of pietism in the mid-18th century, in such a place as Ronald Knox's *Enthusiasm*, we can also check the plausibility of that bit about popularity and fashionableness.

Disbelief, in Williams's sense, is with us; learnt, it cannot be unlearnt. We have seen now that all the church's statements are propositions which in the hands of a master are good, and which become distorted when they pass through popularity to vogue. The Bible is certainly of this kind. I believe in my Lord, but what sort of belief do I offer to a printed page which seems to invite me to hate my father and mother, or which portrays the Master as cursing a fig tree for not bearing figs in April? Is the belief I accord to 1 Corinthians 13 the same as that which I accord to the passage about women being silent in church and wearing hats because of the angels? I am coming to that in my third section, which is almost due. But I want to sew this one up first because it's in danger of falling apart. I may indeed have allowed my grip on Williams's notion of disbelief to slip. I do not want to lose sight of that more distant meaning of disbelief which I surely hear in St Peter's 'Depart from me'. If we are committed to seeking for maturity ourselves and resisting attempts to frustrate it in others, then we must realise that the more we approach maturity, the more we approach the intolerable beauty. The more mature, the more vulnerable. Up there on Everest they find it difficult to breathe. 'And they saw the God of Israel: and there was under his feet as it were a pavement of sapphire stone, like the very heaven for clearness / And he did not lay his hands on the chief men of the people of Israel. They beheld God, and at and drank.'

Eternal Light! Eternal light!

How pure the soule must be
when placed within thy searching sight
   it shrinks not, but with calm delight
   can live, and look on Thee!

  O how shall I, whose native sphere
   is dark, whose mind is dim,
before the Ineffable appear,
   and on my naked spirit bear
   the uncreated beam?

I'm sure the Charles Williams Society is composed of hymn-haters: but there, in the words of Thomas Binney, a Congregationalist who was moved to write them in 1829, is a transcendence of disbelief.

3. We must now get to my third point, which is just conceivably about what Williams called the 'Alteration in Knowledge'. No – that may be too high a claim: but still I make it. You will surely think I have been too kind to the puritans. I now want to indicate the point at which I think most of them failed to follow their chosen ideal through. I want to mention the thing which I feel sure most of them missed: the very thing which Williams supplies. It has to do with what we now call communication: with the nature of that conversation which takes place in that garden. It's a difficult point to make but I will try it out on you. I think I will approach it through an experience which my American residence has given me. C. S. Lewis is the object of a cult in America, and if you want to see displays of his books, you go to what we call the South. That means the South-East, or what's familiarly called the Bible Belt. Lewis has been largely appropriated by the fundamentalists, the people who promote a naive and literalist cult of Christ.

Why has Williams been spared these grotesque accolades? Lewis is asking Williams the question at this moment, and Williams is trying to change the conversation because it's impossible for him to reveal his secret. Well, I hazard a guess at what the secret is. Imagine two quite different activities. In the first scene I am asking one of you to lend me a pencil for a moment. Your response is to move the pencil towards me, to retain your hold of it until I have got hold of it myself, and only then to let it go. Throwing it to me would be bad manners. On the other hand consider a group of people playing with a ball out of doors. They throw it to each other. Suppose that instead of throwing it to me, you walked up to me and passed it to me as you had earlier passed the pencil. What is that but an insult? You have made it clear that I'm not in the game because I am incapable of catching it if you throw it. (In my own case you were actually right, but you were still unkind.) One kind of communication is pencil-passing. That's the communication I expect of the telephone directory. I don't want to be told that the exchange is the square of 26 and the private wire the cube of 13. I want to be told 676−2197 which information I use and then discard. But another kind of person says to me:

> at the round earth's imagin'd corners, blow
>   your trumpets, angels and arise, arise
>   from death, you numberless infinities
> of souls, and to your scatter'd bodies go,
> all whom the flood did, and fire shall o'erthrow.
>   all whom war, dearth, age, agues, tyrannies,
>   despair, law, chance hath slain: and you, whose eyes
> shall behold God, and never taste death's woe.

Normally I use that illustration when I am lecturing on aesthetics to distinguish between what is art and what is not: and I use it if I lecture to preachers or liturgists. I hold that the communication of Christian truth is more like Jonne than like the telephone directory. Now in that matter of 'disbelief', this seems to me to be crucial. Moreover I think that this was a truth which the puritan at his best stumbled on but never gave himself time to work out. Conversation is throwing balls, not passing pencils. 'Evensong is a conversation which began long before you were born and will continue long after you are dead.' Yes: come and join in the ball game when you feel you want to. But don't stand there ridiculing the game. I am quite clear myself that the church's liturgy is a ball-throwing, not a pencil-passing activity: and that the Bible does the same thing. 'Without a parable spoke he not to them'. 'Parable' − look at the word: its second syllable is the Greek for, precisely, throwing a ball. You might say that when a ball comes in from Charles it has plenty of top-spin on it. But it's perfectly obvious that Charles is the teacher whom one can trust, not only because he wrote *He Came Down* and *The Descent* but because he also wrote *Taliessin* and *Seed of Adam*. I am also disposed to suggest that C. S. Lewis has fallen on evil days in America (though his heirs and assigns are doing very nicely) because he has, through no fault of his own, been mistaken for a pencil-passer. People who organise Christianity into a series of quite practicable demands have found, they think, an ally in him because he talks in prose. (They don't know his poetry: a southern audience was bowled over when a Scottish minister of great distinction read them the poem 'The Late Passenger' in 1979: they thought they had Lewis boxed in: I suspect that when the shock wore off they returned to their assurance.)

But – disbelief? Why, what it really is is a man or a woman saying, 'I am ready to join in the ball game'. The way an artist communicates is by assuming that whoever hears or reads or sees his work is ready to reach up and confidently anticipates that they'll catch at least some of the balls. But you must not walk up to the player and put the ball in his hand. And that is, I venture to say, what the puritan knew but never followed through, and what the modern church, so deeply corrupted by evengelicalism, is bent on doing. You won't understand this, so we'll translate it into the language of the business letter or the newspaper story. You have no faculty for appreciating the language of any other age, so we'll give you that of your own. We will retranslate 'et cum spiritu tuo' as 'and also with you'. Ah yes, and while we are about it, since you won't understand 'You cannot serve God and Mammon' we'll retranslate it 'You cannot serve God and money'. You won't mind the tendentiousness of our translation: you'll thank us because we've made it easier. You might find it difficult to understand 'Peter was grieved' – at the third question about love presented by his Master, so we'll say 'Peter was upset'.

I don't know if it has occurred to many people that the condition to which the church has been reduced in our time is the consequence of a conspiracy to separate poetry from theology, or to bring theological speech in the congregation as close to the telephone directory as it can come. Now the sizzling vivacity of Charles Williams's exposition of doctrine and history in the books I have been using for reference here suggests that he knew of no other way of communicating truth than throwing balls. He makes most other theologians look like carpenters − apprentice carpenters at that. And his top-spin has, so far, kept him out of the hands of the fundamentalists. Well, in this he is a puritan. More than that − he's what the puritans at their best wished they could be. The weakness of the puritans (the best of them) was that their horror of make-believe inhibited their artistry. It meant that they took 500 pages to get anything said. Bunyan was an exception, we might say; Milton, goodness knows, another; Baxter, I would insist, a third when he was writing verse −

> Christ leads me through no darker rooms
>   than he went through before:
> he that into God's kingdom comes
>   must enter by this door....

> As for my friends, they are not lost;
>   the several vessels of thy fleet,
> though parted now, by tempests toss'd,
>   shall safely in thy haven meet.

Henry More too, and Henry Vaughan the Silurist − puritan poets despite themselves. But if we want to uncover the secret that unlocks the problems of being, of belief, and of communication, this is the area in which we look for the key. For the Church has never really attempted to evade the huge enigma of death. How could it? What is the church's tradition but a *traditio* − which is the Latin for a handing-over, and possibly a betrayal. Tradition and betray have the same root. Here is a second century instructor catechizing a new convert. At the baptism the convert renders back (*redditio*) what he has been given. But it's the young convert who will be sixty-two one day and passing on the secret. The teacher must leave it with him. He must take no precautions to see that the convert doesn't drop the ball. Any time he does, any time he passes it instead of throwing it, the ball's *dead*. I say this to preachers; I'd say it to authors if I ever spoke to them. The poets know it.

I think it is characteristic of Charles Williams that he should write a book about church history which uses as a ground base the most enigmatic epigram ever coined by a Christian mind: 'My eros is crucified'. It is equally characteristic of him that the first time he quotes it he makes it clear that it can mean more or less anything. Each time he introduces it it means something different, and that makes him like a master composer. 'He doesn't want us to *be* anything'. 'We may be astonished at the self'. 'The shame of Adam becomes the shyness of the saints'. One who is with the Lord pressed *He Came Down From Heaven* into my hand in 1939: this and much else he taught me to read. But for him I might never have opened a book of Charles Williams – or of St Thomas Aquinas. I remember as if it was yesterday the sense of fire and tumult that the prose of that book, and of *The Descent of the Dove* communicated. Forty years later I am sure I haven't caught more than a fraction of the balls these books throw. But what I think I do know is that this is real conversation: conversation in a garden: civilised and bracing and shaming and exalting conversation.

Chapter Four

Doctrine and Mystery in the Prose of Charles Williams and Lancelot Andrewes

Ralph Townsend

There is a correspondence in thought and expression between Williams and Lancelot Andrewes. They are both concerned with matters of theology and their expression in such a way that their prose has a distinctive method and character. Their use of language and concept, methodical but not enslaved to system, is a blend of the analytical and the poetic, the discursive and the contemplative.

Charles Williams was a High Anglican in spiritual allegiance. Glen Cavaliero in *Charles Williams – Poet of Theology* has explored the relationship between Williams as poet and Williams as theologian.

The theologian must answer a series of prior questions. Did the person of Jesus ever live: was he born as our records assert and did he suffer death on the cross? Did he, again as the records assert, think and speak of himself as the Messiah, the Son of God? These plainly are questions of history the answers to which depend on the weighing of documentary evidence, exactly as in the case of any other recorded event of the past. To this extent the truth of the narrative may be granted without commitment to any supernatural creed. The real problem of Christiantiy begins with a question of a different order: when Jesus thought and spoke of himself as the

Messiah, the Son of God, was he what he proclaimed himself to be or was he suffering a delusion? This also is a question of fact, but obviously the answer is to be sought otherwise than in the mere weighing of documentary evidence. We pass from the province of history to theology.

The Catholic approach to Christian doctrine may be described as the insistence that the final and clinching proof of the Christian faith, which raises probability to certainty, for intellectual and simple alike, lies in verification through simple first-hand experience of God in Christ, and of Christ in the Church and the sacraments. It is not solely in the statement of dogmatic propositions that theology discovers itself, but in the authentication of these propositions in experience. It is perhaps for this reason that the English tradition of theology discloses itself as much in poetry or prose as in dogma, canon and systematic argument. For poetry and prose are organic in themselves, processes of reflective experience; personal, because they are the imaginative construction of the writer, yet incorporative in their appeal to a body of doctrine through which the human experience of God may be interpreted. The prose of Charles Williams and Lancelot Andrewes entails at once an unfolding of the writer's own self-persuasion to faith, and an invitation to the reader to give assent in faith by engagement in that process of persuasion and appeal to reflection upon his own experience. It is the individual's persuasion to the corporate truth of Christian tradition and doctrine.

In order to explore this theme I shall compare Williams's *He Came Down From Heaven*, which is his most coherent working-out of the implications of the doctrine of the Incarnation, with the Nativity sermons of a key figure in seventeenth-century English, and in the whole of the English tradition, those of Bishop Lancelot Andrewes. T. S. Eliot says of Andrewes' sermons that 'they rank with the finest English prose of their time, of any time'. Different as they were as men, different as their historical contexts were, there is a bond between them which is a pointer to the character of the wider tradition to which they belong.

The doctrine of the Incarnation is a thing approached by Williams first and foremost as a mystery; a constructive, fulfilling mystery, not mystery as mere baffling wonder.

Williams is aware that we cannot understand all that is involved in God being God, nor can we expect to understand why he is God or how he can succeed in being God. We must be content to accept the mystery of his being God, because we have kindled within us the faith and the awareness that he is God. We understand him not in the structure of his nature but in what he has done. So, for example, Williams points out, the experience of pardon is a way into the reality of the Incarnation. Pardon, he says,

> is the name now given to the heavenly knowledge of the evil of earth; evil is known as an occasion of good, that is, love. It has always been so known on the side of heaven, but now it can be so known on the side of earth also. What mankind could not do, manhood did, and a manhood which was at the disposal of all men and women. It was therefore possible now for mankind itself to know evil as an occasion of heavenly love.

We understand the mystery of the Incarnation as an unfolding of God's loving and responsible activity, 'not by infusing grace only, but by himself becoming what himself had made'. Lancelot Andrewes shares this powerful sense of the constructive mystery of the Incarnation. His theology centres upon the idea of Christ as the head of redeemed humanity, of the Church as his body, of Christians as those who live in him. The purpose of God's taking flesh was that we might be incorporate in Christ. The nature of this mystery is one that effects a change in us. 'The manifestation of God in the flesh,' says Andrewes,

> the Evangelists set down by way of an history ... a man may hear a story, and never wash his hands, but a mystery requireth both the hands and the heart to be clean that shall deal with it.

This is the mystery of glory which is the master-theme of the writings of Andrewes and Williams. The Incarnation is not the mystification arising from loose talk about love; still less is it the muddle arising from romantic escapism indulging in fantasies about love. It is concerned with the concrete presentation of the mystery seen in its fullness as the embodiment of the forgiving God in the crucified man, and experienced in its beginnings by every human being who has begun to share the interchange of love.

The essence of this mystery, then, lies in a mutually-related pattern of giving and receiving. This pattern Williams called co-inherence, a theme of the writings of the Greek Fathers on the Trinity and in developing his principle of co-inherence he quarried the deep recesses of the doctrine of the Incarnation. Andrewes also enunciates a theology of co-inherence as a way at once of probing and preserving mystery. Of the nativity he says this:

> And here now at his word, 'made of a woman', He beginneth to concern us somewhat. There groweth an alliance between us; for we also are made of a woman. This now is full for the union with our own nature, to be 'made of a woman'.

Co-inherence has to do with persons. The pattern of the humanity of Jesus, God Incarnate, was determined by the obedience of love expressed in love. This was perfectly matched by the pattern of divinity which is transcendent love likewise expressed, in relation to history, as the service of love. The doctrine of the Incarnation, that Christ is two natures in one person, recognises that the love of God and the love of man come to the same thing. When God, who is truly love, and man, who can find his true reality only in love, express their true selves in history, it comes to the same person. Jesus Christ is the person who is the perfect pattern of the human service of love and the divine service of love. 'The union of history and the individual is', says Williams,

> like that of so many other opposites, in the coming of the kingdom of heaven, historic and contemporary at once. It was historic in order that it might always be contemporary; it is contemporary because it was certainly historic.

Because we are confronted with the co-inherence of patterns of love, we encounter in the end a personal union. God is the loving man: the man is the loving God. Andrewes assembles the pattern of co-inherence thus:

> And now, if we will put together *natus* and *Servator, Servator* and *Christus, Christus* and *Dominus, Dominus* and *natus*; 'born and Saviour, Saviour and Christ, Christ and the Lord, the Lord and born', take them which way you will in combination, any of the four, then we have his two natures in one Person. In *Servator*, His Godhead; none but God is a Saviour. In *Christus* His Manhood; God cannot be anointed, man may. In *Dominus*, His Divine again, 'the Lord from Heaven'. In *natus*, his human nature directly, born of a woman; both ever carefully joined, to be joined together.

We see here that the Incarnation reveals through perfect love the height and depth of personal union. The existence of Jesus Christ depends wholly on the living God, while the existence of Jesus is expressed wholly as the loving man. Williams projects this pattern of personal co-inherence revealed in the Incarnation into the collective human world:

> Into the chaotic experience of good as evil the first pattern of order is introduced; every man is to answer for the life of his brother. As the Omnipotence so limits man, it limits itself, and for the first time characterises itself by limitation − the everlasting covenant between God and every living creature of all flesh that is upon the earth.

The reality of the transcendent God is expressed in terms of total involvement in the events of history. This co-inherence holds together the transcendence and the immanence of God. Williams locates here an absolute definition of poetry:

> The union of flesh and spirit ... is credible everywhere; indeed, that union which so much poetry has desired to describe, is understood as more profound and more natural, than the dichotomy, of experience of expression,

which has separated them. She is inclusive of both, and exclusive of their separateness.

And so, 'it is a result of the Incarnation that opened all potentialities of the knowledge of the kingdom of heaven in and through matter'.

For both Andrewes and Williams, then, the mystery of the Incarnation is elucidated by reflection on the co-inherence of material and spiritual, immanence and transcendence. This leads to another common theme, the experience of mystery evoked in worship. It is in worship that we are faced with both the offer and demand of transcendence, of the immeasurable distance which goes with the intimate closeness of the living God whose life is love. For both writers, worship is the practice of the response of love to the love of God, who in the infinite openness of his love is endlessly and gloriously worshipful. 'And what is it to worship?' asks Andrewes:

> Some great matter sure it is, that Heaven and earth, the stars and Prophets, thus do but serve to lead them and conduct us to. For we all see ends in *adorare* ... the Scripture and world are but to this end, that He that created the one and inspired the other might be worshipped ... *Tanti est adorare*. Worth the while, worth our coming, if coming we do but that, but worship and nothing else.

Worship is different from mere ceremony. 'A ceremony', says Andrewes,

> represents and signifies, but works nothing; a mystery doth both. Beside that it signifieth, it hath its operation; a work it doth, else mystery is it none.

Williams makes the same point when he suggests that the Bible 'is concerned with *what happened*, the Rituals with *what is happening*. There is a ceremony of word and movement, thought and language, invoking the experience of worship and belief. Religious prose runs parallel to liturgical worship, as Williams suggests in this passage: 'The "sweet reasonableness" of Christ is always there, but it is always in a dance, and its dancing hall is from the topless heavens to the bottomless abyss. Its balance is wholly in itself ...'.

In Andrewes's *adorare*, in Williams's dance, there is a contemplative gaze. There is a great deal that is to be said about belief, a great deal that is communicable, but the core of the matter is something you must apprehend for yourself. For belief is concerned neither exclusively with the truth of certain doctrines, nor with the validity of a certain way of life, but with the response of worship to the revelation of God's glory, a response that involves an orientationof our whole being, a way of life, and the articulation of that glory in doctrine. Both Andrewes and Williams engage in a prose of contemplation, fot it is in contemplation that faith and experience, theology and spirituality, co-inhere. Yet contemplation is not something acquired but given, our response to God's loving gaze, a gaze centred on and concentrated in the mysterious co-inherence of God in man, of life and death. For Williams it is again expressed in the image of movement:

> It is as if, from moment to moment, he withdrew and returned, swifter than lightning, known in one mode and another mode and always new ... the coming and the going one, the going and the coming one, and all is joy.

It is only in worship that we can encounter the reality of the Christ to whom we respond in love. Worship limits a tendency for Christ to become domesticated, one who is merely familiar, in the hearts of those who love him; and also a tendency for the prevenience of God's grace to become simply an abstract pre-supposition. God is not merely sovereign, but one who comes; he *has* come and *does* come. And what he was in Christ, self-emptying, defenceless, sustaining an irrevocable love for men, that he really is.

These themes demand of the writer prose which somehow demonstrates and contains within itself the contemplative ingredient of worship. Faith is not so much analytically and systematically proved as contemplatively received. This is the approach to religious inquiry that characterizes the tradition in which Andrewes and Williams think, feel and write. In his essay on Lancelot Andrewes, T. S. Eliot quotes F. E. Brightman on the structure of Andrewes's prayers:

> ... the structure is not merely an external scheme or framework: the internal structure is as close to the external. Andrewes develops an idea he has in mind: every line tells and adds something. He does not expatiate, but moves forward: if he repeats, it is because the repetition has a real force of expression; if he accumulates, each new word or phrase represents a new development, a substantive addition to what he is saying.

Eliot provides a gloss on this in a well-known passage:

> Andrewes may seem pedantic and verbal. It is only when we have saturated ourselves in his prose, followed the movement of his thought, that we find his examination of words terminating in the ecstasy of assent. Andrewes takes a word and derives the world from it; squeezing and squeezing the word until it yields a full juice of meaning ...

In a passage which closely echoes this, Williams argues that in an approach to the study of the Bible

> it is precisely good literary criticism that is needed, for those of use who are neither theologians, higher critics, nor fundamentalists ... the illumination of phrase by phrase, by the discovery (without ingenuity) of complexity within complexity and simplicity within simplicity ... to extract the utmost meaning out of words.

At the heart of this tradition is a concern for and awareness of the way in which language serves religious inquiry. Images, perhaps especially, as Andrewes and Williams suggest, the images of the Bible, are more than just concepts, to be apprehended by the analytic intellect alone. Andrewes's sermons demonstrate again and again that even the simplest words can operate on many levels at once – informative, emotive, evaluative – so that images touch the whole personality down to the very deepest levels of the psyche, and involve our bodily life as well. Religious language customarily comes to us in a context of actions loaded with significance; and we receive its meaning not just mentally but sacramentally. Andrewes is able to take the name of a place, for example, and give it elevated significance by associating it with Bread:

> We speak of the *transeamus usque Bethlehem* ... That we may even locally do and never go out of this room, in as much as here is to be had the 'true Bread of life that came down from Heaven' ... the Church in this sense is very Bethlehem no less than the town itself ... Not till this Bread was born there, which is *Panis Angelorum* ...

The images of religious language are also symbols of a larger non-verbal reality, and come alive only where that total reality is involved in our openness to the truths which they mediate. It is precisely because of this quality that religious language can exercise a healing and unifying influence on the whole personality and act as a means of grace.

It is clear from Williams's writing that he is aware of the difficulties of religious language. If we apply words to God in their ordinary literal sense, then we all too easily make God in our image and fall into idolatry; if we use them in an entirely different sense, then we have no reason for using one word rather than another, and we are lost in agnosticism. One way of handling this problem is to apply the principle of analogy to what we say about God. Williams does this in each of the seven essays of *He Came Down From Heaven*. Our ideas are based on the perfections and excellences we can see in God's finite creatures. It is because these are real perfections and excellences, reflecting and communicating something of the goodness and nature of God, that God is known to us at all. 'The God of nature', says Andrewes, 'is not bound to the rules of nature'. 'The kingdom came down', says Williams, 'and was incarnate; since then and perhaps (because of it) before then, it is beheld through and in a carnality of joy':

> The beloved − person or thing − becomes the Mother of Love; Love is born in the soul; it may have its passion

there; it may have its resurrection. It has its own divine nature united with our undivine nature.

It is in connection with this matter of the language of belief that Cavaliero makes one of his best insights into the theological books of Williams. 'To use doctrine as myth', he argues,

> is to put it to its proper use; it relates to the responsive imagination. He recognizes that people have an emotional need for metaphysics; but he insists that metaphysics, inevitably, involves the use of imagery. Like poetry, it is a way of seeing, not itself sight or knowledge.

The essays in *He Came Down From Heaven* show religious language to be poetic without suggesting that religious beliefs need have no definite content. To say that all religious language is inadequate, or to say that we are dealing with images and symbols of a transcendent and ultimately inexpressible reality, does not mean that anything goes. Williams is clear that doctrinal models are pointers, pointing in certain directions and not in others. We may not be able to gather all that they include, but we do know that there are quite a lot of things that they exclude. The mystery of the Incarnation, a pattern or ceremony of co-inherence, the Word making demands upon language: Andrewes and Williams recognise the necessity of both a scientific (i.e. analytical) method *and* the findings of poetic intuition. In Cavaliero's words they 'will have no schism between the two, for both are methods of discriminating among connections which make reasoning life possible'.

In the pattern of the Incarnation is ultimately an invitation to glory. Williams dedicates *He Came Down From Heaven* 'to Michal, by whom I began to study the Doctrine of Glory'. In the true worship of the true God which is the way to fulfilment, to the glory of man, grace must be scientific. To be human and personal, as God is to be human and personal, is to be open to whatever is given, to all data. We are in the image of God, but this describes our potentialities more than our present realities. Our potentiality is glory. 'The word glory', says Williams, to English ears, usually means no more than a kind of mazy bright blur. But the maze should be, though it generally is not, exact, and the brightness should be that of a geometric pattern. It is this which becomes a kind of key problem — what is the web of the glory of heaven as a state? It may be said, roughly, that certain patterns in the web are already discernible; the recognition of the good, the reflection of power, the exercise of the intellect the importance of interchange, and a deliberate relation to the Centre ... knowledge of good, knowledge of joy. The glory is the goodness, but even the goodness is not he.

We must not think of God in *our* image. We must not be trapped in any symbol, picture or definition of God. The mystery of God is yet unfinished: we await the day of the Seventh Angel. 'Then shall the mystery be finished', says Andrewes, 'when He that was this day "manifest in the flesh", shall manifest to the flesh the fullness of his mystery. His eternity, glory and bliss'. The *image* we have of God is never a decisive definition of God. Similarly, no present theory of the universe must finally shut in our understanding of that universe, of our place within it, and of the reality of the God who is making us for himself in and through history. 'Glorify God with your bodies', preached Andrewes, 'for Christ hath now a body with which to do him worship with our bodies. Williams re-expresses this principle of carnality in his scheme of Romantic Love:

> Here, surrounded by angels, prophets, evangelists, virtues, Romantic Love is seen to mirror the Humanity and Deity of the Redeemer.

'The glory is apt to dazzle the beholder', says Williams, 'unless he already has a mind disposed to examine the pattern of glory ... The effort after the pattern makes the difference'. Theology is 'the effort after the pattern'. The mind disposed to examine the pattern must be at once scientific and poetic, in a word, theological. Such minds we find in Andrewes and Williams. We must not be trapped in mythology, theory or fragmentation: rather, we must seize every opportunity of hopeful openness to the future. The key signature of *He Came Down From Heaven* is Glory as the ambience of the Incarnation. Andrewes boldly signs the stave of the sermons on the Nativity:

> Glory to be first, and then Peace. There is much in the order.
> Glory to be first, else you change the clef, − the clef is in
> Glory, that the key of the song ... no *Pax in terris*, unless it be first considered how it will stand with *Gloria in excelsis*.

If it is true that the fulfilment of our human nature lies in union with the nature of God, then we can never suppose that we have reached the end of meaningfulness. The Incarnation of God is a sufficient statement of our hope and definition of our direction. As Williams put it:

> The appearance of the glory is temporary; the authority of the glory towards pure love is everlasting; the quality of the glory is eternal, such as the heavens have in Christ.

There is a definite relationship between the religious prose of Lancelot Andrewes and Charles Williams. There may even be a direct influence. The relationship suggests a common theological tradition, the character of which discloses itself particularly in their approach to the doctrine of the Incarnation. Theirs is a way of doing theology which at once probes and preserves mystery; understands divine creation through a principle of co-inherence; expresses itself in worship and contemplation, aware of the limitations of religious language; and which sets as its goal a vision of the glory of God in man and man in God.

Chapter Five

The Figure of Cressida

John Heath-Stubbs

What I propose to talk about has, perhaps, only a contingent relationship to Charles Williams and his work, but
Shakespeare's *Troilus and Cressida* was a play which he
held to be important and which he deals with in the title
Reason and Beauty in the English Poetic Mind. What he saw
Shakespeare exploring in it was the theme of the abolition
of identity, the contradiction between Troilus's Cressida
and Diomede's Cressida. When, in the play, Ulysses brings
Troilus to witness Cressida's unfaithfulness, the young lover
cries out bitterly: 'Think we had mothers.' Ulysses, the man
of unimaginative reason, replies: 'Why, what has she done
which could dishonour our mothers?' and Troilus answers:
'Nothing at all, unless that this be she'. This abolition of
identity, this bitter negation of the Beatrician experience
was a motif which CW explored both in his poetry and in
his novels. In the Palomides poems of *Taliessin Through
Logres,* the blatant beast:

> scratches itself in the space between
> the Queen's substance and the Queen.

This is Palomides's experience when his vision of the Queen
Iseult seems contradicted for him by his realisation that her
love is given not to him but to Tristan.

But Shakespeare did not invent the story of Troilus and
Cressida, and I thought it might be interesting to follow

49

the development of this character from her origins in the medieval Chaucer to her treatment by three of our greatest English poets and one very notable Scottish poet. More recently there is also the operatic treatment of her story by Sir William Walton to a libretto by Christopher Hassall but about this I will not have much to say. This relating of a theme or a character in one poet to the work of others is something which CW liked to do. His view of poetry was, I think, almost that images and characters had an existence independent of the individual poet's imagination. The image of the forest which he describes, among other places, in the opening pages of *The Figure of Beatrice* – the forest of Brociliande in the Taliessin poems is, as he once said in answer to a question I put to him, only his own small portion of that great forest. Therefore, to follow the changing fortunes of Cressida as it were through the various poetic imaginations which have dwelt upon her, may, I hope, not be irrelevant to the understanding of CW's own interpretation of Shakespeare and in accordance with the spirit of his own approach to poetry.

The story of Troilus and Cressida is part of the tale of Troy but it is not to be found in Homer or in any of the classical Greek and Roman authors. It is a medieval story and first appears in the *Roman de Troie* by Benoit de Saintmaur. But stories are not created simply out of nothing. If you will pass back your mind to Homer's *Iliad*, you will recall that the theme of that poem is the wrath of Achilles and that it begins with a quarrel over a woman captive. Menaleus has taken Chryseis, the daughter of Chryses, priest to Apollo. Her father begs the King to release her but is churlishly refused. He prays to his god and Apollo sends a plague into the Greek camp. The Greeks therefore persuade Menaleus to give up Chryseis but he demands Briseis who has been assigned in the booty to Achilles as compensation and it is this demand which causes the wrath of Achilles and his withdrawal from the war until he is persuaded once more to take part in the fighting in order to avenge his friend Petrochles and kills Hector. All this brutal treatment of women as mere chattels to be exchanged and owned is quite appalling, of course, and it represents, no doubt, the reality of war in ancient times. Simone Weil, in her splendid essay on Homer, shows the universality and the truth of his writing about war – how he shows that war reduces people to mere objects and, though we are a long way from the early feudal society which Homer describes, that truth is still with us.

The figure of Cressida, as she appears in the literature of the Middle Ages, seems to have arisen from a confusion of Chryseis and Briseis. Her name, in fact, represents the Greek accusative form of Chryseis's name – Chryseida. Furthermore, Chryseis's father, the priest Chryses, has been confused with Calkas, the soothsayer, who accompanied the Greeks to Troy. Cressida, or rather, Criseyde (the French form of her name which Chaucer also used) first appears, as I have already said, in the *Roman de Troie* of Benoit de Saintmaur in the thirteenth century. For the medieval poets, the story of the siege of Troy, together with other matter taken from classical antiquity, notably the story of the siege of Thebes and the romantic account of the adventures of Alexander the Great formed part of the 'matter of Rome'. This was one of the three 'matters' – legendary material on which the medieval poets traditionally drew. The other two were the 'matter of Britain' (the whole Arthurian cycle) and 'the matter of France' (the legends of Charlemagne and his Paladins) but all three are in a certain sense matters of Rome and as such hark back to the imperial ideal, the idea of Christendom as a unity providentially ordained by the establishment of the Roman Empire. The kingship of Britain was supposed to have been established by Brutus the Trojan, the great grandson of Aeneas, the founder of Troy. Moreover, Arthur was Emperor and not merely King for he was supposed to have conquered the Roman Empire challenged by Lucius Iberus, consul or Emperor of Rome. Arthur's conquests, in fact, probably represent the ambitions of Henry II towards an Anjovin Empire which should include a unified Britain as well as his hereditary lands on the continent.

Arthur's imperial conquest, first told by Geoffrey of Monmouth, make him no less a valid Roman Emperor than Charlemagne who historically was crowned by the Pope as Caesar Augustus and did seek to establish a real European Christian unity. The basis for the legend of Arthur's imperial conquest would seem to be the historical bids made for the Roman Empire from a British base by Constantine and by the usurper Maximus who appeared in Welsh legend as Maxenwledig, Emperor of Rome, although the real Maximus, a Spanish adventurer, was, in fact, ignominiously defeated. These historical reminiscences seem to have been combined with primitive myths of Arthur as a hero who raids an Otherworld which is both a supernatural place and a western island thought of as a home of the dead. Lucius Iberus, in fact, is probably Lugh, the Irishman, an ancient Celtic god who appears in earlier Irish sagas and whose cult probably extended over the whole Celtic world; he must have been the titular divinity of Lyons or Lugdunum in Gaul. He may originally, in fact, have been a Lynx totem.

The story of the siege of Troy as it appeared to the Latin middle ages was different from that which we know from Homer. There was, it is true, a standard medieval school text book called *Homer* which was, in fact, a Latin abridgement of the Homeric material, but in late antiquity had appeared two accounts of the siege of Troy attributed to Dares the Phrygian and Dictys of Crete respectively. Both these fictitious authors claimed to be eyewitnesses of the Trojan war and were therefore taken to be more reliable than Homer. The works attributed to Dares and Dictys were, of course, spurious, though it has been suggested that, in some cases, their real authors may have drawn on early traditions which might even have gone back beyond Homer. Both these accounts are written from the Trojan point of view and hence it is, that, for the Middle Ages, the Trojans, who were, after all, through Aeneas, the ancestors of the Romans and of the founders of other European nations including Britain, are treated more sympathetically than the Greeks. This heroic view of the Trojans still subsists with us in such a common phrase as 'to work like a Trojan', and Hector, along with Julius Caesar and Alexander, was traditionally numbered among the nine Worthies.

Benoit's story of Troilus and Cressida begins with the parting of the lovers and the going of Criseyde to the Greek camp. It is her wooing by Diomede which forms the main love motif and this wooing of Diomede was transferred by Boccaccio to Troilus's wooing. Boccaccio's telling of the story of Troilus and Criseyde is the subject of his Italian poem *The Filostrato* which is Chaucer's immediate source. Chaucer attributes the story to 'Myn Auctor Lollius'. It was a common convention in the Middle Ages to give a fictitious source for one's work − a trick which Cervantes, incidentally, plays very effectively in *Don Quixote*. It is possible that the name Lollius, can be taken to mean 'big mouth' which is the actual meaning of the name Boccaccio. The medieval concept of authorship was not ours. A medieval work (Malory's is an extreme example) can at the same time be a translation and thoroughly original. This is likewise true of Chaucer, most notably in his *Troilus and Criseyde* with which my survey must really begin. The most important changes that Chaucer made was in the figure of Pandaro or Pandarus who is Boccaccio's invention, although Pandarus, prince of the Lithians, does occur in Homer. In Boccaccio's poem, Pandaro is not Criseyde's uncle but her cousin, a young man of Troilus's own generation. In Chaucer, he becomes a figure of humour and worldly-wisdom. The wooing becomes much more subtle than the light-hearted seduction described by Boccaccio.

The Criseyde of Chaucer (and of Boccaccio) is not like Shakespeare's Cressida, a young and inexperienced, sexually unaware girl, but a youthful widow. She is in an equivocal position in Troy since her father Calkas has defected to the Grecian camp. She is not without sexual experience and is aware of her own sexuality. This is very much brought out in the scene where Troilus first sees her, in church, as it happens. The story of Troilus's wooing with the assistance of Pandarus, is told by Chaucer with delicacy, frankness, humour, and, at one point, passion. There is nothing of such psychological subtlety, in narrative English as opposed to drama, for perhaps another 400 years.

Troilus and Criseyde, the title, has been described rightly as a psychological novel, but Chaucer calls it a tragedy. Medieval critical theory did not necessarily associate tragedy and comedy with dramatic presentation. It seems to have been thought that in antiquity, tragedies and comedies were mimed while someone read the narrative from a pulpit − this perhaps may represent an actual practice in late antiquity but we do not know. But Troilus and Criseyde is a truly tragic work. The medieval definition of tragedy which is given by Chaucer in the prologue to his *Monk's Tale*, is, to our way of thinking, perhaps a simplistic one. It is concerned basically with the concept of fortune's wheel. The hero begins in the state of felicity and is plunged by the turn of the wheel into one of misery. And this is true of the story of Troilus and Criseyde. It is mere chance that an exchange of prisoners is arranged so that Antinor, who has been captured by the Greeks, is to be returned to Troy and Criseyde sent to join her father Calkas in the Greek camp. This might have led to her felicity but, in fact, puts her in an even more unprotected position in the Greek camp where she is unable to resist the pressure put upon her by Diomede and becomes unfaithful to Troilus. She is not like Shakespeare's Cressida, a wanton, but her character, her very feminity and gentleness, has a fundamental flaw of weakness in it which does, in fact, make the story a tragedy in the sense that those of us who have read Aristotle (as Chaucer had not) can appreciate.

It is also an ironic tragedy. For me, one of the most poignant moments in the poem is where Troilus waits in vain by the gates for Troy for her return and then 'Troilus to Troy homeward he went'. In a way unusual in Chaucer, there is a sort of pun. We are made aware of the relationship of Troilus's name to that of the city of whose king he is the youngest son, and the equal doom which is prepared for both. But because the story of Troy is part of the 'matter of Rome', part of a greater plan of destiny, Troilus and Criseyde are actors in a drama whose full scope they cannot understand. When Troilus is finally slain, his spirit rises to the celestial spheres where it laughs seeing the folly of the human life that he has been leading and Chaucer begins one of his most famous passages, his exhortation to 'yonge, freshe folkes, he or she', to turn from the folly of earthly loves to Him who will 'falsen no man'.

The next poet to take up the story of Criseyde was the fifteenth century Scotsman, Robert Henryson, schoolmaster of Dunfermline. In his *Testament of Criseyde*, we are in a world subtly different from Chaucer's, the world of the very end of the Middle Ages. Europe had been devastated by plague, and, partly contingent on this, there was a general social disintegration. It was the age of the Peasant

Revolts and of the break-up of the old feudal structure of society. The 'dance macabre' or dance of death is one of the great images of the fifteenth century and variations of it pervade the poetry of that period. The greatest of European poets in that Age was Francois Villon whose work is in the form of a testament, a convention which was becoming widespread in English literature. There is a rather depressing period between the greatness of Chaucer and the first beginnings of the Renaissance proper in the work of Wyatt and Surrey. This is partly due to very rapid shifts in the language which caused metrical uncertainty. I suspect that this is directly connected with the break-up of the feudal system. It was impossible in practice for people to remain tied to the land. Populations, therefore, became mobile, speakers of different dialects mingled with a consequent breaking down of inflections. But in Scotland, though in this period it was equally torn as England by the feuding of the great nobles, the system was perhaps not so obviously breaking up and the heritage of Chaucer which for poets south of the border seemed almost too heavy a burden to take up, was fruitful in Scotland. Henryson's poem, as he tells us in his Prologue, arose directly out of his reading of Chaucer's *Troilus and Criscyde*, thinking that Chaucer had not told all, he attempted a sequel.

Criseyde, deserted by Diomede, returns to the house of her father Calkas, but there appears before her a procession of the seven planetary gods, each of which reproaches her for her lack of fidelity. Last comes Saturn, the bringer of melancholy, old-age and disease, and as a punishment, he smites her with leprosy. Shakespeare had perhaps this incident in mind when, in *Henry V*, Doll Tearsheet is described as a 'lazar kite of Cressid's kind'. Leprosy indicated here by the word 'lazar' is probably syphilis; the two diseases had some symptoms in common and were confused, but for Henryson writing in the middle of the fifteenth century, it is too early for syphilis. Criseyde joins a company of lepers bearing a begging bowl and a clapper. They wait at the gates of the city and Troilus comes through riding to his death. He gives alms, particularly to the young leper who is Criseyde whose face seems faintly familiar. Criseyde asks the others who it was who had given her the alms, for her disease apparently had blinded her, and they tell her it was Troilus. Then, stricken deeply with remorse, she makes her testament which gives its title to the poem and dies. It is a powerful poem though Henryson, the schoolmaster, judges Criseyde in a way which Chaucer and, I think Shakespeare, do not.

Shakespeare's *Troilus and Cressida* will, I suppose, for the majority of us, be the most familiar treatment of the figure I am dealing with. But Chaucer's poem is a masterpiece whilst Shakespeare's play is a problem. The editors of the first folio indeed seemed to be uncertain whether it should be regarded as a tragedy or a comedy. Its affinities are with the dark plays which Shakespeare wrote around about 1600 with *Hamlet* but more clearly with *Measure for Measure* and with *All's Well That Ends Well* — the dark comedies, or problem plays, as they have been called. The American critic Wylie Cypher in his very interesting book titled *Four Phases of Renaissance Style*, relates these plays, along with other works of roughly the same period in English — the tragedies of Webster and Ford, the early poetry of John Donne and others — with the mannerist movement in Renaissance painting. The mannerists had exhibited a kind of failure of nerve coming between the confidence of the high renaissance and the confidence of the baroque, oftern associated as it was with the triumph of the Counter-Reformation. In mannerist painting, not only are the actual images dark, but the figures are distorted — the design of the picture uncertain so that the centre of interest does not come where we would expect it to come, and something of the same happens in the poetry and drama I have cited. Wylie Cypher has pointed out that there is perhaps a relationship between this development in the arts and what was going on in the same period with regard to cosmology. Contrary to what is often said, the Copernican system, with its mathematical simplicity and elegance, was for the most part received gladly. The sun, the visible image of God, was now seen to be at the centre of the universe, and the earth, so far from being the lowest point of the cosmos, as the oldest Ptolomeic system postulated, is now taking part in the great dance with the other glorious planets around this central fire in mathematical circles. But it

was disturbing when Keppler showed that the planets moved
not in perfect circles but in elipses and confidence was only
to be restored with the new synthesis of Newton.

We may experience *Troilus and Cressida* as an anti-heroic
play. When I first read it in the thirties it seemed to me to
be astonishingly contemporary, and I think it may still do
so for the young with its sexual frankness and its anti-war
feeling. The down-grading of the Homeric heroes in this
piece is partly in the tradition of Dares and Dictys which
I have already alluded to.

But it is also partly deliberate for Shakespeare had read
Homer — Chapman's translation had recently appeared. It
is notable that Ulysses appears, perhaps for the first time
since Homer, as a noble and wise character, though of limited vision. He is quite incapable of understanding Troilus's
crisis, his problem over the division betwen Cressida and
her identity. For since Homer, in Euripides, for example,
and Sophocles and in Virgil, the character of Ulysses, the
supreme politician, had been progressively blackened. The
later Greeks and perhaps the Romans had learned to be
disillusioned with politicians. Incidentally, I cannot resist
mentioning, in passing, the remark of John Addington
Symonds that, of the two principal heroes of the Homeric
epic, Achilles represented the Greeks as they wished to see
themselves, while Ulysses is a picture of the Greeks as they
really were.

In a certain sense, the tragic centre of Shakespeare's play
is not in Troilus at all, but in Hector, the one truly noble
character (still in accordance with the medieval tradition).
On the last occasion I saw this play, the actor playing Hector
made the fatal mistake of treating this character also as a
mere braggart. The real tragedy is using the death of Hector.
Troilus, disillusioned, is left alive at the end of the play:

Sit, gods, upon your thrones, and smile at Troy!

Shakespeare, I am sure, knew Chaucer well, and he had been
haunted by the story of Troilus and Cressida at least since
the time when he wrote *The Merchant of Venice*:

The moon shines bright: in such a night as this,

When the sweet wind did gently kiss the trees
And they did make no noise, in such a night
Troilus methinks mounted the Troyan walls,
And sighed his soul toward the Grecian tents,
Where Cressid lay that night.

Cressida is mentioned here along with the tragic heroines of
ancient story – Dido, Medea and Thisbe. But in his own
play, which may possibly be a re-writing of an earlier one
dating from about the time that he composed *Romeo and
Juliet* (the two plays have some points in common), the
figures of Pandarus and Cressida are downgraded along with
the Homeric heroes and this must be deliberate. Pandarus
becomes merely the pander – the word is, of course, derived
from his name – he is a dirty-minded voyeur, but also a
kind of cousin of the nurse in *Romeo and Juliet*. The shift
is swift from innocence and inexperience to the girl who
makes eyes at all the soldiers as soon as she comes into
the Grecian camp. She succumbs to the seductive wiles of
Diomede with very little resistance yet her portrait is not
just that of a wanton. Her frailty is part of her humanity.
Sir Walter Raleigh, the Edwardian critic, interestingly relates
her to two other characters of Shakespeare – to Cleopatra
on the one hand and on the other to poor Doll Tearsheet:

Come, I'll be friends with thee, Jack: thou art going to
the wars; and whether I shall ever see thee again or no,
there is nobody cares'.

There is one final treatment of the story of Troilus and
Cressida and that is the re-working of Shakespeare's play by
John Dryden. At the period he did this re-working, Dryden
was becoming disenchanted with the rhymed heroic plays he
had championed a few years earlier and was beginning to
re-consider Shakespeare as a model from whom he might
learn. Two of his plays exhibit this renewed interest in
Shakespeare. One of them, *All For Love* is a masterpiece.
It is a re-telling of the story of Anthony and Cleopatra in
Dryden's own terms, but not in any sense an adaptation
of Shakespeare. It is, perhaps, the only English play which
can challenge comparison with the tragedies of Corneille and

Racine. *Troilus and Cressida, or, Truth Found Too Late*, is another matter altogether. It is not an original play but a re-working of Shakespeare. Many of Shakespeare's scenes and characters remain unaltered but new scenes are added and, as we shall see, the ending of the play is radically different. It may seem shocking that Dryden should have the temerity to re-write Shakespeare, but this was a common-place in his day. It should be remembered that adaptations of *King Lear*, the first one by Nahum Tate and then by David Garrick, were the normal stage versions until well into the nineteenth century. The actors and directors of that century, although they did not actually tamper with the text, except for a notorious Bowdlerisation of Shakespeare's language, were nevertheless almost equally free in the way that the plays were presented. The Beerbohm Tree's production of *King John*, for example, included a long scene, in dumb show, of the signing of Magna Carta, a document nowhere referred to in Shakespeare's text, and his *Hamlet* ended with the death of the prince and Horatio's words:

> Goodnight, sweet prince,
> And flights of angels sing thee to thy rest!

whereupon the audience was actually treated to the sound of the celestial choir.

When I consider recent productions of Shakespeare at our two most prestigious theatres, I do not think that we, in the twentieth century, have any reason to take a superior attitude to the nineteenth or eighteenth or seventeenth centuries. It could be argued that Dryden's version of *Troilus and Cressida* is a better acting play than Shakespeare's and it might be worth a revival, though I cannot think that anyone would have the courage to try this (an authentic Shakespearian *Troilus and Cressida* is too much of a rarity anyway.) Ulysses remains an important character in Dryden's version and, in fact, has the last word after the death of Troilus with a typical Restoration mono-logue advocating passive obedience to the monarch (a moral which there does not seem anything very much in the play to justify). But the character of Cassandra, one of Shakespeare's most striking creations, is cut. Dryden also added as a *tour de force*, a quarrel scene between Hector and his brother Troilus on the occasion of the decision of the Trojans to hand Cressida over to the Greeks. This scene is modelled on the quarrel between Brutus and Cassius in Shakespeare's *Julius Caesar*. But Dryden's imagination could not accept the paradox of the contradiction in Cressida's character. In effect she remains faithful to Troilus but on the advice of her father Calkas (Dryden also disliked priests) merely pretends to accept the advances of Diomede as a delaying tactic since Calkas intends to escape from the Grecian camp and to take his daughter with him. It is this deception which Troilus witnesses. Later on, when she learns of her repudiation by her lover, Cressida commits suicide. This finally convinces Troilus, but too late, of her truth. The suicide then, an innovation of Dryden's, is a deed that neither Chaucer's Criseyde nor Shakespeare's Cressida could have brought herself to, I think. As a function of the play, it is an heroic act. In Sir William Walton's opera, the librettist also makes Cressida commit suicide in the end. This suicide seems to me to be pointless and to savour too much of nineteenth-century romantic operatic cliche but I have not heard this work and must suspend judgement.

There is, as far as I know, no other re-telling of Cressida's story, though she does appear at the very end of Walter de la Mare's remarkable romance *Henry Brocken*. In this book, the hero rides out, as it were into the world of English literature where he encounters various familiar characters and at the very end of his pilgrimage he meets Chaucer's Criseyde, still longing for Troilus but still remembering Diomede.

I hope this tracing of the fortunes of Criseyde may have held some interest and it is not, I submit, wholly irrelevant to an understanding of Charles Williams's attitude to poetry.

Chapter Six

Arms and the Man: The Place of Beatrice in Charles Williams's Romantic Theology

Charles A. Huttar

One of the epiphanic moments alluded to in the title of Charles Williams's first novel, *Shadows of Ecstasy*, occurs when Philip Travers, holding aloof from the conversational 'chatter' surrounding him, glances at his fiancee, Rosamond Murchison.

> Sometimes he understood it [his friends' pleasure in small-talk], sometimes he didn't. But he never understood it as now, suddenly, he understood Rosamond's arm when she leant forward to pass a plate to her sister; somehow that arm always made him think of the Downs against the sky. There was a line, a curved beauty, a thing that spoke to both mind and heart; a thing that was there for ever. And Rosamond? Rosamond was like them, she was there for ever. It occurred to him that, if she was, then her occasional slowness when he was trying to explain something was there for ever. Well, after all, Rosamond was only human; she couldn't be absolutely perfect. And then as she stretched out her arm again he cried out that she was perfect, she was more than perfect; the movement of her arm was something frightfully important, and now it

61

was gone. He had seen the verge of a great conclusion of mortal things and then it had vanished. Over that white curve he had looked into incredible space; abysses of intelligence lay beyond it. And in a moment all that lay beyond it was the bright kitchen ... [1]

The beauty of a feminine arm was an image that captivated Williams over the better part of his writing lifetime, an objective correlative, so to speak, having, however, a significance far different from that of the arms imagined by T. S. Eliot's Prufrock, 'braceleted and white and bare/(but in the lamplight, downed with light brown hair!)' – 'arms that lie along a table, or wrap about a shawl'. The sensuousness of Eliot's image is deliberately univocal; the insecure Prufrock is threatened by the rank sexuality of the world which it represents to him. Williams's image is equally sensuous yet at the same time metaphysical in the strictest sense; the insecure Philip is somehow comforted and enlarged, not threatened, by its intimations of an unknown world of mighty but unseen realities. *Shadows of Ecstasy* was written about 1925,[2] and lines Williams wrote in the early 1940s shed light on the nature of this image. He speaks here, it appears, of an experience he himself has had.

> O arms, arms!
> everything sensual and metaphysical there
> rides together: ... ...
> ... I saw it so once;
> everything is in the body – source and measurement:
> I am the most material poet that lived
> since Lucretius ... [3]

Around the same time he wrote in a letter to his wife:

> But as Milton said of you –
> Grace was in all her steps, heaven in her eye.
> – O I babble & quote: 'tis nothing. I could still cry a little in your arms, kissing them first; they are the chains of heaven. Without such chains, heaven itself pales.[4]

Earlier he had given another fictional character, Palomides, an experience parallel to that of Philip Travers.

I saw the hand of the queen Iseult;
down her arm a ruddy bolt
fired the tinder of my brain
to measure the shape of man again;
  . . .
Blessed (I sang) the Cornish queen;
for till to-day no eyes have seen
how curves of golden life define
the straightness of a perfect line,
till the queen's blessed arm became
a rigid bar of golden flame
where well might Archimedes prove
the doctrine of Euclidean love.[5]

Like Philip's vision, that of Palomides is fleeting:

Relation vanished, though beauty stayed;
too long my dangerous eyes delayed
at the shape on the board, but voice was mute:
the queen's arm lay there destitute,
empty of glory . . . (p. 36)

There, however, the resemblance ends. Palomides responds to the loss of his vision in a way that is very nearly disastrous, bringing him (as we shall see) to the brink of damnation before a change of heart enables him to grasp the doctrine of love radiated by the queen's arm.

Palomides should at least not be blamed for obstinately rejecting something obvious. 'The wonder, the thrill, of a shoulder or hand,' Williams wrote in a review published in 1939, 'awaits its proper exploration. At present we [the institutional church] have simply nothing to say to anyone in a state of exaltation, watching for 'meaning' . . . The hungry sheep look up for metaphysics, the profound metaphysics of the awful and redeeming body, and are given morals . . .'[6]

The challenge of these texts to us in the present study is threefold. Though much has been written about Williams's concept of the so-called Dantean or Beatrician experience and much too about his materialism − on both of which these extracts form a representative mini-anthology − his

views on these matters are not yet as widely understood as
could be wished. Therefore our first task is to clarify this
aspect of Williams's thought. In the process of doing so, we
will look closely at some of Williams's Arthurian poems, and
thus the study should lead secondarily to new interpretative
insights on these difficult texts. Third is the closely related
question of the origins and modifications of Williams's
ideas, for though the usual critical way of talking about
it seems to suppose a Dantean source, Williams himself
wrote to a correspondent, 'I developed my own view of
romantic love by myself, and not through reading Dante.'[7]
Yet Williams did make the Dantean link, to the point finally
of manifesting in a substantial study[8] how central it had
become in his thought. We will ask, then, when and how his
views developed and what new insights his study of Dante
contributed. Such an inquiry, touching as it necessarily does
on biographical matters, will be greatly aided by new information which has only recently become part of the public
record on Williams's life, and may in turn contribute to a
better understanding concerning the questions raised by the
new documents.

II

What is destructive to Prufrock in his imagining of women's
arms is his inability to permit them to betoken anything
beyond a threatening sexuality. His state of mind reflects –
accurately enough as concerns *one* spirit of the age – a
despair of transcendence. But other contemporary visions
bring us closer to Williams's view of the matter, and Lawrence
and Yeats are worth quoting here because Williams himself
quoted them appreciatively; their phrases evidently were
absorbed into his mind. D. H. Lawrence, poet of sexuality as a vehicle of transcendence, wrote words that very
nearly (but for 'blood') might have been Williams's: 'The
soft outstretching of her hand was like the whispering of
strange words into the blood, and as she fingered a book
the heart watched silently for the meaning.'[9] Yeats, a votary
of the spirit (and a fellow-initiate with Williams in the
Rosicrucian mysteries),[10] spoke of love more wistfully as

an agonizingly inadequate approach to a spiritual world to which it invites us:

> All that ever loved
> Have loved that way — there is no other way.

> Yet never have two lovers kissed but they
> Believed there was some other near at hand,
> And almost wept because they could not find it.[11]

Forgael, the second speaker in this dialogue from Yeats's play, goes on to insist that 'What the world's million lips are thirsting for/Must be substantial somewhere.' Williams's epigraph for his first book of poetry, *The Silver Stair*, ended with the first quotation, as if to make his own claim more affirmative by contrast: a claim, based on the doctrine of love expressed in his sonnet cycle, that the transcendent 'other way' is not, after all, inaccessible.[12]

Williams's mature Romantic Theology[13] is rooted in the principle that 'if the doors of perception were cleansed every thing would appear to man as it is, infinite';[14] in its Beatrician aspect, this principle would refer more particularly to every *person*. One way of cleansing the doors of perception is being in love, which gives one a double vision of the beloved, seeing through his or her ordinary humanness to the glory of a restored *Imago Dei* in that person. This does not mean some ethereal substitute but real, corporal beauty. 'The body of the beloved appears vital with holiness; the physical flesh is glorious with sanctity — not her sanctity, but its own.'[15] But also implicated in this revelation is an awareness of the Deus behind the Imago.[16] Thus, one's perception is enhanced both of the beloved and of existence itself, in what C. S. Lewis (p. 116) regards as a recovery of prelapsarian awareness. Such epiphanies, while not the whole of the Beatrician experience, are its necessary starting point and continuing nourishment. For distinction's sake we can usefully apply to them the term 'Beatrician moment.' Besides its immediate emotional and perhaps physical impact, the Beatrician moment produces in the beholder two effects, intellectual and moral: the inchoate 'revelation of an "unknown mode of being"'[17] and an infusion of humility and *caritas*. In both respects, a 'new life' has been imparted.

In another sense, however, this *vita nuova* is only beginning, and what characterizes the 'Beatrician experience' as a whole is the role of the beloved in the lover's pilgrimage toward eventual salvation – 'a state in which those first Beatrician encounters, ... full of such a thrilling *tremendum*, seem almost paltry ... compared to the massive whole of single and exchanged Love.'[18] This is the state to which Beatrice has brought Dante by the end of the *Divine Comedy*. The 'beatitude' whose irruption is announced to Dante at the age of nine (*Vita Nuova* 2) is thus a double reference, to the blessedness of that first Beatrician moment and to the bliss of heaven which is the end of the experience.[19]

In his prose and poetry Charles Williams presents several characters who undergo, or who inspire, Beatrician experiences. The latter – for example (from the quotations at the beginning of this article), Rosamond Murchison, Queen Iseult, and Mrs Michal Williams – may be referred to as instances of the 'Beatrician character.' This term, however, has been used rather indiscriminately and hence confusingly in the critical literature, so that we must now turn briefly to a clarification of it. It is important to distinguish the Beatrician character from another bringer of salvation, the Christ-figure, though these two types have some similarities, and to complicate matters some of Williams's fictional characters belong to both types at once. But one's relationship to Beatrice is based on being in love; to Christ, on being loved, with a love that goes beyond desire and even beyond sympathy to identification. Beatrice is passive: the lover receives something from her[20] (revelation, strength of purpose, salvation); Christ is active and gives the other something. The salvation known *through* Beatrice begins with knowledge and involves the lover in acts of the will; it is a salvation to be 'worked out.' The salvation given *by* Christ begins with faith and requires the recipient to accept passively – 'it is God which worketh in you' – and to act not reciprocally but in a new direction, becoming Christ, in turn, for someone else.

The Beatrician experience does not depend on Beatrice's returning the love, or being aware that she has given anything, or even herself possessing the knowledge which is revealed to the lover through her: she is a God-*bearer*. In Williams's novels, the Beatrician characters in this sense are Rosamond in *Shadows of Ecstasy* and Damaris in *The Place of the Lion*.

The Christ-figures who give themselves to others and vicariously for others, quite apart from the others' 'being in love,' are Chloe in *Many Dimensions*, Sybil in *The Greater Trumps*, Peter, Margaret, and especially Pauline in *Descent into Hell*, and Lester in *All Hallows' Eve* in her relationship with Betty. The idea of their being a medium of revelation is not totally absent, just as in Christ the Father is seen, but Sybil is the only character of those six in whom Williams emphasizes that aspect of the Christ-figure.

There are other characters, however, in whom the two figures are fused. When Beatrice returns love, she adds to her passive role an active one which, in varying degrees, resembles the redemptive act of Christ. Sometimes the return of love is virginal, as with Beatrice herself in the *Divine Comedy* and both Taliessin and Dindrane in Williams's *The Region of the Summer Stars*.[21] More often, for Williams, it includes the full range of love that belongs to a successful marriage, or to a relationship which is in the process of becoming a successful marriage. Examples in the fiction of this Christ-who-is-still-Beatrice or Beatrice-who-has-become-or-is-becoming-Christ are Isabel in *Shadows of Ecstasy* (in whom the element of identification is emphasized: see the last half of chapter 10), Barbara in *War in Heaven*, Nancy in *The Greater Trumps* (and Henry too, in the scene where he is the Hanged Man), and Lester in *All Hallows' Eve* in her relationship with Richard.[22]

Examining the paradigmatic Beatrician experience in detail, we find that Philip Travers and Palomides each illustrate several of its aspects, but not many of the same ones. Philip's vision of glory in Rosamond's arm is a Beatrician moment in which transcendent 'beauty' and transcendent meaning issue their call to his very mundane self. It involves an intellectual awakening: having 'suddenly . . . understood' her arm, he knows what 'abysses of intelligence' still beckon him. The moral aspect is present as well: confronted with a sort of mental double exposure, his sense of Rosamond-as-infinite jostled by his realistic memory that she has annoying faults, he is obedient to the love born of that moment (and previous such moments)[23] and refuses to be annoyed. Only later, when we have read on to pp. 60–2 and 134–6, do we appreciate the magnitude of this victory in view of the undoubted shallowness, bad temper, and general unworthiness of Rosamond. But Philip's love, strong enough to keep a firm 'repose and certainty' (p. 101) and even to endure a snub by Rosamond comparable to Beatrice's refusal to speak to Dante, is nurtured by further Beatrician moments founded on the mere memory of her beauty (pp 76–7) and of the dimly glimpsed reality 'of which Rosamond was a shape and a name' (pp. 84–5; cf pp. 99, 102). One has the sense that, entirely without any intention on Rosamond's part of playing such a role, Philip is growing spiritually and she is somehow responsible.

Quite different from Philip's situation is that of the knight Palomides, who appears not as a lover but as a stranger. In the first of two poems devoted to him, 'The Coming of Palomides,' he is given the Beatrician vision of Queen Iseult almost upon first seeing her. He is a master of 'music-craft'[24] and of rational system in general. He also, as a Saracen, 'denies the Incarnation'; for, explains Lewis (p. 124), Islam 'stands for all religions that are afraid of matter and afraid of mystery, for all misplaced reverences and misplaced purities that repudiate the body and shrink back from the glowing materialism of the Grail.' Palomides journeys from the domain of the scimitar with its 'sharp curved line' (line 7) — the enforcing rule of law and also the analyzing reason which defines and divides asunder but has no place for Coinherence. He knows well the lessons of reason, 'the measurement of man / that Euclid and Archimedes showed' (lines 2–3), but beyond the Pyrenees he encounters an offense: not a single line but a doubled figure — crosses, in fact, everywhere in Gaul and Italy. Here he confronts new 'gospels trigonometrical' which 'measured the height of God-in-man'; in other words, Trinity and Incarnation, classic expressions of Coinherence. Interested in neither 'magic' nor 'mystery,' he decides to travel on to a country where they have been dispelled (he supposes) by Roman civilization: 'Julius pierced through the tale of ghosts,/and opened the harbours of the north.'

But a surprise awaits him in Cornwall in the form of 'an outstretched hand'. The light flaming from the queen's arm shakes his belief in the dissecting reason, firing his mind 'to measure the shape of man again' (and 'measure' is now a musical as well as a geometrical term). The paradox that 'curves of golden life define/the straightness of a perfect line' makes him wonder if the line of the scimitar blade was not, after all, imperfect. The one-dimensional geometry of pure reason may define laws, but not the ultimate law of existence. 'The letter killeth but the spirit giveth life,' and it takes 'curves of golden life' to go beyond Euclid (was Williams thinking of the post-Euclidean curved universe?), beyond legalism, and discover 'a perfect line.' For the ultimate law is love −

> till the queen's blessed arm became
> a rigid bar of golden flame
> where well might Archimedes prove
> the doctrine of Euclidean love.

Palomides sees

> fiery circles leap
> round finger-point and shoulder; arc
> with arc encountering strikes a spark
> wherefrom the dropping chords of fire
> fashion the diagram of desire.
> There flames my heart, there flames my thought,
> either to double points is caught;
> lo, on the arm's base for a sign,
> the single equilateral trine!

The imagery now turns to triangles, and for the next verse paragraph 'intellectual power' sees 'triple angles, triple sides,' the suggestion in 'the queen's arm's blissful nakedness' of 'unions metaphysical,' a 'unity' that is community 'triply obedient, each to twain . . . in the true equilateral ease.'

And O what long isosceles
from finger-point and shoulder flies
towards me, and distant strain my eyes
along the twin roads, there to prove
the doctrine of Euclidean love;
let the queen's grace but yield her hand
to be by such strong measure spanned —

With that punctuation, Palomides's song 'suddenly' breaks off, for he has made a near-fatal mistake. 'Down the arm of the queen Iseult/quivered and darkened an angry bolt,' and 'the sign withdrew.' Palomides has been confronted with mystery, he even recognized it as mystery and as good, yet by a lifetime of intellectual habit he is unprepared to respond except by seeking to bring it, too, under his control. The decision he makes is to turn his back on the effort required truly to understand 'Euclidean love' (line 98). In the Beatrician moment Love has offered itself to him, but he can, or will, know love only as possession. 'I caught her arm in a mesh of chords,' he boasted earlier (line 52). Now he asks the queen to 'yield her hand' to be 'spanned' by his craft, his 'strong measure' — as if he would comprehend the light that shineth in darkness. But the arm eludes his craft, and all Palomides succeeds in doing is making the arm 'destitute,/empty of glory.' The trinitarian vision shines a moment longer, growing more distant, and is gone.

Through his fault, not Iseult's, and not of its own mere transiency, Palomides's Beatrician moment passes. Once 'the queen's identity' (line 10) or 'substance' (line 132) has been sundered from the queen's earthly presence he cannot — as Philip could — continue to believe in the mystery of their essential unity: 'Relation vanished' (line 111). Beautiful she remains, but no longer infinite. The desire to possess implied already a denial of her infinity; the failure to possess can only transform the Beatrician energy into a jealousy that feeds his pride, obsesses his life, and severs him from the chivalric community, as is shown in the second Palomides poem, 'Palomides Before His Christening.'[25] His one Beatrician moment abides in his memory — not for bliss, however, but stinging (because he remembers it as humiliation): 'bees buzzed down Iseult's arm in my brain' (line 25). Life is essentially competitive, a quest to win by force of arms what he thinks will restore to him the queen's favor. When he finally catches the beast he has hunted, however, through exhaustion of both body and spirit he lets it escape; and this seeming failure is followed by another vision, not Beatrician this time but nevertheless holding the beginnings of redemption. Not Iseult's beautiful arm he sees, but bones, arm bones and thigh bones 'loving' each other (line 57), 'longing' to be wedded together (so the phrase 'bone of its bone' suggests). 'Spirit' is present also – the whole scene that Palomides imagines evokes Ezekiel's vision in the valley, yet it lacks the prophet's triumph. Palomides's ingrained rationalism will not yet allow a full union of body/'skeleton' with 'spirit' (nor let him admit that the cross-figure has any special significance – 'the Chi-Ro is only a scratching like other scratchings'). Still, the vision has awakened his imaginative life to the point where, upon remembering something Dinadan once said to him, he can recognize his spiritual danger on the brink of hell, come to himself, and determine to be baptized.[26] This decision marks his acceptance both of the materialism of Christianity, in the sacramental rite, and of humility ('why not look a fool before everyone?') – the lesson he had rejected at the palace in Cornwall. But he has not yet quite absorbed the other Beatrician virtue, love; not till he relinquishes the negative desire to possess can he begin on the positive side. There are signs of such a change in his new respect for Dinadan, the 'lord without a lady' (line 98). Palomides, then, relates to Williams's Beatrician doctrine on three points – he is granted the 'moment,' he flunks the 'experience,' but he illustrates finally the fact that salvation may be possible by a different way.[27]

Even Philip and Palomides together do not give us the whole range of the Beatrician experience, of which another important aspect is the physical union of the lovers. It is not essential, of course: Dante did without it and was even married to someone else, and Williams's Taliessin represents the choice of a virginal mode of response to the Beatrician vision. But Williams equally, in keeping with his incarnational theology, emphasized the rightful place of the body as the focal object of the Beatrician moment[28] and exalted the sacrament of marriage as 'a unique opportunity of following [the Dantean] way.'[29]

One of the three Grail knights is a married man, whose addresses to his wife make up two of the poems in *Taliessin*. 'Bors to Elayne: on the King's Coins' (pp. 42–5) presents the married state as an epitome of the City. Bors has just come from the court, where the new mintage of coins has been perceived to hold both promise and danger for the life of society, the political economy; at home, he looks upon Elayne in her role at the centre of the household economy, her 'hair ... the colour of corn' (line 9), her hands distributing bread as an act of domestic love. Here ordinary life, conducted in accord with the Beatrician vocation to virtue, becomes sacramental, redeeming neutral things, whether coins or bread, so that it is their promise not their danger which is fulfilled. The concluding question about the coins – 'can the dead king's head live?' (line 101) – echoes Ezekiel's question about the dry bones and thus hints that the answer must be affirmative. 'Can the law live?' Bors also asks (line 100) – yet another link with the themes of Palomides – and the answer is that it depends on how well the citizens give it life by means of their faithfulness in love.

In 'Bors to Elayne: The Fish of Broceliande' (pp. 24–26) the emphasis is more on the sexual aspect of the conjugal state. Bors brings Elayne a gift, a fish he has caught in a stream. It is a memento of a song he heard about the mysterious sunken forest of Broceliande. The 'song meant all things to all men, and you to me' (line 9). Song and wife are identified in his mind as the vehicles of an elusive but all-important glimpse of ultimate meaning, of which both fish and forest are also symbols. 'Your arm,' he tells Elayne in words reminiscent of Philip Travers's reverie, is 'the piercing entry to a land' safe from mortality (lines 16 ff.). 'No net can catch' this fish' intensely real, it is nevertheless a mystery beyond rationalism. Dropped into her hand,

> it darts up the muscles of the arm, to swim
> round the clear boulder of the shoulder, stung with
> spray,

and down the cataract of the backed spine leaps
into bottomed waters at once clear and dim,
where nets are fingered and flung on many a day;
yet it slides through the mesh of the mind and sweeps
back to its haunt in a fathomless bottomless pool.

The last two lines signal that the Beatrician moment is
over − yet not over, for the fish has been absorbed into
the permanent Beatrician experience which Bors knows in
Elayne through their marriage. There is, thus, one way after
all in which the fish can be − if not possessed, at least sum-
moned. Its 'name,' an anagram of spirit and sense,' can be
known (though it be the ultimate in folly to think so). 'A
twy-nature only' can call it forth, that is, the one flesh of
husband and wife − but also the incarnate God-man, the
grand antitype to which all lesser instances of Coinherence
answer. The fish, traditionally a monogram for Christ who
definitively links 'spirit and sense,' symbolizes in addition
two other things: the sexual consummation of the sacrament
of marriage and the bodily resurrection implicit in the sacrament of baptism. It leaves in its wake 'double tracks':

one, where the forked dominant tail
flicks, beats, reddens the smooth plane
of the happy flesh; one, where the Catacomb's stone
holds its diagram over the happy dead
who flashed in living will through the liquid wish.

III

The system which has just been described and illustrated
did not spring into being complete in Williams's mind
nor continue unchanged. Some of its key elements were
there already by his early twenties, but the explicit identification with Dante was a later refinement, out of which
emerged new emphases that became prominent in the final
formulations.

Only in the context of Williams's life can this course
of development be understood, however; to approach it

as a merely literary or academic phenomenon would be a mistake. The subtle interplay of art and life is well recognized: it is essential to the artist's integrity that what he creates has a stamp of confirmation from his own experience – yet one's experiences are often understood, and sometimes even fashioned, according to paradigms of meaningful behaviour that are made available among one's real-life acquaintance or else through some art medium – journalism, biography, history, cinema, theatre, novels, poetry, and so on. One's experience of life, then, is in some sense a creation already, a deliberate or unconscious making, and not mere raw, unworked data. To trace the development of Williams's Dantean system involves us in several questions that cannot be fully answered. To what extent are his romantic convictions made firm through the validation found in his experiences? But to what extent was his understanding of those experiences shaped by the theoretical patterns – or even the experiences themselves caused to occur through the imitating of theoretical models? On the other hand, to what extent did those particular models attract him because they 'fit' his prior experience? So the questions can go on, one inside another, and they are worth asking, even if the secrets finally elude us, because some better understanding may in the process be divined.

Further, they are essential questions on this particular inquiry because the issue was a central one for Williams himself. It was important to him that the Beatrician experience possess some universality; not that all lovers must encounter love in that way, but, first, that Dante himself have written of a real experience, not just made a fashionable fiction, and, second, that his experience not be unique, for then it could hardly be generalized into a theology. 'It appears that this is an experience which has occurred to a large number of young people besides Dante.'[30]

There is strong evidence that Williams could say this because he considered himself one of that 'large number.' But only in retrospect, it seems, did he give his experience that precise shape. At the time he met his 'Beatrice,' Michal (*nee* Florence Conway), in St Albans around Christmas 1908 and fell in love, aged about 22,[31] he had other guides to help him give words to his unfamiliar experience.

Words he gave in abundance: a sequence of eighty-two sonnets[32] in which is traced the uneven progress of Love. The genre may be Elizabethan, but the implied narrative is not that of a self-assured lover's success in winning the lady; rather, of Love's conquest over *his* doubts, fears, and hesitations. The sequence begins with 'the predestined lover, ignorant of love' (Sonnet 1) who inquires from outside about this phenomenon but then suddenly must come to terms himself with 'the power of Love' (9) encountered in the woman's person:

> All breaking and all making of all laws
>> Surely from one face hath looked forth on me,
>> Who have not uttered nor my heart hath known
> Desire of woman.

Finally, he makes his commitment to this new master in a 'profession of love' (15), which concludes Book I but is only the start of a journey to deeper understanding. The road is not straight. There are 'Love's enemies' to cope with − Mammon (29), Time (31), and even The Cross (33). The lover enters a stage of diffidence and fear. He is convinced 'that we know not yet what it is indeed to love' (38). The claim of the body to its proper role in this experience evokes both desire and dread (40−2): the prospect of sexual union is at once exalting, as the initiation to a world of conjugal joy, and threatening, a kind of death of the lover in his separateness:[33]

> a little door,
> narrow, low-arched, and carven thereabove:
> 'Through me by losing shall a man find love.' (44)

He sees two ways of serving Love, through celibacy or through marriage (45), and struggles between them, still unable to accept that 'alleys cool/Of corporal pleasaunce' can coexist with 'gardens spiritual' in the marital relationship (46). Finally, however, these doubts are resolved, and he declares himself to the woman as a suitor (56). He repents of what he now sees as the shallowness of his earliest love experience; he has realized that it is a fatal error to

suppose (as Williams was to put it later) 'that it is sufficient
to have known that state of love.'[34] Having made the descent
into this hell he is now able gradually, moving on through
the sixteen sonnets of Book III, becoming aware of the pain
of love and the 'Passion of Love' (73–8: a phrase rich in
ambiguities),[35] to grow somewhat toward an understanding
of the higher dimensions of the love experience. Finally he
can celebrate 'in the fullness of Love' (82) — though in fact
there is much yet to learn.

Already in these sonnets several features of Williams's
mature system of Romantic Theology are present. The
woman's physical beauty — 'the moving hands, the neck's
smooth bend ... the wondrous head, the body's grace'
(50) — is to the lover a vehicle of transcendent awareness.
'All breaking and all making of all laws' is in her face (9),
her 'serene presence is/The world's epitome and genesis'
(16). Through her there is access to the divine (17); 'for
every man a woman holds the secret of salvation' (22).
The young man's life has been irresistibly invaded by a
new master, Love, and, since he knows that the God Love
is one, not divided (34), it must be the Christ already known
in worship and devotion who is thus laying claim to his
life — summoning him as he had Matthew to 'leave all and
follow Me' (43), repeating his gospel warning that only in
losing one's life can one save it (44). These references are
not mere clever analogies; the god Love *is* Christ. If, as the
lover believes, marriage is a sacrament, he may anticipate
married life as a genuinely religious experience.

Who were the guides who had taught Williams to say
such things about love? We cannot know when he first met
Dante's Beatrice; we must, unless it were quite incredible,
respect his own statement that she did not enter into the
making of these beliefs, nor would significantly for another
eight years at least. The task of proof reading introduced
him to the *Divine Comedy* in 1910.[36] By 1913, perhaps
sooner, he had pasted in the front of his notebook of
Arthurian studies a passage from the *Vita Nuova* which
not only seems to declare his own 'self-dedication to a
life's work' as a poet but also suggests that Michal was
to be his Beatrice in the sense of inspiring that work;[37] but
that is only one small, separable part of the Dantean love

system. Michal Williams gives a partial list of the books and authors that were frequent companions in the early days of their courtship.[38] Dante is not included.

John Donne and Coventry Patmore are, and they could easily account for the ideas in *The Silver Stair*.[39] Donne, who had written of his wife that 'here the admyring her my mind did whett/To seeke thee God'[40] and on whose love poetry sometimes falls a hushed sense of holy attainment in the union of the sexes, and Patmore, whose Catholic sensibility had explored the sacramental nature of marriage in all its aspects with astonishing boldness, were among the acknowledged doctors of this theology of love and marriage.[41] Patmore himself had drawn heavily on Dante (going beyond him as regards the association of sexual love with the theology of the Incarnation), and thus it would be an easy step later for Williams to assimilate to his system new elements direct from Dante when the time came to do so.

Despite these debts, however, Williams insisted on his originality. 'I developed my own view of romantic love by myself.' Though recognizing Patmore's mighty achievement, Williams felt that in some respects he had gone beyond it.[42]

Williams's next three volumes of poetry touch on a variety of subjects, but where they deal with love they continue to develop the ideas found in *The Silver Stair*. In *Poems of Conformity*,[43] dedicated to Michal and published in the year of their marriage, he now can write of a love which has deepened and matured over the years,[44] but the beloved is still the epitome 'of all beauty' and the embodiment for him of transcendent principles (Sonnet 10, p. 40) and 'lend[s] the whole creation/An awful holiness' (p. 50). Although like Philip's Rosamond she has enumerable faults (p. 37), she is his Zion (pp. 40, 52–4, 70), his avenue of salvation (p. 33) – as he in turn, according to his doctrine, is hers (p. 127). In this spiritual achievement the lovers' bodies prove instrumental: 'Symbol and dogma that sufficed/Dully the story of the Christ/Grey living in a kiss' (p. 126). Yet body alone has not done this, but the sacramental union of flesh and spirit[45] in a knot so intricate with 'implications' that neither can be given priority:

Of her body or her ghost
Who knows which is native most?
My soul to her lordly face
Fac me salvum ever prays;
Yet my most of earth delights
In her soul's more dainty flights.
Which for wear did th' other don
To bring down salvation?[46]

Another poem, where we read, 'Instincts, our bodies' depths
that dredge,/Grow teachers of salvation,' concludes with
an audacious echo of the Athanasian Creed – 'Love, of
the reasonable soul/And human flesh subsisting!' – and
indeed is presented as a 'Commentary' on that text (pp.
60–1). Likewise characteristic of the system of Romantic
Theology as Williams has developed it to this point is an
identification of Michal with the Church (pp. 47, 51, 67–71)
and the Virgin Mary (pp. 44, 56),[47] and of their love with
Christ in his earthly career from birth through death and resurrection (pp. 72–7). For one of the themes of this book,
continuing from *The Silver Stair*, is the expected death of
love – betrayed in the course of day-to-day living by such
realities as anger or desire (pp. 45–6); yet equally the poet
has faith in its resurrection.

In *Divorce*[48] the themes of Romantic Theology continue,
though with some change in emphasis. The glorious vision
is still with him: he remembers how her image gave 'form'
to the 'unruled chaos' storm' of his 'dispersed heart';
'the gospel [her] bright forehead told,' her 'eyes' new
covenant,' he has held 'long hid within' (p. 58). Her
body is a cathedral, 'more shining, mortared with diviner
stuff' than any stone house of worship however 'wonderful' (p. 71). She is the epitome of creation (p. 78),
the Virgin Mary (pp. 78–80), the sacred Host of the
Eucharist (pp. 26–7, 73–4).[49] Marriage has brought, in
exchange for the glory of first love, deeper satisfactions:
'Ah, sweet procrastinator, thou/Hast kept the good wine
until now!' (p. 57). Yet more often this collection strikes
the opposite note. Williams stresses the loss of love to
such a degree that one critic speaks of *Divorce* as a
book focused on the Negative Way – 'Neither is this

Thou' — rather than the Affirmative.[50] This logic should not be pressed too far, however, for *Divorce* is still centred in the romantic experience, which in Williams's thought from the beginning, as we have noted, had somehow to embrace loss. A. M. Hadfield, while careful not to confuse poetry with autobiography, presents a cogent discussion of these darker poems (*Introduction*, pp. 50–3) as reflecting both a basic pessimism in Williams's personality, not limited to matters of love, and also a difficult time in his marriage. She finds in more than one poem a sense of 'defeat of the very capacity for married relationship itself' (p. 52). Her conclusion, however, that for all its disturbances Charles's and Michal's marriage was 'a living one' (p. 53) nicely echoes Anne Ridler's description of it as 'a tempestuous and a true one' (p. xviii).

One may conjecture, as a possible source of tension, a disinclination on Michal's part always to play the roles — even, one may say, to assume the identity — being created for her in her husband's mental exercises. His mind revelled in abstraction, hers did not, and what in his view was doing her high honour may have seemed to her more like being reduced to theology, which one would naturally resist — especially if the theology was offbeat enough to not only arouse one's scepticism but also give colour of orthodoxy to the resistance. Such an attitude would account for her 'delay' described in the 'Epilogue' to *Poems of Conformity*:

Still must that daring heart delay
To find in me, in me, the way,
In me the truth, the life;
And where alone it hath its peace
Must still invent and still increase
Its consummating strife.[51]

It appears that she is, understandably, refusing to be absorbed into his intellectual system. Such reluctance may be part, at least, of what he refers to in 'After Marriage' (*Divorce*, p. 59) as her 'withdraw[ing]' her presence and thus returning him to the 'pain' and 'chaos' of the time before the vision of her had wrought creatively in him.

To take up such biographical questions in the context of reading his poetry seems a valid and even necessary procedure, in the light of what Williams wrote to a friend near the end of his life: 'Nobody will understand my relations with my wife who has not given the full place to that early verse.'[52] Further, we recall Williams's basic premise that it was important to view Dante's writing as rooted in real experience – and the same principle he would apply to his own. Still, it is important to keep in mind the distinction between the beloved as a construct of Williams's theological imagination and the beloved as she was in real life.

Looking ahead, we may anticipate these developments as we continue to trace Williams's ideas about love: (1) personal experiences in the late 1920s and beyond will force him to give still greater attention to the darker side of Romantic Theology, (2) Dante will provide new paradigms enabling him to understand these experiences and to redeem them from utter negativity, and (3) the flowering of his mature expression of Beatrician theology will run parallel with a revitalization of his marriage to Michal. We must first, however, conclude our survey of his earlier writings and the version of Romantic Theology they embrace.

By the time of *Windows of Night*,[53] his fourth book of poetry, a son has been born. Domestic life seems more satisfying, perhaps (as Mrs Hadfield suggests) because Williams has reduced his idealistic demands.[54] There is a greater variety of subject-matter in this book, and while several poems 'reveal ... innate and unrelenting pessimism,'[55] that mood is associated with other matters than love. But 'in a world of shadows and lurking dread, marriage becomes an assurance.'[56] Toward Michal he is tender and affectionate, with recognition of what she means to him – 'In a world insignificant thou significant wholly' (p. 126) – and testimony to the continuing recurrence of a vision which could 'Nimbly transmute a cheek or hand/Into a bright eternal thing,/A landmark on our wayfaring' (p. 38). 'Night Poems' I and II (pp. 38–42) present a concept of the oneness of mature lovers, as in the phrase 'our twined souls,' in a tone of tranquil triumph reminiscent of Donne's 'The Undertaking.'

In the meantime, Williams had written his first treatise on Romantic Theology, the never-published 'Outlines.'[57] The ideas presented there were essentially the ones already embodied in the poetry we have surveyed: that Love is Christ, and that the conjugal life is a form of the imitation of Christ – including pain, death, and renewed life – by which ordinary people are transmuted into a sacrament of divine glory. There is a sense in which sexual love is a communion of 'the Real Presence of the Most Sacred Body.'[58] But such a life is difficult, frequently endangered. To be aware of the ideal is no guarantee of attaining or keeping it.

These ideas must still have been very much in his mind while the manuscript of 'Outlines of Romantic Theology' went around the publishing houses, as Williams turned his hand to fiction and wrote the passage with which we began this study.

Dante, though not wholly absent, is still very much in the background. Williams knows the *Vita Nuova* by now; he 'looks at' it in 'Outlines,' Mrs Hadfield tells us (p. 44) but without indicating what difference, if any, that look may have made; and earlier, in *Divorce* (not in a love poem, however) he had clearly referred to it in the phrase, 'the Burning Heart of Dante' (pp. 32, 34). Yet 'Outlines' seems to have little to say about the glorious vision and the invasion of Love as a master, ideas which are central in the Beatrician system. The name of Rosamond in *Shadows of Ecstasy* suggests the rose imagery which is prominent in Beatrice's Paradise – but it equally suggests the symbol of Eternal Beauty in Yeats's rose poems of 1893 (including 'The Rose of the World'), some of which had become old favourites; however, I think both these associations represent false trails. The primary association of the name Rosamond, as the one through whom her lover Philip glimpses divine glory, is more probably the Zoharic identification of Shekinah as 'the rose of the world,' as recorded in a book Williams is known to have studied carefully.[59] In connection with Rosamond there is, however, a more credible allusion to Dante.

She was a kind of centre, and all the others vibrated in peculiar poses on the circumference. She herself had no circumference, Philip thought, ignorant of how closely he was striving after St Augustine's definition: 'God is a circle, whose centre is everywhere and His circumference nowhere.' (p. 36)

Williams was to cite this aphorism again much later,[60] remarking on its close similarity to a line in *Vita Nuova* 12. Here Love rebukes Dante for a life not truly lived in the 'center' where all points of the 'circumference' are equidistant. I believe the same perceived parallel is already implied in *Shadows of Ecstasy*, for Philip's situation is similar to Dante's. He is made aware of the idea of centricity and at the same time made to realize that he is ec-centric.

Still, despite these glimpses of Williams's growing knowledge of and interest in Dante, his system in 1925 was fundamentally Patmorean, with some additions and special emphases of his own (reflecting other influences). Not yet was it a theology that could claim the epithet 'Beatrician.'

In the *Vita Nuova* Williams had read of Dante's second, rival love; he was soon to encounter it as part of his own experience. In his early poetry he had taught that the loss of love may be inevitably a part of the whole experience, and in Dante he had found this loss related first in Beatrice's snub and then in her death; but not, apparently, until he himself felt a comparable shock did he appreciate the potential of the Dantean experience as a precise paradigm for his own.

Even at first, when at forty he fell in love with a young woman of twenty-five, a fellow-employee at the Press, he thought not in terms of Dante but of seventeenth-century poetry, bestowing on Phyllis Jones the name 'Celia' and on the moment of transcendent vision, when the beloved's person is perceived at once in its actuality and its infinity, the term 'the Celian moment.'[61] That the returning vision should have a different woman as its vehicle did not trouble him. Even though he could speak of Celia as a 'full well in a thirsty land,' bringing him abundance of life,[62] he did not see the situation as one calling for any forsaking of his marital commitment. His larger allegiance was to

Love, as a master to be obeyed – not in sexual union but in a heightened creative life and an acknowledgment and celebration of its source. When Phyllis, after an initial return of love, declined the role of Celia, preferring more ordinary romances, Williams would, in a sense, not allow her the choice, insisting that to him she was Celia and always would be. But her rejection, soon apparent and within two years or so inescapable,[63] was a great blow to him and meant that his experience of Celia would be essentially one of loss, even of betrayal, for which, however, out of his own loyalty to Love's vision, she must not be blamed. That sense of loss, the 'Impossibility' which has to be accepted as fact though one's whole being cries out against it, was to be a continuing theme in Williams's writing from about 1930 on to the end. It is especially intense in the first half-dozen years,[64] but later work shows that he continued to brood on it as one of the paradigmatic human experiences and finally to transmute it into a doctrine of the necessary connection between the highest love and suffering.[65]

This experience must have brought home to Williams the inadequacy of the Patmorean model of Romantic Theology. Both there and in Donne, an understanding of love's transcendental significance is something belonging to the shared life of the man and the woman. (Donne, desolated by his wife's death, did surely face an Impossibility; but as a source for a complete system, Donne offers only sketchy hints.) With first 'Michal' and now 'Celia' not all that interested in his theories, Williams needed new insights in order to come to terms with his own crisis. The alternative, to abandon faith in his doctrine, would mean himself betraying the master Love whom he had vowed to serve.[66] He feared the 'mid-life silence,' resulting from 'some interior wound,' which 'has killed some poets,' but took heart from Shakespeare, Milton, and Wordsworth, who recovered.[67] It was through Dante that he learned how to bring his own experience more firmly into his system of thought. In his reading of Dante he found a Beatrice who fully rewarded her lover's devotion, whose very snub was salvific, and who in the *Divine Comedy* (now dead, the real Beatrice could not reject the role Dante created for her) moved in love to bring about her lover's salvation. He encountered three fruitful concepts, the Death of Beatrice, the Second Image, and the Re-assertion of Beatrice,[68] by means of which it was possible to talk more fully about aspects of the whole experience which, if present in his earlier system, had not· been carefully enough examined.

In Dante the Death of Beatrice is a real death; but generalized, it might also be the 'disappearance' of 'the particular glorious Beatrician quality.'[69] Its central meaning for Williams is the obligation to remain faithful, even in the face of dispiriting loss, to Love's call to a life of *caritas*. The Second Image is likewise a concept which Williams broadens beyond its immediate place in Dante's story.[70] What if the renewal of the vision occurs in another woman, Williams asks, and 'Beatrice is not dead' except 'in the sense ... that the Beatrician quality has been withdrawn?' He answers that the Beatrician experience need not be the 'unique thing' it 'was felt at first to be.' Rather, 'such a perfection' as first appeared in Beatrice 'is implicit in every human being.' In the fullness of paradise Dante is permitted to see 'the light of all the saints ... united with that of Beatrice.' We may wonder if Williams is hinting here that a second falling in love, far from being inherently a sin, might without infidelity to the first be a foretaste of Paradise insofar as we shall attain there a 'universalism' of glorious vision. Certainly it can lead to sin, and 'the Christian Church has insisted that certain conditions are necessary for the carrying out of that great experiment of marriage.... The physical union which is permitted, encouraged, and indeed made part of the full 'saute' of that first experience is to be forbidden to any other.' Yet Williams sees the Second Image as a 'great opportunity' – often thwarted, unfortunately, by jealousy or misguided zeal – to serve the kingdom of 'primal Love' not through 'physical union,' which belongs to the first, but through 'separation'[71] – what he extols elsewhere as the way of virginity, involving only 'intellectual nuptials.'[72]

It is in this framework that the place of sex in Williams's life and thought has to be considered. Sexual union in marriage he considered a way of serving Love and, in that vocation, one of the proper loci of bliss. It should not be considered a 'consummation' but 'at best ... the channel by which a deeper marriage is instituted.'[73] And there was a period of 'months and months,' in the first shock of the Impossibility, when he abstained from 'any kind of married intercourse.'[74] Sexuality he considered a core aspect of human identity, but physical intercourse only one expression of it, and not an end but a means. Though he rejected, because it served self-love and not Love, the enterprise of Nigel Considine in *Shadows of Ecstasy* to bend sex along with other energies toward the monomaniac quest of personal immortality, yet the idea that sexual energy might be abstention by transmuted into spiritual power was one that fascinated him. It gave him the eloquence to extol chastity in his famous spellbinding Oxford lecture on Comus.[75] It lies behind the lengthy, still, unerotic embrace described by one of his young female disciples[76] (an imitation perhaps of the *Subintroductae* whose 'great experiment' received unwonted prominence in his history of the Church)[77] and the curious rituals involving another one.[78] It is shown in a sinister light in the anointing of Barbara Rackstraw's body in *War in Heaven* and more positively in the *post mortem* feelings of Lester Furnival in *All Hallows' Eve* as they centre upon her genitals. To dismiss these passages in the novels as pornographic[79] is to overlook completely Williams's seriousness of purpose in exploring the theology of sex.

The first exposition of Williams's Romantic Theology in its fullness, with the new emphases from Dante and the Dantean reorientation of the whole, came in 1938 with *He Came Down from Heaven*. Significantly, this book was dedicated 'to Michal by whom I began to study the doctrine of glory.' It is possible, of course, to stress the word 'began' and read the dedication as an implicit slur: began, but any progress in the study required Celia. But it is truer to one's sense of Williams's character to read it without irony, as a genuine outward expression of the renewal in his marriage which we are told was taking place about this time.[80] It is truer to his doctrine as well, in which the adoration of the Second Image in no way devalues the first. As he modified his Romantic Theology to give due place to the figure of Beatrice, it appears that he reaffirmed Michal's place as his Beatrice, the first awakener of a lifelong devotion to Love; nor did that reaffirmation need to entail the denial of Celia.[81]

In another publication of 1938, *Taliessin Through Logres*, both paths of response to the Beatrician vision are, as we have observed, given their due: the conjugal way in Bors and Elayne and the virginal in Taliessin and Blanchefleur. In both Bors and Taliessin, Williams mirrors aspects of his own experience. 'Taliessin's Song of the Unicorn' (pp. 22–3) reflects a deepened self-knowledge: he now understands that he, in a way, is Taliessin the poet,[82] the 'unicorn' ill-suited to love a woman in the ordinary fleshly way, attracted by her but 'to her no good.' Understandably, she will reject him. Thus perhaps, with a decade's perspective, he can coolly estimate his relations with Celia (though the coolness has not been attained once and for all). It is possible, though, for an unusual woman to respond differently to such a 'snorting alien love.' It takes 'cunning' (line 21) and Christ-like suffering (lines 23–9) if she will accept the unicorn as her 'paramour,' but the union ('intellectual nuptials') results in 'her son the new sound' and she becomes 'the Mother of the Unicorn's Voice.'

Both these 1938 publications are evidently still in his mind a year later as he addresses to Michal a poem he has composed in the train 'coming down from London.'[83] He speaks of his own life, which

> owes through all the years
> its energy to you, whose cares
> provided it with freedom, peace,
> and room for doctrine to increase.
> Therefore the first that held it even
> and swore that it *came down from heaven*
> I with your name sealed to the earth
> since once from you it had its birth,
> madonna; and your first-born Son
> was Love, and that your youngest one –
> threefold a mother! look and see –
> God, Michael, my capacity.
> Few, blessed one, the women are
> who wear so sharp a triple star:
> much, as I know, though you have spent,
> beheld the spreading increment! (58)

Regarding the 'intellectual nuptials' of Taliessin, C. S. Lewis comments (p. 114), 'Would Beatrice have borne *The Divine Comedy* to Dante if they had been married?' But Williams is Bors as well as Taliessin, and his wife thus goes beyond Beatrice in being the mother of the poet's flesh-and-blood child, Michael ('with [her] name'), as well as the Mother of Love — that is, 'God'[84] — and of the poet's Voice; the star she wears is 'triple.' The inspiration of his life's creative work he traces (in the same poem) to 'that first incalculable break/of glory' when they walked together in St. Albans and her 'head/a double weight of glory shed'; then it was that 'my future sprang.' 'Our great vocation' he tells her, was 'opened ... through you alone.'

Williams came to recognize several different ways in which Michal helped make his creative work possible. One was by the stability which her moral character gave to his existence. It seems very possible that such support from her was what brought him, and their marriage, through the difficult early 1930s. There is a hint of the penitent in his general remark about 'the extreme generosity of temper' which wives display.[85] Absent from her in wartime, he confided to a friend his discovery of how much he 'depended' on his wife's 'steady, unnoticeable nourishment and repose.'[86] After twenty-odd years of marriage, she is still his 'Zion,' for whom from Oxonian exile he longs (180 [cf. above, p 20]). He calls her 'a tower of strength.... When I think of what this last year would have been like if you hadn't had courage, resolution, initiative, thrift, and laughter: besides sympathy, sweetness, intelligence, honour, unselfishness, and tact — I shudder at the idea' (23).[87] 'If you were not what you are,' he writes her late in 1939, 'I could never be comfortable' (58).

'What you are' includes an intelligence and sympathetic critical judgment which also made their contribution to Williams's creative career. From Oxford he reported to Michal Basil Blackwell's praise of her 'masculine ... intelligence' (143), and he was willing to have her substitute for him in reviewing a book manuscript for a publisher (249). It had been with her encouragement that he accepted the commission for the 1936 Canterbury play (186). 'You & victory,' he wrote her in April 1940, 'may restore poetry to me;

I have had to begin the Whitsun play [*Terror of Light*] in prose!' (132). The next month he was following her advice in revising it,[88] a situation that recurred with his last novel, *All Hallows' Eve*.[89]

From 1938 on, as his writings include fewer pot-boilers and more of what he considered his best work, and as he grows in the literary world's esteem, Williams conveys a sense of having arrived finally where he belongs – or rather, he and Michal, for he calls it 'our great vocation' (58). He looks forward to the day when she 'will be attended' by 'great minds' – he mentions Lewis, Eliot, and Tolkien – who will 'walk round you, & admire, & say "This was the Origin of all, and the continual Friend and Supporter" ' (114). If Auden is indebted to Williams ('He has gone all Christian and is composing verse under your husband's influence – he sends me four poems and says so'), his partner deserves a share of the credit. 'Thus we – you & I – "move the minds that move the world" ' (217). He tells her: 'My distinguished admirers – from Alice Meynell to C. S. L – always admire you. Lewis says it would be fatal for a great man's wife to read him; I said that you, as unique in that as in all, read, admired, mocked, and left me free to play at my own job' (48).

The ending of that statement shows Williams's appreciation for another facet of Michal's intelligence, her tendency to be sceptical of his theologizing. From this may derive his observation in *The Figure of Beatrice* (p. 182) that 'in the actual facts of life' it may be Beatrice's function to 'see that the poetry ... is not overdone,' and that probably 'the actual Beatrice would have been both charming and intelligent about, but fundamentally indifferent to, the *Commedia*.' 'You may eschew metaphysics,' he writes to Michal, 'but then your metaphysics are in your vitality. It would have been fatal to my genius had you been other ...' (70). Of his teachings he is sometimes compelled to 'labour to convince you' (277) – and not always successfully (238), even in the case of so important a doctrine as Exchange, although 'it was your remarks about not being separate from people that aided me along the lines' (249). He finds it 'odd' that the one who has inspired his ideas 'should scorn your own children' (134).

Especially her child is Williams's Beatrician system. 'All my critical statements about these high subjects (you must let me say it again) derive from your permanent existence' (23); she has become 'the basis of Romantic Theology at Oxford' (105), and her presence has contributed to the making of *The Figure of Beatrice*.[90] This is strong support for the view I am putting forward that the Williamses' marriage was revitalized over the closing eight years or so. She is 'the cause of poems on marriage as the Good Life,' he tells her (referring probably to the 'Bors and Elayne' poems of 1938); 'everyone else observes the relation' and therefore she should not complain (209).[91] He has become an apostle of marriage, teaching that 'a wife & marriage are – after God – the most important things in a man's life' (277) and that 'it ought to be easier to live from God or peace in marriage than anywhere else' (209). When invited to give a talk on marriage, he has but to describe Michal (224). He acknowledges her 'the absolute Fact of my life. . . . There is not even a choice; it is merely *so*' (272). It is with his attitude toward marriage in mind (the institution of marriage, and his own) that we should weigh the emphasis Williams gives in his unfinished 'Figure of Arthur' (pp. 49–51) to the high place of marriage in the early courtly love treatises.

The vision of glory founded upon the body is still with him,[92] both contemporary and in memory. The memories were especially important, as when a dull and unpleasant evening in Oxford as reclaimed by a memory of 'meeting you in the dark nights of the last war,' that is, during their courtship; for he had a Wordsworthian view of 'such fundamental recollections as power' (211). To others who are sceptical of his enthusiasm regarding marriage, he would 'hurl our St Albans days in their faces, and . . . say there is *no* disillusion, there is *never* disappointment, there is no break in that mystery, because it is divine' (224).

These quotations convey Williams's strong sense of a continuity over the whole course of his romantic life. In many and obvious ways they resemble the ideas about love expressed in his early poetry. Less clear to the observer, perhaps, is the continuity overall; we may fancy that we see instead an initial vision, a slow breakdown, a Celian interlude, and then a return or closing of the circle. Yet

Williams could see it all as a whole, taught by Dante the place that a seemingly antithetical movement could take within a larger single pattern, the 'scattered leaves' of substance and its various accidents 'in a single volume bound by Love' (*Paradiso* 33.86 ff.). That unity is perhaps easiest to recognize in his creative life, for the torments of his forties not only energized a great burst of writing at the time but also contributed to the more profound wisdom contained in the works of his fifties. To the Beatrice through whose glory he had first been overmastered by Love he now owes also his rescue from the dark wood. As a result, he stresses the human person's divine potential not in the glorious vision alone but, even more, in suffering and forgiveness. The theme had been present in his writing from the first but appears now with a new emphasis. In this, as in his exaltation of marriage and of the simple domesticities of life, he is making good the promise of his earliest work. But his range is wider. He appreciates Michal in her many roles on the stage of his life – to use a metaphor from an apparently late poem – whether they are roles of his making or not. He is delighted with her gamut of contrasts – the wild, the exalted, the everyday. Her 'white arms' have something of the old radiance, and he sees her 'Fair as the moon, clear as the sun, / Terrible still as a host with banners.' Yet the other side is simultaneously present: she is 'the Millamant of domestic manners.'[93] As Williams himself might have put it: Dante never thought of calling Beatrice *that*.

Notes

1. (1933; rpt. Grand Rapids: Eerdmans, 1965), p. 56.
2. A. M. Hadfield, *Charles Williams: An Exploration of His Life and Work* (New York and Oxford: Oxford Univ. Press, 1983), p. 45. Subsequent references to this work will use the simplified title *Exploration*.
3. 'Poem at Night' (unpublished), quoted by Hadfield in *Exploration*, pp. 200–1. I follow the text given earlier by Mrs Hadfield in *An Introduction to Charles Williams* (London: Robert Hale, 1959; hereafter cited as *Introduction*), pp. 176–7. Where it differs (in the singular 'measurement'), she has kindly verified the reading for me from the MS.
4. Undated MS letter to Michal Williams, No. 8 in series of

1939–1945 wartime correspondence (Wade Collection, Wheaton College). The allusion is to Eve in *Paradise Lost,* 8.438.

5. 'The Coming of Palomides,' in *Taliessin Through Logres* (London: Oxford Univ. Press, 1938), pp. 34–5.

6. 'Sensuality and Substance,' *Theology*, May 1939, rpt. in *The Image of the City and Other Essays*, ed. Anne Ridler (London: Oxford Univ. Press, 1958), pp. 74–5.

7. Quoted by Hadfield, *Exploration*, p. 34.

8. *The Figure of Beatrice* (London: Faber & Faber, 1943).

9. *The White Peacock* (London: Martin Secker, 1927 rpt.), p. 387, quoted by Williams in 'Sensuality and Substance,' p. 73.

10. Humphrey Carpenter, *The Inklings* (Boston: Houghton Mifflin, 1979), pp. 80–1.

11. *The Shadowy Waters*, in *the Collected Poems of W. B. Yeats* (New York: Macmillan, 1951), p. 410.

12. Williams returned to these lines in the essay on Yeats on *Poetry at Present* (Oxford: Clarendon Press, 1930), p. 64, and read them more positively, calling Forgael's reply 'piercing and prophetic.'

13. The fullest analysis of Williams's system is Mary McDermott Shideler, *The Theology of Romantic Love* (Grand Rapids: Eerdmans, 1962). The best exposition of its larger theological context and implications is Dorothy L. Sayers, 'The Poetry of the Image in Dante and Charles Williams,' in *Further Papers on Dante* (London: Methuen, 1957), pp. 183–204. Other useful studies are by C. S. Lewis, 'Williams and the Arthuriad,' in *Arthurian Torso,* ed. C. S. Lewis (London: Oxford Univ. Press, 1948), pp. 116–20; John Heath-Stubbs, *Charles Williams,* 'Writers and Their Work' 63 (London: Longmans, 1955), pp. 15–27; Ridler, pp. xlii–ix; and chap. 4 of R. J. Reilly, *Romantic Religion* (Athens: Univ. of Georgia Press, 1971). His own exposition of it, with an emphasis on the Beatrician aspect, first appeared as chap. 5, 'The Theology of Romantic Love,' of *He Came Down from Heaven,* 'I Believe,' 5 (London and Toronto: Heinemann, 1938). According to Hadfield, *Exploration*, p. 165, this 'contains the core of his unpublished *Outlines of Romantic Theology,'* which had been composed in 1923–24. Further restatements and refinements appeared in the pamphlet *Religion and Love in Dante* (London: Dacre Press, 1941) and in *The Figure of Beatrice*.

14. Blake, *The Marriage of Heaven and Hell,* in *The Portable Blake*, ed. A. Kazin (New York: Viking Press, 1946), p. 258. Of the English Romantic poets, Williams more commonly used Wordsworth as a reference point on Romantic Theology, since his *Prelude* treats the ideas more directly in relation to personal experience and also more comprehensively, including in its paradigm both stages, revelation and loss.

15. Williams, 'The Figure of Arthur,' in *Arthurian Torso*, p. 55.

16. Reilly, p. 180, quotes a particularly interesting parallel statement by Martin Buber about seeing 'in the *Thou* of [the beloved's] eyes . . . a beam of the eternal *Thou.'*

17. Williams, *Figure of Beatrice*, p. 14.
18. Williams, *He Came Down From Heaven*, p. 91.
19. Pointedly absent from both Dante's account and Williams's is the Platonic metaphor of the ladder, which would imply an unacceptable opposition between the physical beginnings and the spiritual end of love.
20. Beatrice is not necessarily feminine: Taliessin has that role in 'The Star of Percivale.' See Lewis, p. 136.
21. (London: Poetry Editions, 1944).
22. Clinton W. Trowbridge, 'The Beatricean [sic] Character in the Novels of Charles Williams,' *Sewanee Review*, 79 (1971): 335–43, in fact includes under this rubric, without differentiation, two Christ-figures, Chloe and Sybil; Lester in her Christic relationship to Betty; and the mixed Beatrice-Christ type as represented by Isabel, Barbara, and Lester in relation to Richard. One can understand the entire omission of *Descent into Hell*, since it contains little about being in love except on the negative side of its double plot, but the failure to explore the significance of Nancy Coningsby as a Beatrician character, after noticing that she 'Symbolizes the emerging Christ' and that she and Henry are the Lovers of the Tarot cards, is curious.
23. In *Shadows of Ecstasy*, pp. 47–9, there are several allusions to his earlier experiences of this sort.
24. 'The Coming of Palomides' (*Taliessin Through Logres*, pp. 33–7), line 41. The following reading of this poem cites lines and phrases pretty much in their sequence; only the exceptions will be identified by line number. My analysis relies heavily on C. S. Lewis's in *Torso*, pp. 123–7.
25. *Taliessin Through Logres*, pp. 64–8. Cf. Lewis, pp. 162–6. Again, line numbers are omitted for quotations easily located.
26. I have condensed drastically the fine exposition of George Every, *Poetry and Personal Responsibility* (London: SCM Press, 1949), pp. 46–7.
27. Cf. Williams, *Figure of Beatrice*, p. 141: 'one could do without Beatrice; one cannot do without the City.'
28. Cf. Lewis, pp. 118–20, 139–41; Reilly, pp. 162–8, 188.
29. *Religion and Love in Dante*, p. 4; quoted at greater length by Hadfield, *Exploration*, p. 202.
30. *Figure of Beatrice*, pp. 20–1. Cf. Williams, *The Descent of the Dove* (London: Longmans, Green, 1939), p. 139: 'Most lovers feel as Dante felt.' On the authenticity of Dante's experience see the discussion by William Anderson, *Dante the Maker* (London: Routledge & Kegan Paul, 1980), p. 74.
31. Michal Williams, 'I Remember Charles Williams,' *Episcopal Churchnews*, 12 April 1953, pp. 13–14; a sizable portion of her account is quoted by Ridler, p. xvii. Bare months earlier he had been, he writes (*Poetry at Present*, p. 69), 'twenty, a poetaster, never in love.'
32. Eventually to be published (1912) as *The Silver Stair* (London:

Herbert & Daniel, n.d.). References in my text, whether to the verses themselves or to their titles, will be by sonnet number. Glen Cavaliero, *Charles Williams: Poet of Theology* (Grand Rapids: Eerdmans, 1983), devotes a chapter, pp. 9–21, to the early poetry. Hadfield's two accounts of it (*Introduction*, pp. 31–66, and *Exploration*, pp. 16–36, 49–52) are largely independent of one another.

33. Cf. comments in Hadfield, *Exploration*, p. 26.

34. *He Came Down from Heaven*, p. 80.

35. Here and elsewhere in *The Silver Stair* is a full anticipation of this central point in Williams's mature theology, that 'the beloved ... becomes the Mother of Love; Love is born in the soul; it may have its passion there; it may have its resurrection' (*He Came Down from Heaven*, p. 81, quoted and discussed by Cavaliero, p. 133).

36. Dorothy L. Sayers, *The Poetry of Search and the Poetry of Statement* (London: Gollancz, 1963), p. 73; essay rpt. in her *Christian Letters to a Post-Christian World* (Grand Rapids: Eerdmans, 1969), p. 163.

37. Ridler, p. lviii and facing photograph. 'It is my hope,' Dante wrote, 'that I shall yet write concerning her [Beatrice] what hath not before been written of any woman.'

38. 'I Remember Charles Williams,' p. 14.

39. Christopher E. Fullman, 'The Mind and Art of Charles Williams' (unpub. Ph.D. diss., Wisconsin, 1954), p. 131, proposes St. John of the Cross as another major source.

40. *Holy Sonnets*, xvii, lines 5–6, in *Poems*, ed. H. J. C. Grierson (London: Oxford Univ. Press, 1933), p. 301.

41. Hadfield, *Exploration*, p. 44. Two of Williams's mentors, Alice Meynell and Frederick Page, were followers of Patmore and must have encouraged his interest.

42. Letters respectively to Phyllis Potter (1945) and Alice Meynell (1917), quoted by Hadfield, *Exploration*, pp. 34, 27.

43. (London: Oxford Univ. Press, 1917). Parenthetical references in my text to these poems, as well as to those in *Divorce* and *Windows of Night*, will be by page number.

44. See 'Marriage' and 'The Christian Year' as discussed by Hadfield, *Introduction*, p. 44.

45. Cf. Sonnet 9: 'From sacramental joys world's pleasures run' (p. 40).

46. 'A Song of Implications' (pp. 33–4). The whole 32-line poem is worth study for its Donne-like and spirit and its paradoxes which 'for joy perplex' the 'riddling intellect.' Cf. the companion poem just preceding, 'A Song of Opposites,' where 'all her spirit is expressed / In all her body's holy charms.' These poems are an early expression of Williams's characteristic doctrine of Coinherence.

47. An identification parallel to that which he is later to note in Dante (*He Came Down from Heaven*, p. 97; *The Figure of Beatrice*, pp. 112, 222).

48. (London: Oxford Univ. Press, 1920).

49. Again, we may note the Beatrician parallel: cf. *Figure of Beatrice*, p. 188; Sayers, pp. 190–2. But where Dante is interested in allegory, Williams comes closer to asserting identity.

50. Cavaliero, p. 16.

51. P. 127. This is one of the texts for that doctrine of mutual salvation mentioned earlier in my account of *Poems of Conformity*. As to the doctrine itself, cf. Sayers's observation, *Further Papers* p. 193, that where Dante presented a woman as instrumental to the man's salvation, Charles Williams went further to proclaim the equality of the sexes in an 'exchange of hierarchies.'

52. Quoted by Hadfield, *Exploration*, p. 233. A similar remark occurs in a 1941 letter to Michal (Wade Collection, No. 277).

53. (London: Oxford University Press, n.d.). Hadfield, *Exploration*, pp. 49 and 239, supplies documentary evidence for a publication date in 1925 rather than the previously conjectured 1924 – a difference of only eight days, however.

54. *Introduction*, p. 64.

55. Cavaliero, p. 19.

56. Cavaliero, p. 18.

57. Hadfield, *Exploration*, pp. 41–5, gives the only extended account available of the contents of this manuscript. *Outlines of Romatic Theology*, edited by Alice Mary Hadfield was published by Wm B. Eerdmans in 1990 shortly after this essay was written.

58. Quoted by Hadfield, *Exploration*, p. 43.

59. A. E. Waite, *The Secret Doctrine of Israel* (London: William Rider, 1913), p. 72 n; see Ridler, p. xxv. (The fact that 'rose of the world' as an etymology for 'Rosamond' is incorrect is not relevant.)

60. *Figure of Beatrice*, p. 24, where he credits it, probably from working on the *Oxford Dictionary of Quotations*, not to Augustine but to Bonaventura. (It was, in fact, already an aphorism by the thirteenth century. See C. A. Patrides, ed., *The Cambridge Platonists* [London: Edward Arnold, 1969], p. 36.)

61. The phrase has broader implications as well. Cf. Hadfield, *Exploration*, p. 74.

62. Hadfield, *Exploration*, p. 129.

63. Hadfield, *Exploration*, pp. 68, 74–5, 83–4.

64. Cavaliero, pp. 25–42, 60, 74–7, traces it in early plays (*The Chaste Wanton* – treated more fully by Hadfield, *Introduction*, pp. 109–11 – and *Thomas Cranmer of Canterbury*), biographies, criticism (especially in his emphasis on the plight of Shakespeare's Troilus), and some novels. By *Descent into Hell* (1937), says Cavaliero, Williams was 'on the far side of [his] confrontation with the Impossibility' (p. 86).

65. In Williams's Arthurian poems such experience centres in Lancelot. His label 'Impossibility' surfaces in a 1943 essay, and in the same year he devotes an essay ('The Cross,' Ridler, pp. 131–9) to defining Christ's crucifixion as the divine answer to the Impossibility, now seen as a universal human experience in an inexplicable

painful universe (Cavaliero, pp. 26–7, 149–51, 97). The link of love and suffering emphasized in his mature theology is a return full circle to the doctrine of *The Silver Stair* (Hadfield, *Exploration*, pp. 225–6).

66. That he sometimes teetered on the edge of this abyss is suggested by words he wrote to Phyllis, in Java, in 1935: 'If you say that all this is my own hobby and not the *you*, I shall hope you are wrong' (Hadfield, *Exploration*, p. 122); and again, 'This effort of mine to create a unity here is, by its nature, bound to failure, anyhow as far as your nature – and perhaps your apprehension – is concerned' (p. 133). See also pp. 116, 134, and Carpenter, p. 197, where Williams is quoted concerning the difficulty of living his 'myth.'

67. Letter to Phyllis Jones, in Hadfield, *Exploration*, pp. 113–14.

68. These are the designations Williams gave to them in *The Figure of Beatrice.*

69. *Figure of Beatrice*, p. 35.

70. Sayers, *Further Papers*, p. 189, observes that in Williams 'the implications of [Dante's] theology are explored in fresh directions and charged with the accrued experience of the intervening centuries.' The point is developed, with examples, through to p. 197.

71. *Figure of Beatrice*, pp. 47–50. See also the discussion, p. 157, of 'the three degrees of all fidelity to the Images.'

72. *Taliessin Through Logres*, p. 23.

73. 'Outlines of Romantic Theology,' quoted by Hadfield, *Exploration*, p. 44. See also her discussion on pp. 45, 105–7.

74. Letter to Phyllis Jones, in Hadfield, *Exploration*, p. 86.

75. See Carpenter, p. 119.

76. Lois Lang-Sims, *A Time to Be Born* (London: Andre Deutsch, 1971), pp. 202–4; see the discussion by Carpenter, p. 106.

77. *Descent of the Dove*, pp. 12–14.

78. See Hadfield, *Exploration*, p. 106.

79. R. T. Davies, 'Charles Williams and the Romantic Experience,' *Etudes Anglaises*, 8 (1955), 298.

80. Hadfield, *Exploration*, pp. 130, 197–202.

81. Cf. the guarded idealism of this sentence in *The Figure of Beatrice*, p. 50: 'If it were possible to create in marriage a mutual adoration towards the second image, whenever and however it came, and also a mutual limitation of the method of it, I do not know what new liberties and powers might not be achieved.'

82. Cf. C. S. Lewis's lucid exposition (*Torso*, pp. 113–14).

83. During the war the Press was evacuated to Oxford and the Williamses were separated. Michal kept the flat in London, Charles roomed in Oxford, and often they could be together only on weekends. They wrote frequent letters; nearly 700 of his survive, in the Wade Collection, Wheaton College. Quotations from these letters are identified parenthetically in the text by serial number. The numbers usually give some indication of chronology, as the great bulk of the collection is arranged in order of date. Nos. 1–25, however, are undated and in many cases fragmentary, consisting only of a single concluding leaf of a letter, or

even of two or more such leaves brought together under one identifying number. For these letters, the numerical designation is an
archival convenience for ease of reference.

84. Cf. above, note 47 and accompanying text. Several Marian allusions are to be noted in the lines quoted.

85. Quoted in Hadfield, *Exploration*, p. 228. We may conjecture
that Michal's behavior, as well as academic theology, went into
the making of his book on *The Forgiveness of Sins* (London:
Bles, 1942).

86. Letter to Thelma Shuttleworth, quoted in Hadfield, *Exploration*,
p. 230.

87. Cautions have been raised about taking the wartime letters to
Michal at face value. (1) Carpenter, p. 180, suggests that the
devotion they express existed more in Williams's imagination than
in fact. He mentions letters to others which extol their beauty and
virtue in 'almost identical terms' to those used toward Michal. But
such generalized compliments are not the same as the statements I
am referring to, in which the focus is on Williams's sense of his
wife's relationship *to him*. There is nothing comparable to these
statements in other correspondence, to my knowledge, apart from
much earlier letters to Celia. (2) How much distortion do Williams's
sentiments acquire by being filtered through the highly abstract doctrinal system in terms of which they are often expressed? This
question is too difficult to answer summarily; indeed, it is an
underlying concern of this whole essay. It seems, however, that
any simple dichotomy between sincere expression and abstract
thinking would fail to do justice to Williams's conviction that
many states of mind considered pure feelings are really dependent
on the will guided (as may be) by reason. (3) Another interpretation would read the letters as aimed at cheering Michal up or
reassuring her, even at the cost of exaggeration. She might well
want cheering or reassurance (cf. Letter 238), under the difficult
wartime circumstances, but statements having such a function need
not be untrue. In some of the letters there is, to be sure, an air of
hyperbole, but in my judgment the overall tone – often including
the wry humor that belongs to Williams's style when he is at ease
– is that of an honest expression of feelings, perhaps now being
felt with a renewed intensity.

88. Hadfield, *Exploration*, p. 191. It remained in prose, however,
uniquely among his plays.

89. Carpenter, pp. 193–4.

90. Carpenter, p. 179. Hadfield's comment (*Exploration*, p. 202) about
the earlier pamphlet *Religion and Love in Dante*.

91. C. S. Lewis called their marriage 'brilliantly happy' (*Torso*, p. 113).
Carpenter (p. 179) believes that he was naively mistaken – and certainly at one time the phrase would not have applied – but.it is
possible that, for the time when Lewis knew them, he was right.
Certainly his statement harmonizes with other evidence.

92. See Letters 163 and 224, and cf. the passage in the chapter 'The

Re-assertion of Beatrice' where Williams, speaking of Dantean parallels in real life, observes, 'Even physically, there is a moment
at which a new highness appears in the adored ... a forehead,
a gesture, a word ... a new strangeness of beauty,' So Dante
proves congnizant of 'our most intimate life' (*The Figure of
Beatrice*, p. 177).

93.   'To Michal: After Marriage,' *The Grasshopper Broadsheets,* ser.
3, no. 10 (Derby: Kenneth Hopkins, 1944). Williams's concluding
stanza, from which I have just quoted, reuses (with the insertion of
'still') the same verse from the Song of Solomon (6:10) which he
had printed in 1917 as part of the dedication to Michal of *Poems
of Conformity* (p. 4), thus bearing witness to his own sense of the
continuity of his Beatrician experience, early and late.

Chapter Seven

Women in the Arthurian
Poems of Charles Williams

Elisabeth Brewer

I

In Malory's *Le Morte d'Arthur*, we see Guinevere portrayed
with increasing realism. As the cause of the divided loyalties
which finally set Arthur against Lancelot and destroy the
company of the Round Table, she has a significant function
in the book. And Malory, the 'knight prisoner', seems to
have lived in the company of these characters as he told
their story, so that he is able to present them in dramatic
interchange, with psychological realism, as they each work
out their individual and corporate destinies.

Malory did not merely translate the French versions and
reshape the old stories: he made them the bearers of his
own meaning, as Charles Williams was to do so long after.
To Malory, the creation of the noble institution and the
gradual process of its subsequent tragic destruction, seems
to have been of paramount interest. How consistently conscious his intentions were it is hard to tell. Charles Williams,
however, makes very clear in *The Figure of Arthur* that
he is very well aware of what you can do with stories,
of the ways in which the author can bring out, or make
implicit, meanings old or new. Of Geoffrey of Monmouth's
Historia Regum Britanniae, he saw that Geoffrey 'seems
to have meant to create ... one splendid and popular

figure' . . . 'he first made Arthur a king' (210). In the
Taliessin poems, Williams uses to the full the possibilities
open to the modern Arthurian writer, to select the form, the
characters, the characterisation, and above all, perhaps, to
give to old material a new significance of special relevance
today. Speaking of Chrétien's Guenevere, he says that she
is 'something nobler' than the Guenevere of Marie de France
in *Lanval* – 'There is in her a touch of the Guinevere she
was to become' in Malory (234). Williams' recognition of
her potential, where Tennyson, for example, seems only
to have seen a corrupting influence, is one of the great
positive qualities which make Williams's Arthurian poems
so impressive. In the medieval stories there was very little
for Guinevere to do or be; she was not allowed to have
a concern for religion, for example, as Williams points
out (237). Though he only allows Guinevere to move on
the periphery of the action, apart from her appearance in
'Taliessin in the Rose-Garden' (139), however, she not only
incorporates a complex of significances but is also presented
with deep human understanding.

Taliessin sees Guinevere, representing 'the feminine
headship of Logres' in the company of Dindrane, and close
to the toil-hardened girl who tends the roses. The romantic
picture of Guinevere, 'Hazel-lithe', with her 'massed fair
hair under the gold circlet' amongst the roses, also shows
us 'the sensuous mode' while it suggests the whole range of
human experience represented by the other figures present.
While Taliessin is making his poem, brooding on the abstract
concept of the Queen's majesty, we are shown how far she
falls short of the ideal, as she talked and laughed, while 'under
her brow she looked for the king's friend / Lancelot'. The shy
glance destroys the image of majesty, as the laughter seems
to trivialise her. Later, Taliessin again formulates her role:

> Let the queen's majesty, the feminine headship of Logres,
> deign to exhibit the glory to the women of Logres;
> each to one vision, but the queen for all.
> Bring to a flash of seeing the women in the world's base.

Meanwhile, she is seen talking 'sideways to Dindrane' and
then asking, trivially, 'has my lord dallied with poetry

among the roses?' How well her inability to fulfil her function is suggested by the implicit contrast with the other women, through the superficial words (becomingly expressed though they are) as well as by the apparently habitual obliquity of her glance. Her faults co-exist with the idea of what she should be. Yet, as in Malory, Guinevere is redeemed. In Blanchefleur's cell at Almesbury, she is at last 'reconciled', able in her lesser way to practise substitution, to allow the wounded and dead king to enter into salvation. 'She was a good lover, and therefore she made a good end', says Malory. But Williams suggests a whole new dimension of love here – love for her husband rather than for Lancelot her lover.

Guinevere, of course, not only fails in the role of feminine headship of Logres, but to be a mother. In 'The Son of Lancelot' (76) we are told that her 'tormented unaesthetic womanhood / alternately wept and woke' when Galahad was conceived. When at his coming, he is laid in the king's bed, she lies thinking of Lancelot's son all night. Williams's sympathetic insight into women's feelings seems to me very apparent here; but the spiritual implications are of greater importance. Guinevere is not simply a frustrated woman – as her fingers tensely grip like claws, the stone fits itself not to the shell but only to its echo, and her thoughts are on death. That she is also *spiritually* barren (*but* that this is not necessarily a permanent or a hopeless condition) is made clear. Unlike Malory's Guinevere, she does not exist as a rounded individual. Though she is a regal figure, magnificently beautiful, because of her limited spiritual potential she cannot take a more dominant part in this Arthurian cycle.

'Taliessin in the Rose-Garden' is in some ways the most interesting of the poems for my present purpose, in so far as it contains a substantial reflection on the nature of women, from its beginning in 'the rosed femininity / particled out of the universe, the articled form / of the Eve in the Adam; the Adam known in the Eve' (142). When Williams says, 'Well are women warned from serving the altar / who by the nature of their creature . . . / share with the sacrifice the victimization of blood' he may offend those who argue for the ordination of women, but he surely makes amends in the passage that follows: 'happy the woman who feels

Galahad, the companion of Percivale, rise/in her flesh, and her flesh bright in Carbonek with Christ'. Williams, though he emphasises the essentially different nature of women, certainly never underrates their spiritual potential. In Malory, Guinevere is virtually without a function, like most of the other female figures; in the 'Taliessin' poems, everyone has a role, according to her, or his, capacity or choice. And the range of possibilities is enormous; even 'The women in the world's base' may be brought to a flash of seeing (and presumably the men too). But strikingly, the best people, the best 'real' people, are almost all women.

In *Williams and the Arthuriad*, C. S. Lewis described the cycle as 'a work devoted mainly to the glorification of the flesh', a remark which at first sight seems extraordinarily inappropriate, though he is surely right to represent the world of the senses — Caucasia — as feminine, whether we like it or not. Guinevere represents the sensuous mode, but in so far as she fails to fulfil her function, she prevents the sensuous from achieving the integration with the intellectual and spiritual which is to be desired, as well as failing to show how such integration can be realised by ordinary people. Nevertheless, in 'Taliessin in the Rose Garden', the figure of Guinevere does give rise to the formulation of a series of insights into the nature of women. They enable men better to know and understand themselves: 'the Adam known in the Eve' (142). Taliessin's vision of women's potential emphasises their nature and innate spirituality: 'women's flesh lives the quest of the Grail ... blessed is she who gives herself to the journey' (144–5). At the same time he emphasises their unique grounds for felicity: 'happy the women ... who feels Galahad ... rise in her flesh ... Blessed is she who can know the Dolorous Blow/healed in the flesh of Pelles, the flesh of women.' (145).

II

The Grail is of course Charles Williams's real subject, though for Malory it was only incidental. 'No invention can come near it; no fabulous imagination excel it. All the greatest mythical details are only there to hint at the thing

which happens.' Naturally, therefore, the selection of characters and the parts that they play in Williams's cycle were
controlled by the focus on the Grail. The topic of courtly
love, so important in many Arthurian stories of the Middle
Ages and also, in a different way, in the nineteenth century,
is necessarily of minor importance here. That is not to imply
that Williams did not consider such love to be significant.
In the *Figure of Beatrice*, he discusses the initial experience
which is an essential feature of love whether medieval or
modern, the moment of revelation which 'presents the lover
with a way of effort towards nobility and sanctity'. He is not
interested in the problems and pains of the lover; we hear
nothing of the sighs and tears, the sufferings and delights
of the courtly lover, for obvious reasons. Though he could
well describe the more sensuous aspects of such love – 'The
body of the beloved appears vital with holiness; the physical
flesh is vital with sanctity – not her sanctity, but its own' –
the obsessive love which blights the lives of Tristan and
Isolde, for example in the traditional story has virtually no
part to play in these Arthurian poems. 'Love, and do what
you choose', we are told; but a higher range of choice, a
more spiritually-oriented range of choice is held out in these
poems than in the other Grail poems, and above all, we see
that it is women who are to choose. These women, from
Guinevere and Blanchefleur to the slaves, thus have a far
greater autonomy than they appear to have in the medieval
stories. They are not simply the passive objects of male adoration; they are not merely presented with moral choices –
between fidelity and adultery, for example – rather, they
are allowed to choose their whole way of life. Some choose
well, others do not.

The Elaynes provide an interesting illustration. We read in
Malory's story of Elayne of Astolat (or Escalot) a touching
account of this young girl's fatal, infatuated devotion to
Lancelot. It begins when he visits her home on his way
to the Great Tournament and leaves his shield with her
so as later to conceal his identity; then when he is seriously wounded, she goes to nurse him. Her brother is also
devoted to Sir Lancelot – the whole episode is designed to
represent him as a charismatic figure, who will nevertheless
help to bring about the downfall of the Round Table. When

he is recovered, Elayne openly says that she wants him to marry her, or if that is unacceptable, to let her be his paramour – anything, as long as she can stay with him. It is impossible, of course – there can only be Guinevere for Lancelot – and so Elayne falls into a decline and dies. When the priest comes to shrive her, she refuses to renounce her love, which she insists comes from God, and so cannot be sinful. Williams understood very well 'the passion that caused the code' (239), but this story, popular with many nineteenth-century artists and writers, was not relevant to his purpose. Instead of Elayne of Astolat, we have Elayne, Bors' wife, who we see only indirectly, as the source of inspiration to Bors, as the beloved should be. In the two poems, 'Bors to Elayne; the Fish of Broceliande' and 'On the King's Coins' we see, not the sterile infatuation that brings death to an innocent young girl, but the suggestion of a love that grows into reciprocity, partnership, and unselfish, positive action. The king is building Camelot, and, says Bors, 'He has sent me to be his lieutenant on the southern coast'. He speaks of Taliessin's song of the 'sea-rooted western wood':

> his song meant all things to all men, and you to me,
> A forest of the creatures; was it of you? no? ...
> and I plucked a fish from a stream that flowed to the sea
> from you? for you? shall I drop the fish in your hand?

He speaks of the imaginative experience; as C. S. Lewis says, 'of course, of course she is Broceliande' (299), and she understands. Unlike the girl in the preceding poem, 'Taliessin's Song of the Unicorn', who 'cannot like such a snorting alien love' as she is offered, Elayne *can* accept Bors' vision: 'everywhere the light through the great leaves is blown/on your substantial flesh, and everywhere your glory frames'. As Lewis says, 'These two must try together that great experiment, must become that double-natured creature, that 'one flesh' which alone can utter the secret name of their love ... when the two lovers become a 'twy-nature' (one organism in two sexes) they are a living symbol of the grand Twy-Nature, Christ ... who alone can utter celestial, as they utter earthly, love'. Together with the poem of the Unicorn, says Lewis, 'Bors to Elayne' introduces us to Williams's doctrine of Love. So, instead of Malory's picture of fatal love, we have through Bors's vision of the Elayne he loves, a projection of the length and breadth and height, as it were, that love can achieve. 'She/translucent, planted with virtues, lit by throes' who 'should be called the Mother of the Unicorn's Voice' in the *preceding* poem, of course represents love on an altogether higher plane, 'by intellectual nuptials unclosed'. This hypothetical woman, who 'date set palms on the point' of the Unicorn's horn, 'twisting from the least/to feel the sharper impress, for the thrust to stun/her arteries into channels of tears beyond blood', can only be seen as the most extreme example of a transcendent spiritual love and devotion.

In 'Bors to Elayne; on the King's Coins', we again see Elayne through the eyes of Bors. Now she is the mother of two children, the mistress of a large household, the manager of estates, 'the sole figure of the organic salvation of our good', he says. We see what love has achieved in the mature relationship of these two. Bors makes explicit the mutuality of their love:

When you saw me a southern burst of love
tosses a new smile from your eyes to your mouth,
shaping for that mind's while the corn of your face
... I am come again
to live from the founts and fields of your hands.

So, though this Elayne can be said to inspire courtly love as a medieval heroine might do, there is something down-to-earth and modern about her at the same time. As Blanchefleur embodies the spiritual ideal, choosing the Way of Rejection, Elayne represents the practical, secular operation of love in the everyday world. She is further defined by the contrast between the form of exchange represented by the King's coins — 'Money is the medium of exchange' — and the values which she represents. Bors says:

I saw you stand,
in your hand the bread of love, in your head

lightness of law.
The uprightness of the multitude stood in your
    figure.

Love, goodwill, generosity, order, plenty, 'organic salvation', are contrasted with 'ration and rule, and the
fault in ration and rule' of 'organisation in London'. 'O
lady, your hand held the bread/and Christ the city spread
in the extensor muscles of your thumbs'. Elayne is no more
than a symbolic figure, seen through the eyes of another,
but the vision of the way of life which she embodies
is splendid in its richness and positiveness and illustrates
women's potential, as well as the scope and importance of
their traditional role.

III

Speaking of Dante in *The Figure of Beatrice* (231), Charles
Williams says: 'It is in a way astonishing (but blessed) that
this great poet should have said so little in the ordinary
speech of Christians', a remark which seems true to a
large extent of Williams himself, too. It is often through
the symbolic women in these poems that he is able to
communicate the deepest spiritual meaning. Sometimes, as
with Guinevere, their traditional role is diminished, while
as others it is increased, as with Elayne, the wife of Bors.
Similarly Nimue, the Lady of the Lake, becomes a far more
significant figure than in the earlier Arthurian literature; she
is 'the great mother and lady of Broceliande' – Nature, as
it were, or all the vast processes of the universe imaged in
a single figure, terrestrial Nature. As Lewis points out, she
has almost nothing in common with Malory's Nimue. For
obvious reasons, she never becomes an individual; indeed,
is little more than a name. As the 'first mother of making',
'time's mother on earth', she might be said to represent the
life-force. Nimue brings all natural becoming to her shape
of immortal being, as to a flash of seeing the women
in the world's base', as 'nature sets before us for our
delight the unfathomable feminine principle which would
otherwise be invisible', as C. S. Lewis puts it. Rather

similarly, her daughter Brisen, sister of Merlin, is also an abstract figure representing space, 'Time and space, duration and extension'. Traditionally she is the waiting-woman who administers the drugged drink to Lancelot, to cause him to beget Galahad. Her enhanced role in Williams's cycle effectively suggests the inevitability of the divine purpose working through her to bring about the birth. Taliessin sees the whole process in his dream in 'The Calling of Taliessin'. Here, Brisen has become 'the engine of the first Mover', whose 'dark and mighty shadow' falls on 'the wide waste of Logres', in the spells of Merlin which reveal the future.

In a quite different way, Williams breaks away from tradition in his presentation of Iseult, a figure particularly fascinating to writers, especially dramatists, from the end of the nineteenth century into the 1920s, as a symbol of sexual love in revolt against the social convention of the loveless marriage of convenience. The passion glorified by Wagner and Swinburne and the romantic elements of the story are of no significance to Williams. Iseult is seen, of course, only in relation to the Saracen knight, Palomides. Her arm is the basis of his vision;

> I saw the hand of the queen Iseult;
> down her arm a ruddy bolt
> fixed the tinder of my brain
> to measure the shape of man again. (52)

In 'The Coming of Palomides', he expounds the complex meaning of what he has seen, 'the doctrine of Euclidean love', but, as Lewis points out, the Saracen knight has a Beatrician experience which goes wrong. He cannot love without desiring to possess Iseult, and we see him debased and distracted, deflected by the Questing Beast. Nevertheless, Taliessin can liken *himself* to Palomides, as sharing in the same vision: 'Palomides and I, see everywhere the hint, in a queen's shape or a slave's; we bid for a purchase'. Iseult's function in the poem glorifies her, for she provides the hint of beauty, of divine perfection. It is her loveliness and what it represents that is significant; though Palomides and Taliessin may experience frustration after each has seen his vision.

Iseult, then, is a rather shadowy figure, presented without either censure or sympathy. That other famous queen of Arthurian legend, Morgause, is a very different matter. 'With the begetting of Mordred and the striking of the Dolorous Blow all is lost', says C. S. Lewis, in a splendid discussion of 'Lamorack and the Queen Morgause of Orkney' (56). The whole poem, he comments, 'marks strongly the difference between the technique of narrative or drama and that of the metaphysical ode.' The symbolism in the two poems in which we encounter Morgause not only leaves us in no doubt of the extent to which she is evil, but also makes apparent the terrible results which are to ensue from her lust, and Arthur's. In 'The Crowning of Arthur', as Logres heraldically flaunts the king's state, and Merlin looks through the depth to the dome of Sophia, where 'the kingdom and the power and the glory' chime, Morgause leans from a casement to watch. Immediately we are reminded of that other evil queen who looked from a casement, Jezebel. (38). Like the other participants in the ceremonial, she is presented in heraldic terms; a sea rises black against the azure of Percivale's sheild, with a red moon on a fess of argent. The images are sinister in the extreme; the crimson of blood, the sterility associated with the moon. They are linked, through Dinadan's dolphin, 'a silver fish under bloody waters', to the shield of Bors which depicts a pelican in golden piety, drawing bloody drops to nurture its young. Morgause is further contrasted with the lovely young Guinevere, whose emblem is rather surprisingly a red chalice on an argent field, perhaps suggesting her spiritual potential and final redemption. But sinister as Morgause seems here, it is as nothing to the vast, cosmic dimensions of the evil associated with her in the second poem, in which she is seen through the eyes of Lamorack her lover. 'There is, if I may so put it, a mineral quality in Morgause', says Lewis, rather uncharacteristically seeming to minimise thereby the effect so carefully built up by Williams. For, in her, Lamorack sees 'the source of all stone/the rigid tornado, the schism and first strife/of primeval rock with itself'. Williams is surely drawing on the *Inferno* in the images of whirlwind and tornado (reminding us of Paolo and Francesca), and in 'the storm's shock', the 'hideous huge forms' hewn in a

cleft of the remote and desolate scenes visited by Lamorack,
as he explores 'the coast of the kingdom towards the Pole'.
(Traditionally, too, the north is a quarter of the compass
associated with evil and the devil.) The images associated
with Morgause, the pre-Adamic sculpture on an ocean rock'
from which his vision of her face rises, also suggest the dark,
formless chaos before the Creation. When Lamorack sees
Morgause in Arthur's hall (seated, of course, on the king's
left hand), he sees again in her long eyes the 'humanized
shapes of the cleft'.

C. S. Lewis has discussed this poem so fully and so brilliantly that there is little more that one can say, except
perhaps to remark that once again, Williams has emphasised the conscious and deliberate evil in Morgause as no
other writer has done, because from her conscious choice
and intention stems 'the web of all our doom'. (58). She
knew what she was doing: 'the eyes of the queen Morgause
were a dark cavern; / there a crowned man without eyes came
to a carved tavern'. She could see, Arthur could not. Later,
she is eyeless, 'a blind woman under a blind man', as they
make the 'beast with two backs', while 'below them both,
the shape of the blatant beast matches the 'cipher of the
Great Ban' above them.

It is a relief to turn from the nightmarish images in which
Morgause is presented to us, to the princess Blanchefleur,
'who walked dropping light'. Her rare face, seen by Taliessin
in a Beatrician moment, is an image of grace, of the grace
which fulfils, completes, brings to perfection and full circle
what is begun in the slave drawing water in the yard when
Blanchefleur arrives with her two brothers. The gold on her
gown symbolises perfection, as the red here suggests her
sacrificial death. We feel her radiance, a radiance that she
owes entirely to Charles Williams, for in Malory she is a
colourless figure, without definite personality. Her life at
Almesbury further defines her, in 'The Son of Lancelot'.
The comprehensiveness of the ideal that is embodied in her
makes her an interesting figure. At Almesbury, Blanchefleur
is among the nuns 'of infinite adoration, of veiled passions,
of sororal intellects'. They are 'earth's lambs, wolves of the
heavens, with heat's pallor's secret within and beyond cold's
pallor'. All these features of the community as a whole go

to define her, but beyond that, of course, she is 'the contact of exchange', to a degree unrivalled by any other. Deep in exchange with the world, she is 'love's means to love', a phrase which sums up her whole function and significance.

The evolution of Blanchefleur is in itself interesting. In one of the early French versions she is the niece of Gournemant, besieged in a castle to which Percival (*not* her brother in this story) comes. He defends the castle, and the two spend the night together and are betrothed. But in the *High History of the Holy Grail* which Charles Williams read later, Blanchefleur, here named Dindrane, is Percival's sister, and it is she who gives her blood to save another lady, as in Malory. Clearly, the story of Blanchefleur in the first version included features much less well suited to Williams's purpose than the story of Dindrane in the *High History*.

Blanchefleur's life of devotion and supreme sacrifice present an ideal and an inspiration, and yet we feel that within the limits imposed by the medium, she is a real person. In 'The Departure of Dindrane', we see her with her two friends, Elayne, Bors's wife, and Taliessin − male and female friends. 'Her nature was sweet to all; no call in vain reached her, but these two she loved', and 'her best arts', we are told, 'changed toils with Elayne and studies with Taliessin'. (To Taliessin, of course, she is much more than an ordinary friend.) Even the slaves in the king's house know her well, indeed she is an eidolon of the slaves.

IV

One of the most striking features of the cycle is the introduction of the slaves, all of them female. Because of their status, and because they have no traditional place in the story of the Grail and do not appear in Malory's *Morte d'Arthur* − they are of course sheer invention on Williams's part − they often seem convincingly human to a greater extent than such characters as Iseult or Morgause can be. In 'The Sister of Percivale', however, the slave drawing water in the courtyard seems little more than a foil to Blanchefleur; and yet in Taliessin's version, each is necessary to the other, since both go to make up the circle of perfection. Without both, the circle would be incomplete, not perfect. The scar on the slave's bent back begins the pattern of circularity as it 'lightens over a curved horizon', and at the same time reveals to Taliessin the 'curved bottom of the world'; but the horizon in the slave's eyes as she swings the handle of the well is 'breaking with distant Byzantium'. Humble though she is, she is capable of vision, too. In the water in her bucket, however, she sees only her own face reflected, while Taliessin in the same moment sees the 'rare face' of Blanchefleur.

In 'The Departure of Dindrane' (147), we have a slave who though nameless, is yet a well-realised individual. 'One of the company, a girl bought in Athens' is seen in a crucial situation, in which she is confronted with a moment of choice. It is, of course, the mere sight of Blanchefleur that enables her to make the vital decision correctly,

> whether with a passport under the king's seal
> to return safe to Athens through the themes;
> or whether with a dowry to wed some friend;
> or to swear herself still of the household, and
>   leave
> what end would to come – and then to grieve
> perchance for all forgone. (148)

Taliessin cannot help her: the decision must be hers. This girl's sensitivity allows her to perceive how painful Blanchefleur's departure is for Taliessin; as well as to understand the nature of her own servitude in the light of the princess's own 'bondage', and to evaluate it more correctly. As she understands the power that comes from discipline, 'at once, in her heart/servitude and freedom were one and interchangeable'. The journey of the cavalcade along the road allows the girl to think out her whole situation in the light of her perception of the implications of Blanchefleur's choice. There is an unreality about the centaur shapes of the cloaked riders in the rain which assists this girl to consider, dispassionately, detachedly, the choices before her, and to know that there is 'no choice then or ever' for her, for 'fixed is the full'. Blanchefleur both enables others to realise their vocation and gives them a yardstick to measure themselves by. We see in this poem, in the representative figure of the slave girl, the complex process of realisation that even lesser natures must go through in order to reach their own certainties and to make their own vital decisions.

Other slaves also illustrate the spiritual potential of the ordinary person; in 'The Star of Percivale' (64), the serving-maid whose 'face is flushed with the mere speed of adoration' as Taliessin plays, is contrasted with Lancelot, whose gaze at the Host 'found only a ghost of the Queen'. In 'The Ascent of the Spear', (66), however, another girl – or perhaps the same one – is in trouble, in the stocks for 'taking a stick/to a sneering bastard slut'. One's sympathy is at once engaged for the sulky, defiant girl whose indignation, one feels, was probably entirely justified, at least by the ordinary standards of this world. Taliessin's gentleness elicits from her a half-sobbing laugh and a blush, as she chokes on her words. Again and yet again in this scene she tries to speak and cannot finish the sentence, but with her last words, 'I was wrong from beginning', she has reached full understanding, and her attitude has completely changed. The psychological realism of the little scene is very convincing; while this ordinary girl's experience makes apparent the difference between the world's order, and heaven's.

The girl in 'The Coming of Galahad' (87), who asks Taliessin what food he had preferred at the coming of the Grail, does not have quite so much personality or individuality as the girl in the stocks, though she, too, has known the hazel's stripes on her shoulders. She is searching for understanding; her function in the sequence is to ask the questions that should be asked, to enable Taliessin to comment on the great event that has just taken place. Yet this unnamed girl, who certainly was and perhaps still is a slave, can break in upon the king's poet's conversation, smile gravely, hold out her hand to be kissed by Taliessin, and finally let cry, 'Lord, make us die as you would have us die'. The presence of such figures as this girl and the other slaves makes clearly apparent the courtesy of the Household, of Byzantium, as well as suggesting the necessity for the discipline without which it could not exist.

'The Queen's Servant', as C. S. Lewis points out, makes even clearer the significance of the slave's status, and of her emancipation for a higher service. This girl, bought by Taliessin in Caucasia, has emerged from barbarism with a fuller capacity for the Christian life. She will be required to read Greek and translate, to manage the building of rose-gardens, and to know how to wait upon her mistress. More than this, she must know the rhythms of ceremony, and of the grand art. However one understands these symbolic accomplishments, they constitute a wide range of desirable faculties, intellectual, practical and intuitive. In the casting off of all superfluities, of her old nature, the girl is pre-pared for her new and fuller life, clothed anew in the beauty and splendour of the roses and wool, with all their sym-bolic undertones. She is made free, in readiness for more strenuous service. Her eyes are now set upon Taliessin, 'com-panion to companion, peer to peer', 'flesh and blood and soul/whole and organic in the divined redemption' under the Protection.

It is such astonishingly poems as *this*, so extraordinarily and so rich in symbolic meaning, that seem to me to make *Taliessin through Logres* and *The Region of the Summer Stars* the most distinguished and important rehandling of the Arthurian myths in the twentieth century. By relating the myths to Byzantium, instead of limiting the setting to medieval Britain, Charles Williams was able to introduce the slaves. And these slaves, presented to us with so much sym-pathy, understanding and psychological realism, are vital to the communication of his deeper meanings, since they help to make apparent the implications of Byzantium in ordinary human terms.

So what conclusions can one draw from all this? Charles Williams's emphasis on the importance of women in the life of the City, obvious enough perhaps in the novels, seems to me even more apparent here. We see that they have many different roles; Helayne the mother of Galahad, of the mother of the Unicorn's voice, are of course special cases, but for every woman there exists the possibility of being the instrument of divine purpose. Blanchefleur is the mother of the *nature* of lovers. Women are shown as – at their best – love's means to love, though Guinevere fails to fulfil her role, and Morgause knowingly brings evil into active life. The City also needs those who, like

Elayne the wife of Bors, have vision and ideals and can bring order and abundance into everyday life, for ordinary people. (It is easy to see why Elayne of Astolat could not serve Williams's purpose.) But with the practical, the spiritual must go hand in hand; mere do-gooders do not have enough to give. Elayne, as Blanchefleur's friend and Bors's inspiration, embodies both the practical and the spiritual.

Charles Williams also asserts, through the women in the cycle, the intrinsic beauty and goodness of the flesh appropriately disciplined, as reflection of the divine beauty, source of inspiration, and constant delight. It is in and through the flesh that we learn: through the scar on the slave's back, through the arm of Iseult. We also see that the life of the City, of the Company, of the Household is open to all, from the princess to the slave. The City can of course accommodate all, needs all, and it offers scope for growth in spirituality, through discipline and service, through the servant's own initiative and through the operation of grace. But by means of such figures as Blanchefleur, so perfectly realised, and the anonymous slaves, Charles Williams ensures that the life of devotion never appears dreary or disagreeably pious. The Grail offers meats of 'love, laughter, intelligence and prayer'; and the importance of the more unexpected gifts of *laughter* and *intelligence*, so characteristic of Williams's teaching (if one can call it that) is, I think, made apparent in these poems. The intelligence of the girl in 'The Queen's Servant' and Blanchefleur's smile are examples. Williams understands *joy*.

It is interesting to consider the way in which women are presented in some other Arthurian works of the 19th and 20th centuries by way of comparison. In the *Idylls of the King*, Tennyson − for his own very good reasons − showed the ladies of the court as contemptible in their coarse superficiality and lack of moral fibre, and Guinevere, at the end, as humiliated, grovelling in acknowledgement of her wrongdoing, a painful spectacle. In *The Once and Future King*, T. H. White understands all, forgives all, and shows Guinevere as a lovable individual. More recent retellings of the story in the form of out-and-out romances, such as Marion Bradley's *The Mists of Avalon* (1983), often take a mildly feminist approach, and tend rather to focus on the sexuality of

Guinevere and other female figures. To do so is usually to trivialise both character and story. But by comparison, Williams in my view can be seen to have greater insight into at least some aspects of women's experience than do many writers, and to represent women, as women, with remarkable fairness. Of course women in the 'Taliessin' poems are important for him as symbols rather than as individuals, and for their spiritual potential rather than as sexual objects, but such recognition as this implies is surely to be welcomed. Women are presented as symbols, without condescension, enabling Williams to make profound observations about the nature of women's experience: 'dying each other's life, living each other's death' (63).

Though Williams fully acknowledges the significance of the body, 'the substantial flesh', he recognises that relationships between men and women are not necessarily always sexual. Women may be friends and equals, the slave-girl with the King's poet, 'slave and squire, woman and wizard' (109). 'Her eyes were set/upon him, companion to companion, peer to peer' (163), we read, of 'The Queen's Servant' and Taliessin. And as Williams also suggests in *The Figure of Beatrice* (182), an interchange of function between men and women is often possible. 'Hell is the cessation of work', to have no function is unbearable. Beatrice requires of Dante that his function should be perfectly fulfilled. We see that in the 'Taliessin' poems, most figures have a function of some kind in the Household. They may be mere slaves, at the other end of the scale from Dindrane and Elayne, but as such they show that many different roles are available to women, according to their gifts and their natures. The household is hierarchical, but the hierarchy does not place women below men as a matter of course.

Williams also suggests in these poems as elsewhere, that women – and once again, especially such women as Dindrane and Elayne who have fulfilled or are fulfilling their spiritual potential – offer like Beatrice a 'way of knowing'. 'Beatrice is the knowing', Williams says (231), and so too is Dindrane. They demonstrate, as Beatrice does, what Love is 'about', what Love is 'up to' (232). The Beatrician moment (which of course can be seen to occur in Williams's poems, as elsewhere in his writing) is as he says, a moment of choice, and his identification and definition of the experience suggest his understanding of psychology. It does happen. The experience may not be literally restricted to a girl and a lover; other relationships may offer such moments of revelation. But perhaps one of the main points suggested by Williams's definition of the 'Beatrician moment' as a moment of choice is that such experiences often occur through human relationships rather than from, say, intellectual effort. The 'Taliessin' poems also take for granted that such experience is possible; the moment of revelation, of realisation can and does change lives. And through the women in the poems, Williams shows significant changes constantly taking place. Symbolic though they remain, Williams's characters are dynamic, and their capacity for experiencing and for initiating change makes the poems themselves dynamic.

Many of the traditional figures who appear in the Arthurian stories make their appearance in the cycle, and with few exceptions, the author has set them before us very much as they figure in the medieval versions. Arthur and Guinevere, Lancelot and Gawain, Kay and Bors and Percivale and Merlin come before us in more or less familiar form, except in so far as the fresh insights which Williams brings to the story enable us to see new facets. But within the traditional framework, women appear who are virtually or entirely his creation, from Blanchefleur − source of illumination and understanding − to the slaves, humble servants and learners. They can show us more of the practical, day-to-day aspects of the spiritual life, I think, than can be learnt from any other version of the Grail story.

(*Page references in the text are to 'Taliessin Through Logres' and 'The Region of the Summer Stars' by Charles Williams and 'Arthurian Torso' by Charles Williams and C. S. Lewis introduced by M. M. Shideler, Eerdmans Publishing Co., Michigan 1974.*)

Chapter Eight

The Role of the Slaves in Charles Williams's Poetry

Brenda Boughton

I think it is worthwhile to begin by asking a rethorical question − "What images are thrown up in the minds of most of us in the latter part of the twentieth century by the word "slave"? Blessedly we have no direct experience of such a person in our society, and we have even come to use the word loosely, not to say misleadingly, in such terms as 'wage-slaves'. Probably we have ideas that coalesce round such images as Spartacus and his uprising, very harsh punishments being lawful and without redress, extremes of luxury being fuelled by slave labour, unremitting toil and sexual subjugation for both sexes. There may be as well a touch of the exotic from the East: Turkish harems of bygone centuries, and unknown horrid practices from the further Orient. Dominating all these in shaping our imaginations, though, is the example nearest to us in the New World barely two centuries ago and most notable in the rigour of its regime.

The essential feature of slaves through all the centuries and in all societies was that they were outsiders. If freedom ever came for slaves it was not until a sufficiency of years had more or less made them insiders. They were procured initially by conquest in war, piracy, kidnapping, punishment for crime or debt, or they were the offspring of slaves or sold into slavery by parents or spouses. Like other parts of the economy, the Christian church was deeply embroiled in slavery and never condemned it. The trade in slaves was everywhere profitable and highly specific. Money could buy you anyone you wanted, of any age, with any skill. There was always some hope that freedom might be gained. However, the rules of manumission varied widely when they applied to all, and were widely disregarded. Christian observance compares unfavourably with that of Islam, which much more meticulously observed the six-year rule laid down in the Koran. A freed slave of more or less the same colour as his owner's countrymen was able to melt into the population quite quickly, but cross-colour ownership gave rise to the ongoing hardship of this being impossible. One's slave origin was betrayed by one's skin, as in North America's southern states. The oft-told tale of Wilberforce and his struggle to outlaw the Slave Trade leaves a warm glow in every Englishman's heart, but tends to obscure the sad reality of widespread slavery in other parts of the world, even today.

When I first began looking into the general subject of slavery, preparatory to thinking afresh about the slaves in Charles Williams's poetry, I was surprised to discover the extent of it in both ancient and modern times: perhaps I should not have been. It is another instance of not seeing what we have not looked for.

There are plenty of disputes in modern scholarship about the detail of conditions in different societies at different times but clear agreement that the word 'slave' must be reserved to describe only that category of person who has been sold or is born into the absolute ownership of another. This condition had virtually no essential variation throughout history but must be kept distant from serfdom. For example the slaves of Anglo-Saxon times, as of others, were regarded as the stock of their owner. In stock inventories that have come down to us slaves and animals are listed together. They had no credibility and no legal rights; their labour and their persons were disposed of at the will of their owner. A slave was a slave was a slave. What seems to us today one of the worst aspects of this was the absolute right of owners to disregard family ties when it suited them between slave parents and their children or

between slave spouses. If a slave achieved manumission
only his or her children born after freedom was attained
were themselves free; the earlier children remained the
property of the owner.

Doubtless individual owners varied in the rigour with
which their slaves were treated, but 'one cannot escape
recognition of the fact that the failure of any individual
slaveowner to exercise all his rights over his slave property
was always a unilateral act on his part, never binding,
always revocable'. (M. Finlay: *Ancient Slavery and Modern
Ideology*). It is proper to emphasise all this because the
term 'slave' must always include what Demosthenes defined
as the greatest difference between the slave and the free man,
which is 'that the former is answerable with his body for all
offences' – which usually meant a flogging or other tor-
turous abuse. But being answerable also meant being 'at
the disposal of' for purposes of sex: 'Horace was not
being satirical when he recommended his own preference
for household slaves, male or female – "I like my sex easy
and ready to hand" ' (Finlay).

Turning to the period in England from the Dark Ages
to medieval times we find that the Anglo-Saxons, like their
Saxon cousins, were accustomed to slave-ownership. Curiously enough, the invasion of the Normans into Britain
accelerated the decline of slavery here. While they certainly
subjugated the Saxons, they were more disposed to free the
slaves they acquired than their former owners. About 10%
of the population of England is recorded in Domesday Book
as 'slave'. In the course of the next few centuries they
declined in numbers and eventually disappeared as varied
forms of serfdom and villeinage absorbed them (F.M. Stenton,
Anglo-Saxon England).

This brings us to the knotty question of how to regard the
'time' of Williams's poems. Written in the twentieth century for modern ears they meditate upon events in Arthur's
time. But what was that? It certainly will not help much
to project our thoughts towards what we know of sixth-
century England, but to live imaginatively in the myth we
need to place them somewhere. I think we have to say
that Arthur's time is inside the poet's head and inside
ours. There resides the historical Arthur, but there also

resides all that has come to us from medieval times 'about' Arthur, notable from Malory. The great names of Arthur, Galahad, Lancelot and the rest cannot be spoken without bringing with them reverberations of their medieval incarnations. Williams's own description of the development of the legend of Arthur and the legend of the Grail (published in *Arthurian Torso*) make it very plain that the story as projected by Malory is, for Englishmen, the important poetic source. There is no mention of slaves in Malory (and I suppose they did not feature in his French sources either) but that need not detain us. Slaves were endemic in the period to which the story of Arthur is assigned and for many centuries to follow, and we may certainly feel that Williams was entitled to introduce them should his purposes demand it. What unifies the two disparate periods is the nature of this poetry – not epic, or primarily narrative, though narrative appears, but sometimes lyric, most often meditative. As he himself wrote: 'The poems do not so much tell a story or describe a process as express states or principles of experience.' It is in the life of the imagination that the real Arthur and the medieval Arthur co-exist.

So what were the poetic purposes that required the introduction of slaves? It would be cheating a bit to tell you what I think they were without first looking at the relevant poems. There are six which cry out for attention, three from each of the two latest books of the Arthurian cycle. In *Taliessin Through Logres* there is only one which positively introduces us to a slave but the two others which precede it present us with a girl whom Lewis has no doubts about referring to as 'a barbarian slave girl' and, who, on this authority, I think must be included. Certainly her position is lowly enough to fit the picture, and she refers to having 'escaped the stripping and whipping' – a very likely punishment for a slave. We will not stop to consider the fascinating question why, if Williams thought of her as a slave, and originally referred to her as such to Lewis, did he obliterate this in the poems as we have them?

The first of these poems, 'The Star of Percivale' opens tranquilly with Percivale playing his harp 'by the magical western door of the king's hall', and Taliessin defining the music with his voice. The attention then moves to the ardent young soul of a maid, at service in the hall, who runs to fall at Taliessin's feet in a passion of obedience. She has had a Beatrician moment. Taliessin very properly warns her to re-direct her devotion away from him ('I too am a man') and goes on to proclaim: 'More than the voice is the vision, the kingdom than the king'. The second half of that line reminds us of what we have already begun to see in 'The Crowning of Arthur' and will see later in the cycle — Arthur's self-absorption in his role and final inability to put the claims of the kingdom above his own. We then see her bright ado-ration acknowledged by the Archbishop, Dubric, and joy exchanged with him as she shows the depth of her under-standing of what is taking place: 'The light of another, if aught, I bear, as he the song of another.' The remainder of the poem falls away from that high moment to take in the general scene and comment on it. It focuses finally on three separate failures, the 'causeless vigil of anger' of Lord Balin the Savage, the nascent hubris of the king, and Lancelot's gaze at the Host whch is found to be actually intent on an image of the Queen.

The next poem opens on the same girl sitting in the stocks. Her bright steps towards Christ's glory have faltered, as Dubric feared they might. She is in the stocks for a fault she freely but very angrily admits. Her sense of worth is outraged; she will not even look at Taliessin as she answers his question:

> Fortunate, for a brawl in the hall, to escape
> They dare tell me, the post, the stripping and
>   whipping;
> Should I care, if the hazel rods cut flesh from bone,

This is defiance. Taliessin meets it by pointing to the sin 'worse than rage, pride of guilt or no guilt' — a sin either way. 'Did we not together adore?' He treats her throughout with high courtesy, but goes to the heart of her obduracy in not deigning even to throw back the mis-siles with which she has been pelted by the onlookers. He leads her to acknowledge her fault and deny pride, and her reward is 'her heart flowed to the crowd', what he calls 'her own poor kin'.

There follows an elegant coda to this. A 'demure' chamberlain comes from Sir Kay, the High Steward, to give Taliessin the option of deciding whether the girl should be released or not. He waives the right and refers it to the girl's choosing. She hesitates, thinking of what may be said of her choice either way, and Taliessin encourages her to 'treat the world's will but as and at the world's will'. His final gesture is to insist that the guard unlock the stocks: it is not for the king's poet to respond 'to the chamberlain's sly smile'.

Now let us turn to the slave, who is named as such in the poem called 'The Sister of Percivale', she who 'was named Blanchfleur in religion'. Lewis finds this to be the most difficult in the cycle and goes on to provide a wonderful exposition of many of the difficulties. Roma King's recent book makes no addition I want to refer to but is useful in providing a further consideration of the complexities. He makes a true comment when he remarks, à propos of this slave, 'No poet is more securely anchored in the material creation. The scarred body represents all Caucasia, flesh, fallen but subject to redemption.' (*The Pattern in the Web*).

We are invited in the poem to contemplate a scene as Taliessin, lying on a wall, watches it unfold. A slave, again a women, is drawing water from the well in the courtyard. As the bucket reaches the surface the trumpet at the gate announces the arrival of the princess Blanchfleur and her two brothers. The poem is dense with meanings that flicker round images involving measurement words such as circle, horizon, hemisphere, axis, plane, diameter, radii, circumference, asymptote, decimal.... Williams's great statement about Hell being 'inaccurate' is supported here by the attempt to glory in the exact relationship of significance between the meaning of the scars of the slave's back and the view Taliessin has of the face of Blanchfleur. In one sense it would be proper to say, as Lewis does, that he is enamoured of both. For his perceptions both are required. What is being made actual before us is 'the organic body singing together' the Empire in fact.

The slave, (and her treatment, the scars) show us, not so much the hurt and shame of discipline but what remains after it has been transformed. The scars are healed and shine white as she labours at the well. At another level of the functional hierarchy Blanchfleur appears. She is a princess, and her 'rare' face is 'the grace at the Back of the Mount'. A description of her dress is calculated to support the overall impression of 'a front of glory', and our last glimpse of her as she smiles and greets Taliessin is of one who can sing 'in one note the infinite decimal'.

It is impossible to consider the slave in this poem without the princess hovering in one's consciousness. The scars of the one and the star of Percivale's emblem (and consequently his sister's) are each perceived to be symbolic of their owners and are linked in glory. The slave as well as the princess is necessary to Williams's invention because his view of the beauty of Order, or as he usually called it, the City, requires those in the various social categories of function, willingly to embrace their duty. As he sees it, only thus can the individual be liberated into the republic of exchange. 'As willed necessity is freedom, so willed hierarchy becomes equality'. (Lewis).

Before moving on to *The Region of the Summer Stars*, this might be a good moment to pause and say something about the Empire, as projected by Williams in the cycle. He uses the image to bring before us his concept of the City, the provinces of this material world laid out in right relationship with one another. He chooses Byzantium rather than Rome to be the centre. Either would have served most of his poetic requirement but he says he chose Byzantium partly due to 'a romantic love of the (then) strange' and partly because the Byzantine Emperor was a more complex poetic image than the Roman.' In some earlier poems the Emperor was 'a kind of sacerdotal royalty'. Gradually he became 'God as known in Church and State, God as ruling men'. He claims that the identification of the Empire with the human organism just 'happened' and was not the result of curious ingenuity on his part. The drawing on the endpapers of *Taliessin Through Logres* illustrates his thinking here; Byzantium is represented by the navel, the centre, and Logres by the head. 'The Empire is the pattern, Logres the experiment.' Several commentators have written eloquently about this.

What has perhaps not been so much remarked is the difficulty of penetrating the mind-set of contemporary readers to the point of convincing them of the value of the fundamental principles of this Empire. It may actually be hard for them to believe in the desirability of an individual embracing necessity when so much political experience cries out for the need of collective refusal of necessities which are injust. Here it is not inappropriate to remember that Williams was 13 when the 19th century gave way to the 20th. His most formative years were lived in Edwardian times before the First World War and his stance vis-à-vis society was, and remained, largely acquiescent. Being fundamentally concerned with spiritual life and the life of the imagination he has little interest or energy for the never-ending struggle to transform society by direct action. A very revealing incident is referred to in one of his letters to Phyllis Jones. The time is Christmas 1927, barely a year after the General Strike. He writes from St Albans that while young Michael is being put to bed he will go and talk to his father-in-law, because Mr Conway wants to talk about the Budget. 'What a lot of people', he writes, 'understand the Budget'! His father-in-law does the talking, while doing some paper-hanging. Charles is amazed at such a hobby. 'As if I should ever want to hang paper on the walls! Or discuss the Budget – which I find my own father is yearning to do! Bless them.' It seems that both Mr Conway and Mr Williams the elder had a grasp of the policy and an interest in the process of its conduct quite absent in Charles. (Hadfield: *Charles Williams – An Exploration of his life and work.*)

There are three more poems that bear directly on this whole subject. Two concern themselves with aspect of manumission, the 'Departure of Dindrane' and 'The Queen's Servant'. In the first we are told that Logres kept the old Levitical law, which freed a slave automatically after seven years and gave him or her some choice of destiny. One of these choices was

To compact again with a fresh heart's love
In what household was sweet alike to past and future.

This framework was very apt for Wiiliams' purposes. He then shows us a girl who, approaching this moment of choice, is brooding on the alternatives but watchful of the scene before her. The princess is preparing to leave after a year's sojourn to take her vows at the convent at Almesbury. The slave is struck by 'the chrism of dedication. Shining already there in Dindrane's brow'. She misses nothing. She acknowledges the high courtesy of the love between Taliessin and Dindrane, who must now part. She knows the willing servitude to which Dindrane now goes

> the shell of her body
> Yearned along the road to the cell of vocation.

The poem hovers over great definitions of the two Ways: the Affirmation and the Rejection of Images, summed in the persons of Taliessin and Dindrane. Each acknowledges the other, and in the heart of the slave

> Servitude and freedom are one and interchangeable'.

On the one hand we are invited to contemplate the ever-changing hierarchy of merit, which reflects our acknowledgement of our masters in particular areas of life – 'we needs must love the highest when we see it' – and on the other hand the stable hierarchy of function. Writing in the person of Eugenio, one of the characters in his 'Dialogue on Hierarchy' in *Time and Tide* (1943), Charles Williams says quite explicitly that he is content to have it so for the sake of the organisation of society. He comments 'It is often easing to the mind to recognise this distinction for one may generously yield to function the respect which one would reasonably deny to incapacity'. Hence the general picture of authority from the top and the slave's relationship to it. The given order is not just to be endured; she has an opportunity to embrace it.

The view of society we are invited to acquiesce in is put neatly though crudely in a quatrain from 'All Things Bright and Beautiful'

> The rich man in his castle

The poor man at his gate
God made them high or lowly
And ordered their estate.

This is the literal reality which is used to substantiate the
spiritual realities. Frankly, it may be hard to hold on to the
subtle distinctions that Williams's poetry gives expression to,
when ringing in the ears of many is that other tradition of
gradual emancipation from oppression achieved painfully
over the centuries, which is summed up in the stalwart cry
of such as the Tolpuddle Martyrs:

We raise the watchword Liberty
We will, we will, we will be free.

Williams had a profound awareness that true freedom
resides in the exercise of choice, and he shows us in 'The
Ascent of the Spear' a slave choosing her redemption. But
the deliberate selection of a temporal environment for these
poems so rife with oppression as must be conveyed by
the very words 'Empire' and 'Slavery' may in the end
be the stumbling block which excludes readers who would
otherwise be receptive of his ideas. It demands from the
reader more than an exercise of historical imagination. One
has to put in abeyance the whole question of how do we
live in a just society and at the same time acknowledge the
undoubted truths of will and faith that are so important for
a right relation of the individual to God and the world. The
slave in this poem is able to perceive a kind of glory not just
in the persons and the manner of the princess and Taliessin
but in the beauty of dedication. The final lines retreat from
the high ground of meditation and drama and give us a
matter-of-fact statement as the slave makes what is by now
for the reader her inevitable choice:

They only can do it with my Lord who can do it
    without him,
And I know he will have about him only those.

'The Queen's Servant' we meet in the process of preparation for that role. She also is a slave of the king's

poet's household, this time a highly accomplished one, and she has just been chosen by Taliessin to fulfil a request from the Queen. It is needful to free her, since

The royalties of Logres are not slavishly served.

What follows is a wonderfully imagined scene of transformation. The slave was bought in Caucasia, standing here not only for the province but as a trope for the flesh. The girl denies memory of the place as described by Taliessin and he tells her she should read 'the maps of Merlin's book, or Ours or the one small title we brought from Byzantium.' Better, because quicker for understanding, is to undergo a rite. He tells her to unclothe, and then proceeds to furnish her with a glorious and magical succession of coverings derived from roses and lambswool. The significances shimmer through the images, and all is carried off with the lightness and charm of courtesy:

> The roses climbed round her; shoulder to knee
> they clung and twined and changed to a crimson kirtle
> The wool rose gently on no wind,
> and was flung to her shoulders; behind her, woven
>   of itself,
> it fell in full folds to a gold-creamed cloak.

'He fastened the cloak with his own brooch'; but also with her old leathern girdle. That, and the shoes from the household's best store will help her to keep 'the recollection of her peers'. Finally he strikes her lightly on the face as the Roman masters used to do and her manumission is complete.

In between these two poems lies 'The Founding of the Company' which is highly germane to this discussion, because it sums up a picture of the true co-inherence of 'the commons and the whole manner of love'. We are led to consider three degrees of dedication. At the bottom are those who:

> 'lived by a frankness of honourable exchange,
> Labour in the kingdom, devotion in the Church

Be the exchange dutiful or debonair.'
'The Company's second mode bore farther
The labour and fruition; it exchanged the proper self
and wherever need was drew breathe daily
in another's place, according to the grace of the
    Spirit
dying each other's life, living each other's death.'

Finally we come to those

Few — and that hardly — entered on the third
station, where the full salvation of all souls
is seen, and their co-inhering.

The poem proposes, in effect, an index of redemption which
runs through the whole company and brings

God's new grace in the street of Camelot.

It spread from the household of the King's poet and

was first nobly spoken as a token of love
Between themselves and between themselves and their
    lord.

Dinadan appears, and meets Taliessin's reluctance to assume
this lieutenancy by assuring him

    any buyer of souls
Is bought himself by his purchases; take the
    lieutenancy
for the sake of the shyness and excellent absurdity
holds.

In that *Dialogue on Hierarchy* already referred to, Williams
declared 'We are not to suppose that the hierarchy of one
moment is likely to be that of the next. The ranked degrees
of intelligence are continually reordered ... Equality is the
name we give to the whole sum of such changes.' His
thinking on this subject was of long gestation. In *Heroes
and Kings*, published in 1930, there is a marvellous sonnet

dedicated to Humphrey Milford which already encapsulates all the essentials. It is called 'On Kingship'

> That in the neighbourhood of mighty kings
> Lives true delight for ever, this I knew
> And tasted all the joy that order brings,
> headship, and ritual, when I looked on you,
> Caesar, amid your officers last night;
> and more than you — the worth of majesty,
> Distinction, place, and courts in motion right
> around the Presence, so the king's head be
> by the crown's self o'ershadowed; for the crown
> not to be too much merited, lest man
> suppose desert deserves it, shows his town
> not less, but more, O more republican
> when great equalities in order fall
> and freedom's self grows hierarchical.

He could so often find an acceptable counterpoint between these two hierarchies — of merit and of function; but it was his willingness to use the Byzantine Empire to carry so much meaning for his Arthurian cycle that I think does constitute a barrier that takes some overcoming.

What richness is here, though. Anne Ridler writes in her Preface to *The Image of the City* about the 'ambivalence of Williams's own habit of mind — between belief and scepticism. It came from his freedom from prejudice where ideas wee concerned, whatever their source.' We could add to that his scrupulous vigilance to go back to the text of what is being considered and not attend too much to the commentators — a trait encouraged apparently by his father who first drew his attention to:

> What slanders still the pious talk
> Of Voltaire and Tom Paine.

I suppose we cannot leave this subject without a reference to the recent publication of Charles Williams's letters to Lois Lang-Sims and her commentary. The somewhat disquieting view it gives of the extent to which by this time he was living inside his myth is bound to arouse defensive explanations there is no need for me to particularise here. The insistence on Lois becoming 'Lalage' is quite in tune with Florence being 'Michal' and Phyllis becoming 'Phyllida' and 'Celia'. It seems to me that Lois Lang-Sims has been remarkably clear and honest in her exposition and is probably right to think that he found it difficult to allow the individuality of another person to be independent of his myth when once they had assumed a place in it. They found themselves dismissed from his thoughts. Glen Cavaliero comments in his very insightful introduction that 'in this instance the real trouble may be that Williams did not know enough of his pupil as she really was. Their relationship was not based on an equality; and "Lalage" was more a figment of his own mind than she was Lois in the fullness of her being.' Nevertheless, she paints a welcome and glowing picture of the effect he had on her while she knew him, and defines very accurately several of the remarkable qualities others have also been struck by.

That he was aware of the difficulties of relationship up and down the ranks of the hierarchies comes out often in his writings. Here is a telling quote from a paragraph about Hadrian VII by Baron Corvo. 'One cannot love downwards, de haut en bas. That is reserved for God. One cannot love when one thinks oneself superior – even if one is superior. Human love is always between equals, and the most sheikh-like of heroes submits to that eventually however often he abducts heroines on camels.'

So what purpose do we think was served by the introduction of these slaves into the Arthurian myth? They are a most notable addition; only the shift to the perspective of Taliessin in the collection as a whole is a more radical alteration. It seems as though it cannot be other than to enhance the paradox he faces us with; that however lowly, however subjected to extremes of treatment, it is always open to the individual to 'choose necessity' and thereby escape the sense of being compelled and come into that harmony of relationships that makes exchanges of love possible. A slave is so absolutely at the disposal of her master that she makes this paradox clearer than had she been a free servant, however down-trodden. And being female of course emphasises this further. And he needs to be able to present us with images at the top and the bottom of this society in order to flesh out the concept of 'the organic body sang together'. It should perhaps be noted, however, that none of Williams's slaves are shown to us in the stress of suffering. (One can hardly regard the stocks in that light, however repugnant and the scars on the slave's back in 'The Sister of Percivale' are, precisely, healed). All have positive outcomes, even (one or two) glorious ones. This looks a bit like skewing the picture if one considers at all the evidence of the realities.

Chapter Nine

'It is Love that I am Seeking': Charles Williams and *The Silver Stair*

Kerryl Lynne Henderson

When Charles Williams was born in 1886, two years before the birth of T. S. Eliot and twelve years before C. S. Lewis, Queen Victoria had reigned for nearly fifty years and was at the height of her popularity. Her son, Edward VII, took the throne in 1901 when Williams was fifteen years old, and was in turn succeeded by George V in 1910. *The Silver Stair*, a sonnet sequence on the subject of love, was written just before the accession of George V, when Williams was in his early twenties. Three more volumes of poetry were written over the next decade. Williams's formative years as a poet thus spanned a period of significant change in the world of affairs and literary creation. He was born at the end of the Victorian era, a period which stressed traditional values and social concerns, and had been writing poetry for some fifteen years before the modernist movement made its definitive, radical break with the foundations of Western culture and thought (Eliot's *Waste Land* and Joyce's *Ulysses* were published in 1922).

Yet Williams's early poetry does not easily fit into classifications such as Victorian or modernist, nor is his work characteristic of the traditional romantic realism of the Georgians. In large part this elusiveness is due to the distinctive voice with which he speaks. Despite adherence to

131

traditional poetic forms, which would rank him with the Victorians, Williams's perspective is anything but traditional. He shares a deep commitment to Christian principles yet refuses to confine himself to a singular view, which puts him closer to the modernists. That is, although he is a man of definite and strongly held views, he continually, in his writings, takes those views and tests them from many angles — head on, obliquely, inside out, by negation, by affirmation, by metaphorical transference, by wrenching, by division, by unity. He is often accused of obscurity and awkwardness of expression because a general coherence fails to emerge with sufficient clarity. Nonetheless, his letters and personal communications do not indicate a man who sees himself darkly confused or in cosmic uncertainty about the nature of the universe. God rests comfortably at its centre.

God also rests *un*-comfortably at its centre. Both views are true, but only together. Neither expression is wholly true, alone. It is the tension between these two recognitions that characterises Williams's writings throughout his life: 'This is Thou; neither is this Thou.' He was not a dualist — darkness was not equal and opposite to the light for him. Light is always better, and the best, and finally darkness will flee before it. But darkness has not fled yet, and as long as we live in a world where darkness is present, it will show us something about the light. Nothing is wasted in the Divine Economy.

Williams does not exalt the natural world with its attendant evils for its own sake, though at times he comes perilously close. Rather, he lets it serve the greater spiritual world, and values it according to its service. This approach led to severe problems with certain critics, such as Theodore Maynard who, while reading *Poems of Conformity*, decided Williams was a satanist and wrote a scathing attack in *The New Witness*, G. K. Chesterton's weekly newspaper (published 1912–1923). (Maynard later retracted his accusations, however, conceding that Williams was an Anglo-Catholic who had 'established for himself a philosophical point of contact between Paganism and the Christian faith.'[1]) Williams's familiar look at evil as it serves the good also set him apart from a common Victorian view typified by his father's published stories and poems and his uncle's fairly orthodox antiquarian books. Love, for them, was an amazing gift from a righteous God, and man's responsibility was to nurture that love despite life's hardships. Williams would have agreed with that view, but for him love was also a tantalising mystery, an exciting quest full of paradoxes and complexities, an abstraction more real and ultimately more knowable than the natural world itself. God, whose name is Love, became less an anchor for the soul and more like a hook drawing Williams towards greater glories but at the risk of greater perils along the way.

Background Influences

Before we look at these themes in *The Silver Stair*, it might be useful to examine in more detail the published work of members of Williams's family, beginning with his father, Richard Walter Williams, who published under the name 'Stansby', a family name. According to Alice Mary Hadfield's biography of Williams, his father was an avid reader and had many books in the house. He spent much time in discussion with Charles about poetry and history. These discussions helped Charles formulate his own views of life. In the poem 'Divorce' (1920) Charles states that, as a young man, he turned for instruction to

> [. . .] such souls as, torn with pain,
> Have proved all things and proved them vain
>   And have no joy thereof,
> Yet lifting their pale heads august
> Declare the frame of things is just,
>   Nor shall the balance move [.]

Such a one was his father, 'Who taught me all the good I knew / Ere Love and I were met':

> Great good and small, – the terms of face,
> The nature of the gods, the strait
>   Path of the climbing mind,
> The freedom of the commonwealth,
> The laws of soul's and body's health,

The commerce of mankind.

The charges launched on Christendom
You showed me, ere the years had come
    When I endured the strain,
Yet warned me, unfair tales to balk,
What slanders still the pious talk
    Of Voltaire and Tom Paine.

What early verse of mine you chid,
Rebuked the use of doth and did,
    Measuring the rhythm's beat;
Or read with me how Caesar passed,
On the March Ides, to hold his last
    Senate at Pompey's feet!

Walter Williams not only read about and discussed these subjects, he also wrote poems and stories which reflected his philosophical outlook. It is not clear when Walter began to write for publication, but in 1876 a 16-page, monthly periodical entitled *The North London Magazine* began circulation in the 'northern parts of London called Hoxton, Kingsland, and De Beauvoir Town' (*NLM*, V. 1, p. 2). The editors invited contributions from 'those of our friends and readers who may wish to contribute,' which, they hoped, would 'greatly add to the interest of the Magazine, and be the means of bringing out the latent abilities of many aspirants for literary fame residing in the locality'. The Williams family resided in the area of North London known as Holloway at this time, and Walter took full advantage of the opportunity. In 1879 his first story, 'Jim', and poem, 'December', appeared in *NLM*, after which he became a regular contributor, publishing nine poems, six stories, and the first five chapters of a serial story over the next year and a half.

Stansby's writings also appeared in several other journals of the day. *Household Words* (1881–1899), under the editorship of Charles Dickens's son, published at least nine poems, the first appearing in 1881 and the last in 1893; *Chambers's Journal* (1843–1956) published one poem in 1894 and another in 1895, both of which were reprinted in the American publication *Littell's Living Age* (1844–1941); and the *Temperance Record* (1856–1907) published a short story in 1904. Walter Williams's writings give us a good idea of his approach to literary creation, which was essentially harmonious with the Christian and humanitarian views of the Victorian editors, characterised by an insistence on high moral standards. *Household Words* was a family journal intended to replace what Dickens called the 'villainous' periodical literature of crime and sensation popular among the reading public of the day.[2] *The North London Magazine* stated expressly that

> The trashy and only semi-moral tendency of much of the light reading of the present day will be avoided, and whilst the contributions, it is hoped, will sometimes be found amusing and humourous, none will be admitted, the morality of which is not of the highest character.

Poems and stories in these periodicals were usually didactic and infused with Christian principles. There was little attempt at subtlety of thought or expression and no ambivalence about the demands of existence. Life, literature, vicissitudes, Scripture, all were readily comprehensible when viewed with a good dose of common sense, folk wisdom, and acknowledgement of the Christian verities. The challenge of life was to conform oneself to the obvious – obvious, that is, if one just took a little time to look and meditate, and then pray.

Take, for instance, Stansby's poem in *The North London Magazine* (1880, p. 28):

PARTED
'With Christ, which is far better.'

Dark as the cloud in stormy sky,
   And chill as winter's breath,
The silent shadow passes by,
   We speak of here as Death.
No home but one day feels his power,
   No home but yields in thrall,
And learns at last, in some dread hour,
   His rule is over all.

And so he takes them, one by one,
　　He turns their life's last page,
Maiden or mother, sire or son,
　　Fresh youth, or hoary age.
He calls them, and they fade and sink,
　　And vanish from our side,
We stand upon the river's brink,
　　But they have crossed the tide.

Oh Saviour Christ! Thou knowest all
　　The bitter sense of loss;
Be near us when the shadows fall,
　　And help us bear the cross.
Though lonely here the path may be,
　　Where pain and sorrow are,
We trust our dear ones dwell with Thee,
　　And that is better far.

Here we see the overt, unselfconscious reliance on Christ to meet our needs as life's sorrows assail us. Again, a selection from opening paragraphs of Stansby's stories gives a sense of the down-to-earth, deep but uncomplicated view of life:

'Only an Old Maid': 'Yes, my dear, you are quite right, I am "only an old maid," one of a class of persons that you young people look upon with, I believe, a mingled feeling of pity and contempt. No; I am not offended with you, though I confess to being a little hurt, not by your thoughtless words, but by the recollection of the past that they bring afresh to my mind. You have sometimes asked me why I never married, and if you would care to hear the story – it is not a long one – I will tell you now.'

'A Strong Temptation': 'Sunshine, sunshine everywhere. On quiet villages and busy towns; on open highways and on narrow streets, the gladdening radiance fell. Wide fields of corn, waving and bending in the summer breeze, took from the beams a deeper tint and richer hue of gold, and sweet wildflowers, on mossy bank and fragrant hedgerow, turned bud and blossom upward to the sky, and drank in warmth and life.'

'For Her Sake': '[. . .] In the shadow cast by one of the boats, a young man was lying resting his head upon his hand, and gazing dreamily out across the glittering sea. His features, if not regular, were pleasing, with a frank, and open expression though there was a lack of resolution and settled purpose indicated by the lower part of the face, giving the impression of one ready to plan, but slow to execute; one who would deserve success, but in nine cases out of ten would lose it through want of energy in action.'

Perhaps the grandest opening paragraph is that to 'Beyond the Grave':

Night brooded over the Imperial city. In his mansion slept the noble, in his hut the slave. Here and there a few revellers broke the silence with their shouts, but, as the hours wore on, these grew less frequent, and at last died entirely away.

As these selections suggest, Walter's stories are characterized by a sensitivity to the human plight, an attention to character, an embracing of the natural wonders of creation. The ideas are highly moral, but seldom obscure or abstract in nature. The general tone is one of acceptance of the world, and resolution to meet its vicissitudes in a morally responsible way. The world is not a place of mystery where we strive to unlock its secrets, but a rational, moral world whose fundamental unknowns (i.e., the mysteries) are an unquestioned part of the greater whole, which is itself not a mystery. God and His universe, as it were, will forever remain in part unknown, and that is not just acceptable, but comforting in its own way; the finite needs the infinite. There is no sense of existential yearning for something just beyond reach, *die blaue Blume*.

This view of the world is clearly shared in a poem by Charles's aunt on his mother's side. Alice Wall, also published in *The North London Magazine* (1880), entitled 'Looking unto Jesus'. The 16-line poem has four stanzas of rhyming couplets and sounds very much like a hymn. For example, stanza three begins, 'If with sorrow life seemed crowded, and the world so full of sin,/Follow in the Saviour's footsteps, peace and comfort thou shalt win.' We know that Charles was relatively close to his Aunt Alice, for in 1911, when he met with Alice Meynell to discuss *The Silver Stair*, Charles wrote a long letter to his aunt describing the meeting. We have no way of knowing whether he was familiar with his aunt's poem, but he was no doubt well aware of the general attitude toward God and the world reflected in it.

Charles was also acquainted with his uncle's writings, although he does not seem to have been as comfortable with his uncle as with his aunt. In the same letter to Aunt Alice, he concludes by urging her to 'Tell Grandma as much as seems good to you: but not my respected uncle. Time enough when the book comes out for his remarks.' By the time of this letter, 1911, J. Charles Wall had published six books, primarily on antiquarian subjects (tombs, shrines, abbeys, ancient earthworks), but also one entitled *Devils* (1904), which looks at the depiction of devils throughout history and throughout the world, in architecture, art, legends, proverbs, moral tales, and natural phenomena. Two features of his works are particularly relevant to our examination of Charles Williams's early poetry. One is the strongly moral and Christian view of the world which emerges in them, a view, as we have seen, shared by Charles's father and aunt, but in the uncle's case, tinged with rather more of a spirit of inquiry or even reluctant scepticism. For example, in discussing the origin of evil in the world in *Devils*, Charles says:

The first man and woman, according to the literal wording of Holy Scripture, were Adam and Eve. It may be an old-fashioned notion and not in accordance with the modern theory of evolution. Just so; but the old fashion of simple faith, as much as it is sneered at now, was a time of happy trust in the Divine inspiration, although it is not civilisation unless we are doubting, and trying to tear away the veil to peer into that which has been hidden from curious gaze; the content of the dark ages, lingering at the present day in Brittany and elsewhere, brought more true happiness. The old fashion will, however, be all-sufficient for the present purpose. (*Devils*, p. 30).

Charles Williams, too, was torn between the 'old fashion of simple faith' and a desire 'to tear away the veil to peer into that which has been hidden from curious gaze.' But he ventured rather farther afield in his explorations than did his respected uncle. A desire to tear away the veil no doubt contributed to his joining the Order of the Golden Dawn in 1917, although his firm grounding in traditional Christianity prevented him from abandoning more orthodox expressions of faith.

But Uncle Charles shared another important interest with his nephew, an interest in things Arthurian. The introduction to his book *Shrines of British Saints* (1905), for instance, begins:

> Long years since, ere the fenlands were drained or the forests of England were so denuded of their majestic wealth of timber and foliage that they became mere plantations, when all locomotion was by foot, horse, or coracle, men and women, fired by divine love, undeterred by the difficulties of travel or the danger of preying wolves, carried the gospel news through the weird loneliness of vast solitudes to the tribes settled in the wildest recesses of the country.
>
> Those were the days of mystic loveliness and poetical beauty, when the Isle of Avalon was regarded as the abode of the spirits of the blest, when the Isle of Ely was held to be miraculously enshrouded and watergirt for the protection of purity. (p. ix)

Or, again, in *The Tombs of the Kings of England*, he states with great forcefulness,

> Treating of the people of these early times we have to confront so much that is mythical. There is an increasing delight in consigning many brilliant characters to total oblivion as never having existed. Such is the case with the famed King Arthur.
>
> That Arthur really lived and reigned is now generally accepted, to doubt which is 'unwarrantable scepticism.' If we doubt the word of Geraldus Cambrensis, an eye-witness of Arthur's exhumation, how can we expect

the writings of to-day to be accepted by future generations? (p. 11)

This book was published in 1891. We know that Charles was familiar with his uncle's writings, because he mentions two of them in his Arthurian notes, written between 1912 and 1917 in a commonplace book with the handwritten title, *The Holy Grail*.

These, then, are some of the influences on Charles Williams which form part of the background to his early poetry. The distinctiveness of his poetry in relation to these writings will emerge as we examine his poems in greater depth. Let us now turn to Williams's first book and its circumstances of publication.

The Silver Stair

The Silver Stair (*SS*) is a collection of 84 sonnets whose primary theme is the experience of love by a young man encountering that experience for the first time. When Williams composed these sonnets, he wrote within a long-established tradition of love-poetry, going back at least to the sonnets in Dante's *La Vita Nuova*. As was common in the earlier treatments, Williams explores love as a spiritual as well as physical phenomenon, and the role of the beloved is key to the coming of love. In Williams's cycle, however, the beloved plays a crucial but not primary role in the lover's coming to terms with his own experience of love. That is, the beloved is a means to something even greater. This overshadowing of the beloved by Love itself is emphasised in the quotation from Yeats at the opening of the volume:

It is love that I am seeking for,
But of a beautiful, unheard-of kind
That is not in the world.

[. . .] never have two lovers kissed but they
Believed there was some other near at hand,

And almost wept because they could not find it.
(Yeats, *The Shadowy Waters*, quoted in *SS*, p. iii)

This view of love was one from which Williams never departed. His late novels and Arthurian poetry are more mature expressions of man lost in a world of love, but Love's operation in the City, the Household, and the Body are already present and fairly well-developed in *The Silver Stair*.

Williams's choice of the sonnet form presented him with particular challenges. Despite its simplicity of structure and singleness of idea, or perhaps because of these features, the sonnet demands a full command of the harmonies of language, powerful concentration of thought, and loftiness of subject matter to achieve the grandeur of which a short verse form is capable.[3] Williams is successful quite often in meeting these challenges. He chose the Petrarchan rather than the Shakespearean sonnet, which allowed him to avoid the epigrammatic effect of the final couplet in the Shakespearean twelve-two line division and take full advantage of the Petrarchan octave-sestet with its bipartite structure of observation/conclusion, statement/counterstatement, question/answer.[4] Indeed, this form is more suitable for the kind of exploration Williams attempts in the cycle, which is often tentative and probing rather than meant to drive home a point. Every sonnet adheres strictly to the *abbaabba* rhyme scheme in the octave, but the sestet varies considerably, with *cdecde* the most frequent structure. Williams uses iambic pentameter throughout, and the turn, or *volta*, is usually signalled by a gap in the text between octave and sestet.

The Silver Stair has a more comprehensive division of the sonnets into three 'Books', each sonnet being given a descriptive title. In an essay entitled 'Me,' written sometime after 1924, Williams explains his intention in each of the 'Books':

The 'story', to call it so, is of a young man [not himself, he states earlier in the essay] thoroughly discontented with the world who suddenly and for the first time falls in love − that is the first book. The second is concerned with the development of that experience; and the particular point about it is that he is discontented with the ordinary result of love. He feels it in a way that urges him *away* from marriage as much as towards it; because he feels *love*. Love as a being not as a name. [. . .] he sets aside the ordinary things and enters (he and his lady) on the path of virginal love. And the third book is a kind of ode in praise of Love as God and Man [. . .].

Book I has 15 sonnets, Book II has 51, and Book III has 16; Book III also includes a set of six sonnets entitled 'The Passion of Love', which deal with various facets of Christ's Passion.

The descriptive titles of the poems ranged in length from quite short ('An Ascription') to rather long and involved ('The predestined Lover, ignorant of Love, declares his Creed'; 'The lover, ending, praises his lady in the fullness of Love'). The two prefatory sonnets are simply titled 'I' and 'II'. These titles apparently were not presented in the original version of the cycle, for, in a letter to Aunt Alice, Williams says of the visit to the Meynells, 'that I promised to make the few alterations Mrs. Meynell had suggested, & to think out a title for each one (which Fred Page is now doing, while I criticise)'. Fred Page, who worked with Williams at the Oxford University Press, was the one who introduced Williams to the Meynells. Most of the titles seem connected (more or less strongly) with the sonnets, but a few seem remote at best. It is at least arguable that the titles tend to become distractions and take away from the impact of the poetry by forcing too much attention on themselves. Nonetheless, the titles do serve to unify the sonnets in such a way that a general thematic development is discernible.

Although Williams was not the first to employ descriptive titles, they appeared only rarely in major sonnet and love poetry collections which preceded *The Silver Stair*. Petrarch, Sidney, Spenser, Shakespeare, Meredith, and Bridges did not use such titles, nor did Dante (in, e.g., Rossetti's translation of *La Vita Nuova*), although he did give short expositions of the content of each sonnet. Yeats, however, has similar titles in, for instance, 'The Wind among the Reeds'. Poem LII is titled 'The Lover mourns for the Loss of Love'; Poem LIII, 'He mourns for the change that has come upon him and his Beloved, and longs for the End of the World.' Rossetti's translations of the early Italian poets also include descriptive titles. For example, Sonnet III by Guido Cavalcanti has the title 'He compares all Things with his Lady, and finds them wanting.' Similarly, Sonnet XVI of *The Silver Stair* is titled, 'God has set the world in his lady's heart; the lover questions of his part therein.' To what extent the titles for Williams's sonnets are Fred Page's contribution rather than Williams's is not known, but Williams seems to have been agreeable to their inclusion, and at least one early reviewer welcomed the titles with great enthusiasm:

> His book is the more readily acceptable because he has set forth the argument of each sonnet in a heading of simple prose. To the expert reader the poems will not seem to need the explanation. But the general reader is not ashamed to confess that he is not an expert. And to everyone the pleasure of a first reading is greatly increased by this kind of courtesy. (*The Tablet*, Feb. 15, 1913, p. 249)

I have attempted to give some idea of the structure of *The Silver Stair*. The circumstances of its composition are not entirely unknown, although we could wish for more details. Theodore Maynard, who met with Williams on several occasions after *Poems of Conformity* was published, states that Williams wrote the sonnet sequence between 'his twenty-first and twenty-third years'[5]; that would be between 1907 and 1909. He met Florence Conway in 1908 at a church Christmas party, and she reports that,

> One January night I went to a lecture. On my way home [...] Charles overtook me. He put a parcel into my hands, saying he had written a Sonnet Sequence called *The Silver Stair*. Its theme was Renunciation. Would I read it and tell him my opinion? [...] There were eighty-two sonnets and I read them all.[6]

It would appear from this statement that the two prefatory sonnets had not yet been written, and the date Florence received the poems was probably January of 1910. It is clear from the tone and themes of the sonnets that Charles had begun to probe his spiritual experience rather deeply, particularly in relation to the experience of Love (both divine and earthly) even before he met Florence. There is no indication that he had fallen in love with anyone prior to meeting her, however. In fact, a number of sonnets describe a young man who has heard and read about (romantic) love, but has so far failed to experience it:

> Yet if in very truth such god there be
> How shall he not reveal himself to me?
>   O Love, O Love, exalt thyself, O Love! (II)

> Nor I the less salute you that no face
>   Hath sent these heart-beats quicker, that no hand
>   Hath e'er touched mine save in due courtesy. (IV)

> Speak, servitors of Love, speak, ye elect,
>   Who hold your stations in his mysteries,
>   Tell us again how sweet the knowledge is! (V)

These sonnets are about love. But how is loved defined? The entire sonnet cycle is itself an answer to that question. Sonnet XXXVIII treats of the meanings which lurk within the word:

> I love her! O! what other word could keep
>   In many tongues one clear immutable sound,
>   Having so many meanings? It is bound,
> First, to religion, signifying: 'The steep
> Whence I see God,' translated into sleep
>   It is: 'Glad waking,' into thought; 'Fixed ground;
>   A measuring-rod,' and for the body: 'Found.'
> These know I, with one more, which is: 'To weep.'

Religion, sleep, thought, the body – these significations by no means exhaust the forms of love. For Williams, whatever can be experienced in life, becomes a means to know love, even 'to weep'. But it is not accidental that he binds love's many meanings, 'First, to religion.' The workings of God and Love are interwoven. Both speak and both command response:

Then rang a great voice, shaking tower and booth,
The beggar's porch, and Love his own high seat.

Men say it thundered; others, that there fell,
  Being falsely built, part of the city wall;
And some few: 'Therein God spake.' Who can tell?
But indeed this may be, if it be,
  O Lord of Love, assure me that there call,
  Thy summons, is not laid on me, not me! (XLIII)

This sonnet is titled, 'To one, sitting at the receipt of custom, Love said, "Leave all and follow me".' But love has its cost, for Love is also 'The steep whence I see God' (XXXVIII), and that steep is the one Christ has already climbed: 'God's feet came up toward us from Nazareth,/Olivet, Tabor, Golgotha to climb' (Prefatory II). In Sonnet XLII he contrasts a garden like Eden, made for lovers, and another garden, where Christ showed to man God's greatest expression of love:

(Hush! also in a garden − O, too hard
The ways thereof that feet have trodden, scarred!
  Too crushed the grass by a prone agony!
But there, at night, by men with faces marred,
  Were olives gathered for Gethsemane,
  Was hewn the wood, shaped then for Calvary.)

This entire sestet is enclosed in parentheses, almost as an after-thought to the joyful affirmations of the octave. The lover is intimidated by this expression of Love: 'In sight of stretched hands and tormented brows   How should I dare to venture or to win/Love?' (XXXIII). He is not, however, always so fearful. In Sonnet XLIV, entitled 'Love said, "He that loveth his Life shall lose it",' the lover stands in Love's house and affirms:

'Surely,' I said, 'none would this house forsake,
Once found; yet still there lacks a thing, to make
Perfect all joy that doth our hearts befall.'

That hour a servant plucked me by the arm,

And showed me near at hand a little door,
   Narrow, low-arched, and carven there-above:
   'Through me by losing shall a man find love.'
  I tremble ere I open, yet am sure
That in his house Love shall meet no harm.

As the lover goes deeper into the experience of Love, he begins to see beyond the pain that is part of love, to the joy which the pain subserves. This affirmation of God and Love is the context within which all else that happens to the lover must be interpreted.

God stands in relation to lesser gods just as Love operates through the lesser loves: they can be a means to the one end, Love, or they can become rivals. One such god is Death, and at the beginning of the sonnet cycle this is the only god the lover acknowledges: 'There is no god, nor has been, nor can be/(Our folly this, and this our wisdom saith),/Who is so strong and pitiful as Death' (III). In Sonnet I, 'The predestined Lover, ignorant of Love, declares his Creed' (title) and advises,

Therefore with equal eyes and steadfast heart
  Tread underfoot all excellent desire;
    Seek no great thing, lest any hope or fear
    Lay hold on thee. So Death, when he draw near,
  Shall find thy soul not slothful to depart,
Nor without ease shall quench a little fire.

So speaks the lover while he remains ignorant of Love. But after he 'questions his Fellows concerning love' (title, II), he cautions against summoning Death, for 'be sure he never loitereth':

 Wilt thou desire him therefore? O be wise,
  Turn backward o'er the trodden path thy face,
  And be afraid to entreat him. (III)

Nevertheless, by the end of the sonnet cycle, death, too, has become transcended by a greater God. In the fifth 'Passion of Love' sonnet (LXXVII), subtitled 'The Death of Love', he describes Christ dying on the cross, and urges us to

[...]: watch beside his sepulchre.
We know not; surely Love may rise again,
Who on the cross of all men's lust was slain.

We can now think back to the poem by Williams's father, 'Parted', and see the difference in tone if not in belief. I quote the last stanza:

Oh Saviour Christ! Thou knowest all
    The bitter sense of loss;
Be near us when the shadows fall,
    And help us bear the cross.
Though lonely here the path may be,
    Where pain and sorrow are,
We trust our dear ones dwell with Thee,
    And that is better far.

Much could be said about the rival, lesser loves, but I want to touch on another question of interest, and that is the role of the beloved in the poems. The paths of earthly love are various, yet each one leads to the greater Love. Thus, in Prefatory Sonnet II, God's voice has ceased from time, but He continues to call in other ways:

His ambush in a pebble's heart, His fleet
    Passage in light and shadow of leaves, O soul,
        Hast thou escaped; wilt thou deny thy clay
    If thereupon He stablish His control
In mortal eyes that snare it, mortal feet
    That treat the windings of salvation's way?

This lover, who has escaped God's ambush in the pebble and the leaves, has now been snared by the beloved. Through her eyes and feet God establishes control. For the lover, the beloved is a means to his salvation, not an end in herself. (One sonnet is titled, 'That for every man a woman holds the secret of salvation.') This crucial but finally subordinate role of the beloved is reflected in the number of sonnets addressed to her: of the eighty-two sonnets with titles, the lover's lady is mentioned in the titles of eight and 'woman' is mentioned in five more, whereas thirty-six have titles concerning love (Love often appears as a personi- fication). Within the sonnets themselves, forty-one (that is, one-half of the total) make no mention of the beloved either directly or indirectly, although many of the rest give sig- nificant attention to her. This omission is not accidental. In the essay, 'Me', Williams says,

> [. . .] I am always told I am too intellectual, and I suppose that is largely true: my verse has been concerned with the things of the mind, or at least with the things of the body considered in some intellectual relationship and form.
>
> [. . .] You may remember I suggested something of the sort with Sir Thomas Browne; he preferred thinking about the image of the thing in his mind rather than its image on earth. It is the reactions and repercussions of a thing in my mind and in those of others with which I have been largely concerned.

Williams goes on to say that in the first love sonnet of *The Silver Stair* (IX) the young lover meets his lady for the first time and

> remarks dreamily that 'All making and all breaking of all laws Surely from one face hath looked forth on' him – this is his first feeling; not that her eyes were brown, or her hair, or the shape of her nose, but a bright little meta- physical notion of that kind. And he goes on in the same way – the lady is a microcosm of creation, she is sig- nificant of a farther Reality, she suggests the possible terrors and delights of this new experience, and so on; but there is precious little description of her – you don't know anything more about her appearance than before she occurred.

Again, we see in Sonnet XXI the lover asserting,

> For no escaping glances, words that fall,
>   For no desire of soft lip or high brow,

For none of these, beloved, do I vow
Love: somewhat yet is hidden in them all.
These are the echo to me, not the call;
   A fair dream, whence is not full meaning now:
   However they be beautiful, and thou
Throned in them as a queen within her hall.

The sentiment expressed in this sonnet is close to that found in the Yeats quotation, which concludes,

Yet never have two lovers kissed but they
Believed there was some other near at hand,
And almost wept because they could not find it.

These lines are spoken by Forgael, captain of a ship whose crew plunders other ships as he sails uncharted seas searching for the deep reality of love rather than for 'its image on the mirror.'[7] Forgael, too, sees the fair dream as more real than the substantial body, but there is a difference between Forgael's dreams and those of the lover in *The Silver Stair*. The world Forgael inhabits is not the same, after all, for his world makes no mention of the Christian God who died on a cross of Love. *The Silver Stair*'s young lover is not despairing in his quest for the greater love; rather, as Fred Page noted, *The Silver Stair* is

A Christian poem which, in the course of a human story, invokes and confesses to the Father, the Son, the Holy Ghost, Our Lady (73, 74, 81) and the Archangels, and the Baptist; a poem which, ever and anon, turns to the life of Jesus Christ as a parable of Divine (?human) love, indeed the incarnate life of Deity, born of a virgin, revealed to disciples (78), slighted and crucified by the world (75, 77), and re-arisen as the Inspirer of human life.

[...] But the poem is to be read as the record of one soul's response to the Divine Love: praising human love even while refusing its usual expression, and refusing this, only to press on to that higher thing to which it is confessedly a first step.

The poet, is, then, reconciled to life by his vision of love, and because he can see something of the purpose of God [. . .]. ('The Silver Stair: A New Sonnet-Sequence')

It is instructive to look more deeply into the significance of the phrase 'praising human love even while refusing its usual expression,' for it leads into an exploration of how Williams treats, in this, his earliest published work, the great themes of the Way of Affirmation of Images and the Way of Negation of Images. In *The Silver Stair* the lover is inspired by, yet dissatisfied with, human love, despite his awareness that the Way of Affirmation is pleasing to God. He longs to know the deeper mysteries revealed only to those who follow the Way of Rejection. (This view contrasts strongly with the more accepting attitude of the late Victorians, as evidenced by Stansby's writings, which we looked at earlier.) The sonnet sequence does not build, as might be expected, to grander eulogies of the beloved; rather, the last Book gives its deepest attention to the Way of Rejection of Images, especially in the six sonnets on the Passion of Christ.

Williams says that *The Silver Stair* 'was meant as a study in and song of virginal love' ('Me'). Florence Conway, as noted earlier, was told by him that its theme was Renunciation. In fact, Sonnet XLVIII in Book II and the penultimate Sonnet LXXXI of Book III both have the same title, 'Of Renunciation'. In Sonnet XLV the lover is given 'two offerings of love' (title) and told to choose:

> But if thou choose love, wilt thou have this gift
>   Fashioned in work of silver or of gold?
> Aureate, bought with toil and holy thrift,
> With filling and with emptying horn and cruse?
>   Argent, with tears, sad hours, and frustrate hold? –
> Or wilt thou enter empty-handed? Choose.

The terms silver and gold do not appear in the first half of the sonnet cycle at all, but in the second half they appear several times, always with the same respective associations. What is curious is that commentators have invariably misinterpreted the meanings. The three primary passages are found in Sonnets XLV, LXVII, and LXXX. In Sonnet

LXVII, 'An Ascription', pertaining to God the Holy Ghost, the lover says, 'The silver and golden stairs are His,/The altar His — yea, His the lupanar.' Sonnet LXXX, 'The Consummation', first describes wedded lovers 'stretched on the golden couch of their delight,' then contrasts another group of people in the sestet, who proclaim:

> Sleep yet! This is our holy day we greet,
>> With notes of silver echoing its fame.
> Sleep! Toward white gates, down many a shouting street,
> Masters of hope and passion and sorrow, we
>> With clash of sword on shield, move and acclaim
> The solemn Feast of Love's Virginity.

In each case, silver is associated with renunciation, the Way of Rejection of Images, and gold is associated with the Way of Affirmation of Images: the silver stairs and the altar, the golden stairs and the lupanar. Yet, despite the overwhelming consistency in the use of the two terms, silver and gold, their associations are frequently reversed by critics. H. N. Fairchild, for instance, boldly asserts that, 'although theoretically Williams seeks only to restore the erotic silver stair to its proper dignity of kinship with the ascetic golden stair, in these poems his personal preference for the former kind of holiness is obvious.'[8] That statement is remarkable for how exactly wrong it is in every way.

I would like to end with a few extracts from reviews of *The Silver Stair* in journals of the day. The favourable response Williams met with was uniform among his reviewers, beginning with Alice and Wilfred Meynell, who were responsible for having the sonnets published. The *Times Literary Supplement* (November 28, 1912) said, 'his verse is [...] full of quiet melody, and his thoughts cultured and refined.' J. S. Phillimore, in *The Dublin Review* (April 1913), extolled the sonnets at great length, beginning his review with, 'To come to Mr Charles Williams's *Silver Stair* [...] is to pass into an atmosphere of wise, deliberate serenity and hear very noble voices. His execution is faultless, his frugality quietly shames the riot of some of the "Georgians"; he realizes perfect freedom of expression without a trace of rebellion or lawlessness: a poet after Patmore's own heart [. . .].' *The Tablet* (February 15, 1913) placed Williams among the great writers of love poetry, with 'an intellect imaginatively free, responsibly submissive [. . .].' Sir Walter Raleigh, who held the Chair of Poetry at Oxford at that time, said of it 'there is no doubt about it; real poetry.' Hopefully, Williams's early poems will again become available for today's readers so that they, too, might explore through his eyes the experience of Love.

Notes

1. Theodore Maynard, 'The Poetry of Charles Williams', *The North American Review* (Sept. 1919, Vol. 210), p. 403.

2. See Anne Lohrli, compiler, *Household Words: A Weekly Journal 1850–1859, Conducted by Charles Dickens* (Toronto: University of Toronto Press, 1973), p. 4.

3. See Sidney Lee, *Elizabethan Sonnets: Newly Arranged and Indexed* (Westminster: Archibald Constable and Co. Ltd., 1904), Vol. 1, pp. x–xi.

4. See John Fuller, *The Sonnet* (London: Methuen & Co. Ltd., 1972), p. 2.

5. Maynard, p. 403.

6. Florence Williams, 'As I Remember,' *Episcopal Church News* (April 12, 1953), p. 14.

7. W. B. Yeats, *The Shadowy Waters,* in *The Variorum Edition of the Poems of W. B. Yeats*, edited by Peter Allt and Russell K. Alspach (New York: Macmillan Publishing Co. Inc., 1940), p. 230.

8. Hoxie Neale Fairchild, *Religious Trends in English Poetry*, Vol. VI: 1920–1965 (London: Columbia University Press, 1968), p. 263.

Chapter Ten

Common Themes Among Inklings

Richard Sturch

I should perhaps make it clear before beginning that I am only proposing to consider what might be called the three quintessential Inklings, Charles Williams, C.S. Lewis and J.R.R. Tolkien (with perhaps a few shy allusions to George MacDonald as a kind of 19th century proto-Inkling). My excuse for treating them together is certain themes which seem to appear quite often in all or most of them, but are not so prominent in all Christian writers or thinkers. The most conspicuous is what for lack of a better word I shall call 'moralism'.

No-one will suppose that this implies asceticism or a neglect of pleasant things. All four were in fact rather fond of stressing the goodness of the senses. 'It is a good thing to eat your breakfast', says the old princess to Curdie: 'The thing is good – not you'. And 'water hot is a noble thing' according to one of the Bilbo Baggins' bath-songs. Sybil Coningsby would have agreed: 'Drinks and baths and changes were exquisite delights in themselves; part of an existence in which one beauty was always providing a reason and a place for an entirely opposite beauty.' Nor by 'moralism' do I mean some sort of theology of 'jus-tification by works', nor an ethical legalism. They do of course present their characters with situations that demand decisions, moral decisions if you like, but they do not see

these simply as the application of law. It might be simplest
to say that they were concerned more with the goodness of
the agent than with that of the act. In the *Screwtape Letters*
the tempters do not discuss whether pacifism or patriotism is
objectively right for the 'patient'; their interest lies in making
him adopt either of them for the wrong reasons, or in using
it to subvert him in his other choices. (It is perhaps significant that Williams, also during the Second World War,
described pacifism as a 'vocation'.) And repentance tends to
be for the faults of one's character rather than for past sins.
(Tolkien is probably the exception here.)

'Moralism', then, as I am using the word, is a passionate
interest in human goodness – and indeed in *all* goodness.
It is interesting that the 'Conversation of Damaris Tighe'
in *The Place of the Lion* turns (like the conversations
of Eustace and Edmund in Lewis's 'Narnia' books) on a
good that is not strictly speaking a moral good at all –
ordinary human love. At the last extremity of her terror,
when the Eagle of intellect is appearing to her, who has
been 'degrading intellect and spirit', in 'old, huge and
violent shape', she calls on her lover. And the same principle of salvation comes again near the end of the same
book, when for a moment the old Damaris reasserts itself.
'The years of selfish toil had had at any rate this good –
they had been years of toil; she had not easily abandoned
any search because of difficulty, and that habit of intention,
by its own power of good, offered her salvation then.' You
will even find something of this in Tolkien; in *Leaf by Niggle*
at least part of Niggle's salvation lies in devotion to something outside himself (which, as the Skeleton in *Cranmer*
remarks, is more than most of us do): 'He took a great
deal of pains with leaves, just for their own sake. But he
never thought that made him important.'

There is a natural tendency to suppose that great stress
on morals by a Christian is likely to go with a light stress
on dogma, and even on faith: a tendency to set St James
against St Paul, as it were. This is perhaps true to a certain
extent of MacDonald, who usually avoided theology; when
he did not, it was usually based on moral principles. 'Understanding is the reward of obedience' – John 7:17 is a
constant theme with him. It is taken up at times by Lewis

(notably in *The Magician's Nephew* and *The Silver Chair*) and referred to with evident approval by Williams in *Flecker of Dean Close*. It was on moral grounds that MacDonald tended to an Abailardian approach to the Atonement. Lewis has, I gather, been accused of doing the same, but surely wrongly: though he avoided adherence to any *theory* of the Atonement ('The thing itself is infinitely more important than any explanations'), the death of Aslan in *The Lion, the Witch and the Wardrobe* is straight substitution (though of course it may well be that he wanted a fairly close echo of the best-known picture of the Atonement, for the sake of his readers).

For Williams, of course, substitution and exchange were absolutely central ideas, and in this company I need hardly expand on this; to him the Cross was 'a central substitution (whereby) He became everywhere the centre of, and everywhere He energized and reaffirmed, all our substitutions and exchanges.' 'What happened there the Church itself has never seen, except that in the last reaches of that living death to which we are exposed He substituted Himself for us. He submitted in our stead to the full results of that Law which is He.' This does not affect Williams's novels directly very much, though it is alluded to in *Descent into Hell*; the most direct appearance of the Cross is, I suppose, in *All Hallows' Eve*, where Lester Furnivall is receiving the force of the spell meant for Betty; 'She was no longer standing. She was leaning back on something, some frame which from her buttocks to her head supported her; indeed, she could have believed, but she was not sure, that her arms, flung out on each side held onto a part of the frame, as along a beam of wood ... The endurance had been short and the restoration soon, so quickly had the Name which is the City sprung to the rescue of its own.'

The central substitution, then, does not itself figure largely in Williams's fantastic writings; but the doctrines that it exemplifies do. When Williams is moralistic, it is with a morality of coinherence and exchange; it is the refusal of these that damns and the acceptance of them that blesses. 'Bear ye one another's burdens' and 'He saved others; himself he cannot save' are key texts; and they imply that we must let others bear *our* burdens at times. That was what saved Damaris − that she was willing to let someone else save her − as even Christ was saved from Herod the Great, by those who died in his place, the Holy Innocents. 'The chastisement of His peace was upon them' (*The Image of the City*, p. 133), 'they suffered unknowingly in direct substitution for Christ' (*Witchcraft*, Meridian Books p/b, p. 118).

It is also possible to *deny* the coinherence, whether by refusing to give or refusing to take. The former is the more obvious. Simon the Clerk is depicted as a 'second climax' of the Jewish nation, yet in the long run he is also like any other sinner: 'It was fame and domination that he desired', not exchange; he would only take, and any giving he did would be merely incidental and contemptuous. There is also the opposite peril, that of refusing to take. It is not so prominent in Williams's writings (it is perhaps rare in actual life), but it exists, and he knew it. It was the first sin of Milton's Satan; it would have been the last sin of Damaris Tighe if she had not been converted. It was the sin, too, in Williams's pleasing 'Apologue on the Parable of the Wedding Garment' (*The Image of the City*, pp. 166−8), where the gentleman of quality, invited to Immanuel's fancy-dress ball, felt that would be beneath his dignity, and was turned away:

He had his own; his own was all
but that permitted at the Ball.

Now central to any moralism whatever must be the notion of choice; and over and over again the books of our four turn upon some character's choice. This is most conspicuous, maybe, in *The Lord of the Rings*, which moves to its climax through a series of such − beginning, indeed, back in *The Hobbit*, when Bilbo has the opportunity to kill his enemy Gollum and does not do so. The main adventure of the later book begins when Bilbo succeeds in choosing to abandon the Ring, and continues with Frodo's choosing to try and destroy it. Much later, in Lórien, each of the Company is offered the possibility of giving up their task in favour of some other good, for themselves or for others; and one of them, Boromir, eventually succumbs to the temptation, trying to seize the Ring for his own glory and his city's needs, though he repents before his death. Also in Lórien, Galadriel, who had set the Company these tests, is herself offered the Ring and the power that it commands. Then there is the choice of Faramir, who passes the test his brother failed, and what the chapter-heading itself calls 'The Choice of Master Samwise'. Finally, in the heart of Mount Doom, Frodo, who has come through such perils to destroy the Ring, declares 'I do not choose now to do what I came to do' and claims the Ring as his own – upon which the first of our series becomes important again, for it is Gollum who seizes the Ring and falls with it into the fire.

Side by side with all this run other choices, hardly less vital to the story. Denethor exemplifies the refusal to take and the refusal to give at one and the same time. If the war is lost, he and Gondor will be utterly destroyed; but if it is won, he, as Steward, will become subordinate to the newly restored King, Aragorn. He is not willing either to give up his power or to receive it from another; he refuses the choice and commits suicide (thereby that much the more weakening the cause he has fought for). Saruman has earlier chosen the way of treason; his armies are defeated and his plans brought to nothing, but when he is offered the chance to repent and rejoin the fight against Sauron in a lesser capacity, he will not. 'Better to reign in hell than serve in heaven' – but his 'reign' is only a venting of malice in petty evils among the hobbits until, defeated even there, he is murdered by one of his own followers. In *The Silmarillion*, which is far more densely packed with sheer incident than *The Lord of the Rings*, and has as a result less exploration of its many characters, choice is less prominent; but it is there, and important. It is the choice of Feanor, first not to give the Simarils to restore light to the world, and then not to receive the warnings of Mandos, that gives rise to the whole theme of the book, and the choice of Lúthien that is the climax to the main subsidiary story.

MacDonald does not deal with choice so often. *Foolish* choices are found all right. Anodos in *Phantastes* makes more than one, in the best fairy-tale tradition of falling into the trap you have just been warned against, like Bluebeard's wife or the one-eyed prince in the *Arabian Nights*; Vane in *Lilith* behaves in a similar way, though out of self-will rather than folly. But MacDonald stresses most the choice that gives an opportunity for obedient trust, the sort of choice that faced Abraham when he was told to leave his father's house. This is found more than once in the 'Curdie' books, for example.

The most conspicuous examples of choice in Williams are I suppose to be found in *Many Dimensions* and *Descent into Hell*, but there are others in plenty. *The House by the Stable*, for instance, turns on one. The moment of choice that forms the climax of *Many Dimensions* is rather a special case; it is not a facing of temptation but a deliberate judgement among possible goods, entrusted to the Lord Chief Justice. 'It is a very dreadful thing to refuse health to the sick – but it is more tragic still to loose upon earth that which does not belong to the earth'.

In *Descent into Hell* the crucial choices are those of the military historian Wentworth; there are three, and each time he chooses the worse. A rival historian is knighted. A momentary pang of envy or resentment would perhaps be natural; but Wentworth likes and cherishes it, instead of (say) regarding the knighthood as an honour to his profession generally or as a chance to 'rejoice with those that rejoice'. Then the girl he is in love with prefers someone else, and he cannot accept this either, preferring a succubus fashioned out of his daydreams, a ghastly parody which is in no danger of showing the independence of the real girl. Finally, he is offered a chance for professional integrity, akin to the 'repentance through non-moral goodness' mentioned earlier. His knighted rival is, we are told, a 'holy and beautiful soul who would have sacrificed reputation, income and life, if necessary, for the discovery of one fact'. Wentworth had already begun to lose that sort of integrity; but he is given a chance to regain it. The uniforms for a play are historically incorrect. He could point this out. He is actually asked to say whether they are all right or not. But he cannot be bothered; he prefers his fantasies. And steadily he loses touch with reality and slides into a mindless damnation.

But it is Lewis most of all who is fascinated by what we might call the mechanisms of choice. Repentance through non-moral goodness is only one such. There is also, for instance, one which was for a time rather a favourite of

Lewis's, that of the 'Inner Ring', which appears in an address at King's College, London, in an essay on Kipling, in the novel *That Hideous Strength*. There the main character, the sociologist Mark Studdock, has begun even at school to feel the lure of the charmed circle, the 'people who really *matter*', and the first part of the book is largely about how this is used by the leaders of the NICE (a kind of hell-born political conspiracy masquerading as a scientific institute) to lure him into their conspiracy. (The Inner Ring can of course be used for good purpose as well, but not in this instance; and it is not perhaps of much moral significance when it works for good.) He is brought into the fringes of one Ring after another until the idea of being left out in the cold − very cold, as the Rings would then be working *against* him − is utterly appalling, the idea of being 'in' utterly absorbing. And so, when first he is asked to do something for the NICE which he knows to be definitely dishonest, 'the moment of his consent almost escaped his notice; . . . . it all slipped past in a chatter of laughter, of that intimate laughter between fellow professionals, which of all earthly powers is strongest to make men do very bad things before they are yet, individually, very bad men'. He does in the end break with the NICE and repent: partly through love of his wife, when he realises that they wish to use her (she has clairvoyant powers); partly through revulsion at what is going on, for 'his toughness was only of the will, not of the nerves, and the virtues he had almost succeeded in banishing from his mind still lived, if only negatively and as weaknesses, in his body'. Also partly because of their efforts to implicate him completely: 'the knowledge that his own assumptions led to Frost's position, combined with what he saw in Frost's face and what he had experienced . . . effected a complete conversion'. He is rescued largely by lingering traces of moral goodness, not only in weak nerves, but in his ability to see that the NICE is evil, at least when seen side by side with his wife, though he had failed to see it with himself.

That Hideous Strength also includes an instance of another kind of choice which is to be found in all four writers − the deliberately perverse choice. We have seen examples of this already, with Saruman and Denethor in Tolkien and with

Wentworth in Williams. It is less conspicuous in MacDonald. There is something of it in the episode (already mentioned) of Anodos in the ogre's house; but its clearest appearance is in the 'Unspoken Sermon' on Freedom: 'The slave in heart would immediately, with Milton's Satan, reply that the furthest from Him who made him must be the freest, thus acknowledging his very existence a slavery ... *Being* itself must, for what they call liberty, be repudiated ... The liberty of the God that would have His creature free is in contrast with the slavery of the creature who would cut his own stem from his root that he might call it his own and love it'.

The normal sinner prefers a lesser good (probably a selfish one) to a greater (probably an unselfish one on the face of it). Perversity has gone beyond this; it rejects known good for something that can hardly even be called a 'lesser good'. Saruman had sought more greatness for himself than he already had by right; but the thing he sought was good, for him at least, and had he come by it honestly might have been used for others' good too. But in the end he chooses a state which resembles his old goal only in its lack of subordination. It is not good for him or for others, and he knows this; but it is the only course left him that is opposed to the course he deserted, and therefore he chooses it. Better be damned than change one's mind. Frost, in *That Hideous Strength*, is similarly placed. The NICE is collapsing round him. He has been a determinist, disbelieving in free choice altogether; and now his theories actually become true in a way, and his mind is a mere spectator with no control over his body, which is now a puppet of hell, of no further use to it and about to be destroyed. But just before he dies he is given an opportunity. 'He became able to know (and simultaneously refused the knowledge) that he had been wrong from the beginning, that souls and personal responsibility existed. He half saw: he wholly hated ... With one supreme effort he flung himself back into his illusion'. If his beliefs had been true, they would have had value; even if not, there would have been value in the intelligence used in coming to them, or the integrity with which they were held. But none of these now apply. The beliefs are false; it is stupid and intellectually dishonest to cling to them; but the idea of abandoning them is intolerable. Saruman will not change his will; Frost will not change his opinions; the result in both cases is damnation.

Instances could be multiplied. Much of Lewis's *The Great Divorce* is a series of 'perverse choices'. But the most extended portrayal of perversity is perhaps Lavrodopoulos in Williams's *War in Heaven*. His original choice is not described, but the result is: 'No mortal mind could conceive a desire which was not based on a natural and right desire . . . But of every conceivable and inconceivable desire this was the negation. This was desire itself sick, but not unto death; rejection which tore all things asunder and swept them with it in its fall through the abyss'.

The perverse choice is typically an act of pride (though Lavrodopoulos is now beyond even that); and our four take that sin very seriously. 'Unchastity, anger, greed, drunkenness, and all that, are mere fleabites in comparison' wrote Lewis: '. . . Pride leads to every other vice; it is the complete anti-God state of mind'. *The Silmarillion* is about little else. Pride first rots Melkor; pride ruins Feanor, 'the proudest and most self-willed of the Eldar, and sends him out into exile and death; as the story goes on pride strikes down one of the heroes after another. Tolkien is merciful; pride brings disaster and death, but not necessarily total corruption, for often the disaster and death follow it too swiftly. Fingolfin, 'the most proud and valiant' of the Elven-kings, challenges Morgoth to a single combat he knows he cannot win, in an act of both pride and despair; but he falls before more harm can be done (except by his loss!). The theme is worked out at greatest length in the story of Turin. He does indeed lead a life darkened by sorrows and malice that are not of his making; but these would not have wrecked him in the way they do but for the folly of his pride. Pride will not let him return to Doriath to face judgement after the death of Saeros − even when he knows that he has been acquitted. It makes him break the concealment of Margothrond and prevent the destruction of its bridge (despite warning); and it is this that leads to the destruction of the city and sets in train the events that culminate in his own despair and suicide. Perverse pride is not analysed in the way it is in *The Lord of the Rings*, but its evil and stupidity are clear.

Even our non-perverse choices (the majority!) can be cata-strophic for others, especially where power is concerned; and this theme keeps turning up in the three Inklings. One is tempted to see this as a reflection of the times they lived in – though the problem of power is as old as mankind! Thus *The Lord of the Rings* is chiefly about the use of power and the Ring of Power. (Tolkien himself said it was mostly about death really; but that is true more of the sub-creation as a whole and his thoughts about it than of the book as it emerged.) The Ring is a corrupted power, evil in origin and in what it effects; but there is no suggestion that power in itself has to be wicked. For the power it gives is not that of authority or leadership, such as that exercised (in very different ways) by the Stewards of Gondor or the Mayors of Michel Delving); it is the power of domination, one will overriding another. Some, such as Saruman and the Lord of the Rings himself, desire this power for its own sake or worse. Others, like Boromir, desire to use it for good ends; but since it *is* domination, such use would corrupt the user and pervert the ends. Gandulf tells Denethor that if Boromir had indeed taken the Ring 'you would not have known your son'; and Gandalf himself, Tolkien said in a letter, would have been a worse Ring-lord than Sauron: 'he would have remained "righteous", but self-righteous and made good detestable and seem evil'.

Most of the cases of legitimate authority in Tolkien are monarchies (there are a couple of elective offices). This is natural in the sort of culture he is describing, and they are monarchies (on the good side anyway) of service rather than domination. It is no accident that the only King of Gondor to usurp the throne turned out to be a tyrant. 'Authority' may turn into 'domination', as the history of Numenor proves; but the two are properly distinct. Writing to his son Christopher, Tolkien said that his political opinions were leaning more and more to Anarchy or 'unconstitu-tional' monarchy; and the Anarchist side of this comes out in his fiction as well as the Monarchist. The Shire is in effect an Anarchy, with hardly any 'government'. Though, as Tolkien remarks in the same letter, the fatal weakness of both systems is that they work 'only when all the world is messing along in the same good old inefficient way'.

In only one of Lewis's novels is power a major theme, *That Hideous Strength*, in writing which he had in mind what he considered a genuine danger: power, specifically over Nature, especially human nature – the power of 'hidden persuaders' and propagandists over people in the mass, and of psychological cunning over individuals. This sort of power is never likely to be used for good ends, for a good man is not likely to be willing to use it. But what Lewis feared was that it would be combined with a rejection of all ethical principles in the name of 'objectivity'. A wicked man may know he is wicked; he may repent, he may die and be succeeded by a better. But if ethical principles (what Lewis called the 'Tao') have disappeared, repentance and improvement are both impossible. There will be no reason for anyone to do anything except that he wants to; and a handful at the top will have the power to enforce what they want. In the end even these will be puppets like their subjects, because their own wants have been predetermined by earlier manipulators. This may sound a mere nightmare. When Lewis wrote it (towards the end of World War II) what he feared was (a) the 'evolutionary moralists' like C. H. Waddington and (b) philosophers of the 'linguistic' schools; but his Riddell Lectures were sparked off by finding the infection in a couple of schools English textbooks. Confined to the scientists and the philosophers, such ideas may be relatively harmless (though still false); it is when they get into the hands of administrators, journalists and politicians that the danger starts. These are the people who turn proposals into facts or prepare the public's minds for this. And it is these whom we meet in *That Hideous Strength*. Most of the NICE staff are administrators, propagandists, or secret police; there are few actual scientists, and there are at least two clergy, perhaps as a warning that it is as easy to take the name of God in vain in such a cause as to take that of science.

Power is a recurrent theme in Williams's novels too; it is absent only from *Descent into Hell* and (as a moral problem) from *The Place of the Lion*. In two of the others (*Shadows of Ecstasy* and *All Hallows' Eve*) the central figure already has power when the story begins; it is only a question of how far that power is to extend, and also in part of the way in which power is to be rejected or met. But in the remaining three the opportunity of power is offered, and the story hinges on the way the characters respond. In a way *War in Heaven*, the earliest, is the most complex, because the instrument of power, the Holy Graal, is being sought for so many reasons. Gregory Persimmons desires power for possession (which is still a recognition of some sort of good); Manasseh desires only destruction; Lavrodopoulos, as we have seen, is beyond even that, 'not fighting but vomiting'. Among their opponents the Duke and Kenneth Mornington are to some extent romantics, and shroud the Graal with papal or poetical associations; they are inclined to treat it as just that which has these associations, and even to think in terms of avenging an insult to God. The Archdeacon is the opposite of the Greek, living by acceptance as the other lives (in a way) by rejection, and is consequently the only one really able to let the Graal return to its Keeper. None of the three wishes to dominate the Graal or dominate with it; but two are still in part devoted to their own ideas. Only one has attained to actual self-denial, where power can best be used by leaving it alone; when it is sought to destroy the Graal by magic, the Archdeacon calls on his friends to pray, but not against anything, even the magic, only 'that He who made the universe may sustain the universe, that in all things there may be delight in the justice of His will'.

Sybil in *The Greater Trumps* is a female counterpart of the Archdeacon, though she is not called on to guard the Tarots, only to rescue her brother from their manipulation by Henry. Nancy, on the other hand, is faced with the need to divert the storm they have raised, and again this is not done by power. Her hands 'moved as if in dancing ritual they answered the dancing monstrosities that opposed them. It was not a struggle but a harmony'. (We might compare the way in which the movement of Mary and the negress Hell in *Seed of Adam* 'quickens and becomes a dance'.)

As far as *Many Dimensions* is concerned, we have in Lord Arglay's judgement there the various attitudes towards the power of the Stone that we have seen exemplified in the other books – selfish use, good use, and renunciation of use. The odd thing is that while here too it is renunciation of use that prevails, no-one was more aware than Williams of the need for power of some sort if order is to exist. Order is sustained by power: we remember the episode in *The Greater Trumps* in which for a moment a policeman directing traffic takes on the Imperial form 'helmed, in a white cloak, stretching out one sceptered arm ...Something common to Emperor and Khalif, cadi and magistrate, praetor and alcalde, lictor and constable, shone before her in those lights'. And this is taken up in the Arthurian poems, where the Byzantine Emperor is 'operative providence' – as near God as you can get without turning image into allegory.

We cannot simply distinguish in Williams between Authority and Domination, as in *The Lord of the Rings*. Undoubtedly Domination is excluded from order; but not all the cases of power, or the seeking of power, in Williams's novels are cases of Domination. The Mayor of Rich, seeking the cure of the sick, was not. We are given a clue in the quotation from Dante which Williams prefixed to *Taliessin through Logres*: 'Unde est, quod non operatio propria propter essentiam, sed haec propter illam habet ut sit', 'The proper operation (working or function) is not in existence for the sake of the being, but the being for the sake of the function'. This is true even of the immortal soul of man. 'Man's end is to know God and to enjoy him for ever' – so; but to know God and to enjoy Him are functions, and apart from them man's existence would be pointless. To Williams the whole of creation presented itself as a vast arrangement of interlocking functions – the cosmic dance of *The Greater Trumps*: 'Change – that's what we know of the immortal dance; the law in the nature of things – that's the measure of the dance ...quick or slow, measurable or unmeasurable, there is nothing at all anywhere but the dance'. It is therefore a mistake to set yourself, or even your own good purposes, against the rhythm of the dance, or twist anything from its proper functions; domination is only an extreme instance of this. Power exists for its own proper purpose, and not for another, least of all for the sake of its possessor. If 'possessor' is correct; elsewhere Williams says that 'power is not something one has, it is something that one is' (*Arthurian Torso*, p. 89), so that to want to *have* it cannot be right. We might compare the picture of the dance of creation in

Williams with rather similar ones elsewhere. The myth of creation which begins Tolkien's *The Silmarillion* depicts the shaping of the potential world, before its actual creation, as a *song*; so does that in Lewis's *The Magician's Nephew*. There is the dance of heaven in *The Problem of Pain*: 'It does not exist for the sake of joy, (or even) for the sake of good, or of love. It is Love Himself, and Good Himself, and therefore happy. It does not exist for us, but we for it'. And there is the 'Great Dance' of all being in *Perelandra* (in which 'each movement becomes in its season the breaking into flower of the whole design to which all else had been directed' and at the summit of whose complexity is 'a simplicity beyond all comprehension, ancient and young as spring'). Side by side with this – forming indeed part of it – comes a principle of hierarchy: 'I believe the authority of parent over child, husband over wife, learned over simple, to be as much of the original plan as the authority of man over beast. If we had not fallen ... patriarchal monarchy would be the sole lawful government' (*Transposition and Other Addresses*, p. 489). We need democracy because we are fallen, including parents, husbands, learned men and monarchs.

Williams's idea of hierarchy, despite his use of the image of Byzantium with its suggestion of rigidity, and his liking for words like 'geometry' and 'diagram', is more flexible. There is no one fixed system: 'we are not to suppose that the hierarchy of one moment is likely to be that of the next' (*The Image of the City*, p. 127). If there are degrees of capacity – as there are – they are relative and changing: 'the Prime Minister must be docile to an expert scullion'. Similarly, 'Each man', said MacDonald, 'has his peculiar relation to God. It follows that there is a chamber in God Himself, into which none can enter but the one, the individual, the peculiar man – out of which chamber that man has to bring revelation and strength for his brethren ... How shall the rose ... rejoice against the snowdrop?' But to Williams this holds everywhere, not only in our relationship to God. (Let me be fair to Lewis: in the Dance in *Perelandra* 'each is equally at the centre and none are there by being equals'.)

Hierarchies of function are more stable than those of merit; they depend on the need for tasks to be done more than on the abilities of particular people to do them. At any given time there will be many who think the current Prime Minister less fit to hold that office than the Leader of the Opposition; but they do not deny her authority. Of course, even the Prime Minister may be subject to the direction of a traffic-policeman; but in general it is true that in function, as distinct from merit, degree and order are to some extent opposed; it is therefore best that high function be conferred from without. The dictator is one who has seized high function, and who thinks it exists for his sake, not vice versa. Lewis's imaginary worlds are mostly hierarchical on the lines depicted in his address on 'Membership'. Narnia and Archenland are 'patriarchial monarchies'; Perelandra will become one. On Malacandra the inhabitants are not fallen, but neither have they overcome temptation to fall; they are therefore under the rule of beings higher than they, the eldila. Williams's subtler views are not so prominent in his fiction, partly because he sees hierarchy at work in, say, the correcting of a mistake, where most of us would not. Hence when Anthony in *The House of the Octopus* is definitely in the wrong, and claims the 'prestige of my priesthood', he is told

there is no prestige in any blessed priesthood, only the priesthood; no prestige in any true thing, but God and the thing itself.

For the moment, the hierarchy of accuracy is the reverse of the hierarchy to which Anthony was used. This is a hierarchy of merit; if we want an instance of hierarchy of function in action, I suggest the 'Judgement' in *Many Dimensions*. Lord Arglay is no doubt wise, but then so is the Hajji, and so in another way is Chloe; but judging is his proper function as it is not that of the others.

Moralism, the problem of power, hierarchy: these form a connected series of themes. We may pick out another one that is important in all our four – that of Providence or Luck. (The two terms are deliberately identified.) No doubt Providence bulks large in all forms of Christianity. Certainly it does so in our group – most of all, perhaps, in MacDonald, especially his non-fiction. It may in effect take the place of predestination in his Calvinist forebears.

Already in his twenties we find him writing to his uncle: 'The conviction is, I think, growing upon me that the smallest events are ordered for us, while yet in perfect consistency with the ordinary course of cause and effect in the world' (in G. M. MacDonald, *George MacDonald and his Wife*, p. 109). At this stage he was thinking of those who serve God (with Romans 8:28 in mind); later all were included, and he thought it necessary 'to believe every trouble fitted for the being who has to bear it, every physical evil not merely the result of moral evil but antidotal thereto' (*The Miracles of our Lord*, p. 44). Williams might have agreed: 'It is certain that (outside sin) the position in which at any moment we find ourselves is precisely the best for us at that moment' (*Flecker of Dean Close*, p. 35). Eventually the whole idea was versified:

If to myself – 'God sometimes interferes' –
I said, my faith at once would be struck blind.
I see him all in all, the lifting mind,
Or nowhere in the vacant miles and years.
Diary of an Old Soul, Jan. 9.

That this did not lead to a complete theological determinism was the result of an equally strong insistence on human freedom, even at the cost of allowing a 'sometimes interference': 'He wants to make us in his own image, *choosing* the good, *refusing* the evil. How should he effect this if he were *always* moving us from within, as he does at divine intervals?' (*Unspoken Sermons*, I, p. 174 *Creation in Christ*, p. 337)). Such an idea of universal providence would be hard to embody in fiction, and I do not think MacDonald tried; it is easier in a play, and in some of Williams's plays we do find something very like this. The Skeleton in *Cranmer*, Mary in *The Death of Good Fortune*, the Flame in *The House of the Octopus* all embody the figures of Necessity which is very much part of Williams's doctrine of Providence. 'Necessity' stands outside the action to comment upon it, but also directs it throughout. They are obviously 'providential' figures, but equally obviously they do leave room for the individual's freedom. In *The Death of Good Fortune* the way is opened for five characters to accept that all luck is good; three do, two do not. This is perhaps an unusually high failure rate; 'Most men', says the Accuser in *Judgement at Chelmsford*, 'when at last they see their desire, Fall to repentance – all have that chance'. I think that for all five, faith and repentance are the natural reaction to a 'clear vision of good and evil as they really are; it needs self-destruction or deliberate perversity to do otherwise, and usually a long period of preparation, as with Saruman or Laurence Wentworth.

There have been attempts to argue that free-will does not in fact exist in the worlds of Tolkien and Williams. Mr Douglas Parker has declared that the world of *The Lord of the Rings* is 'totally deterministic', and that at the end 'free-will has not been restored; it never existed in the first place' (*Hwaet We Holbytla, Hudson Review*, Vol. 9, 1956–7, esp. pp. 603–4). This is false. There is no doubt a general programme for history: the Third Age is undoubtedly ending, whatever succeeds it, and the Elves are undoubtedly fated to leave Middle-Earth or 'dwindle to a rustic folk of dell and cave'. And at times a more particular providence is at work. At the end of *The Hobbit*, Gandalf says to Bilbo: 'You don't really suppose that all your adventures and escapes were managed by mere luck, just for your own benefit?'; and later he tells Frodo 'Bilbo was meant to find the Ring, and *not* by its maker. In which case you also were meant to have it. And that may be an encouraging thought'. ('It is not', said Frodo.) And other passages could be quoted. But of course they only make sense in a context in which things are not 'meant' to happen; if all things are directly planned by Ilúvatar, then it is no encouragement to think that one particular event was planned by Him. And it may be possible to frustrate the plans even of Providence, temporarily. This is quite common in Lewis. In *That Hideous Strength*, the Studdocks were to have had a son who should 'turn the enemies out of Logres' for a thousand years; but they had decided against having children. Williams, again, says of the failure of the Jews as a whole to accept Christ that it had been intended that their nation should become 'almost unbearably august', yet it did not happen. What does happen is that God brings some other good, or achieves His ends in some other way. Adam's fall was a *felix culpa*.

And this is to be found in Tolkien too; at the last moment on Mount Doom Frodo after all his heroic struggles falls and claims the Ring. The plan is frustrated – and changes to meet that frustration; it is another, the unhappy Gollum, who seizes the Ring and falls into the fire with it.

This theme is made more explicit in *The Silmarillion* (not available to Mr Parker when he wrote). Melkor, in the *Ainulindale*, tries to drown the angelic music with his own theme; but 'its most triumphant notes were taken by the other and woven into its pattern', and the bitter cold of his work in the actual world produces the snowflake. It is undeniable that words like 'fate' and 'doom' are common in *The Silmarillion*. But Ulmo declares that 'in the armour of Fate (as the Children of Earth name it), there is ever a rift, and in the walls of Doom a breach, until the full-making, which ye call the End' (*Unfinished Tales*, p. 29), and that rift or breach has its origin in freedom – the freedom of Ulmo himself, one of the greatest of the Valar, or of an insignificant hobbit. The real answer to Mr Parker's notion is the emphasis made on choice, already discussed. Galadriel 'passes the test'. Saruman's decision comes to 'the balance of a hair'. When Eomer asks Aragorn: 'What doom do you bring out of the North?', the answer is 'The doom of choice'. There is Providence but not Predestination.

Mr Gunnar Urang (*Shadows of Heaven*, p. 89) inclines to believe that freedom is unreal in Williams, on the grounds that freedom is bound up with the idea of time, and that Williams sometimes treats time as unreal. But freedom is simply a negative – the absence of anything settling our decisions independently of ourselves – and as such is not time-bound. There is one place where Williams does seem to query freedom, in Anthony's thoughts on the edge of the pit in Berringer's house in *The Place of the Lion*: 'How could there be choice, unless there was preference, and if there was preference there was no choice'; but the debate is not ended one way or the other. (It can be taken further. If I am invited to take something I should like – prefer – and abstain for another's sake, then, if I can be said to 'prefer' abstention, it is because I have *chosen* to prefer it ...). The reality of freedom in Williams is shown up by the description of Sybil in *The Greater Trumps*, who really *is* no longer free, by her own deliberate surrender to the divine will.

In *Miracles*, Lewis tried to describe *how* Providence and freedom could co-exist, suggesting that our normal view of physical nature as constant and human volitions as variable is no more true than the converse: that it is equally true (though equally misleading) to regard the whole of nature as adapted by God to the free choice of human beings. I do not think this will do. Laws and states of nature can be described (though incompletely) without reference to human decisions; the reverse is not the case. I cannot choose to vote for Smith unless Smith, and voting exist; more, my choice cannot even be described unless they do. Not even God could make Smith or elections dependent on my decision to vote for Smith. This is not to say that Providence is impossible; only that it cannot work in quite that way.

Now if Providence is a reality the ancient Problem of Evil arises in a particularly acute form. All theists are faced with an apparent need to make God ultimately responsible for the existence of evil; but a 'providential' theist seems to make Him *directly* responsible for it. How do our authors deal with this?

Tolkien we can be fairly brief with: as we have seen, freedom is real, but God can turn misused freedom to good. Meanwhile, as far as this Middle-earth is concerned, we are given a kind of dualism; there is a perpetual battle going on between good and evil. Evil often seems the stronger; but this is misleading. Even in Mordor Sam is able to realise that 'in the end the Shadow was only a small and passing thing; there was light and beauty for ever beyond its reach'. Heaven does not normally intervene directly, and therefore seems weaker; most of the time its cause is waged by us lesser beings, Men and Elves and Hobbits and the like. Sometimes we fail; and when the failure is of someone great it seems to those in his shadow that the world itself has been ruined; but it has not.

MacDonald, while of course acknowledging that we can fall into evil despite the will of God for good, believed strongly that the evils we suffer are in the long run good. 'What we call evil', says Anodos in almost the last sentence of *Phantastes*, 'is the only and best shape which, for the person and his conditions at the time, could be assumed by the best good'. Hell itself is for MacDonald first and foremost a *curative* place. Evil 'must be destroyed one day, even if it be by that form of divine love which appears as a consuming fire ... That which is fire to them which are afar off is a mighty graciousness to them that are nigh. They are both the same thing' (*Adela Cathcart*, 1890 ed. p. 147). Chapter 25 of *Lilith* is a concrete example of the MacDonald hell at work.

Once a soul has repented, past offences no longer matter (cf. Ezekiel 18:22). Much the same applies, it seems, to natural evil as well; the whole creation is ultimately to be redeemed, and this must include all sentient life. If so, all suffering by anything 'is not to be compared with the glory that shall be revealed'. Not that this is developed; MacDonald always sought to be practical, not theoretical, and what he wanted was for his readers to respect and love the creation, and believe that God did so too.

Williams's attitude towards evil was of course quite different, in fact containing several different ideas intertwined. His picture of the Fall in e.g. *He Came Down From Heaven* is almost MacDonald in mirror-image: to MacDonald what seems evil will turn out to have been good, to Williams what is now good may be seen as evil because we insist on seeing it wrongly. The 'free candour' of the Adam's nakedness was known as undesirable, because they had insisted on knowing evil as well as good. Part at least of our redemption must then consist of another alteration in knowledge — the realisation that 'all luck is good'. This may not be easy; it may be 'heaven's kind of salvation, not at all to the mind / of any except the redeemed, and to theirs hardly' as Williams said in another context. Williams himself said that Christianity did not come easily to him, that it was a matter of conviction, not of instinct, and there is a thread of what might be called a pessimism of the emotions, especially in some of the earlier plays and poems. (Do you know that rather horrifying poem in *Windows of Night* called 'Domesticity' — what Chesterton, and Tolkien after him, called 'Recovery', but in a kind of dark inversion?) Lionel Rackstraw in *War in Heaven*, when he says 'let us pray only that immortality is a dream. But I don't suppose it is' was echoing feelings of his author.

In some way this has to be resolved. (Even Lionel is offered 'the annihilation which is God'). But the resolution was harder to describe than the conflict it would resolve. It is clear that Lester, at the end of *All Hallows' Eve*, is entering beatitude and glory; but it is even clearer that she is parting from her husband in a far more final way than she had by death; almost her last words to him are 'I did love you'. MacDonald would not have approved. 'Shall God be the God of the families of the earth, and shall the love that he has thus created go moaning and longing to all eternity; or worse, die out of our bosoms?' (*Unspoken Sermons*, series I, p. 242). Not that Williams asserted either of these: only that 'of any future union, if any were to be, she could not even begin to think; had she, the sense of separation would have been incomplete, and the deadly keenness of the rain unenjoyed ...without him, what was immortality or glory worth? And yet only without him could she even be that which she now was'.

In the meantime this life is almost unendurable, an 'infinite distress'. Ordinary apologists, like Lewis, will say God permits evil without willing it Himself; to Williams, God must have known the consequences of creation before creating, and still chose to create. 'Shall there be evil in a city, and I the Lord not have done it?' as the Archdeacon quotes from Amos somewhat to his hearers' bewilderment. Williams's answer to all this, or part of his answer, is in the essay on *The Cross*, 'Ought not the Christ to have suffered these things?' 'Yes, He ought ...But then also He did.' To introduce this into plays or novels is another matter. The submission of God to His own system belongs to one particular period of history, and so does not make appropriate material for imaginative fiction. The nature of evil can be depicted, and its defeat in the individual; but the ultimate reason why it can be defeated can only be referred to, not depicted.

In his *The Problem of Pain*, and also in some of his other writings, Lewis takes very seriously the idea of the devil. This is not true of the other three – or not in quite Lewis's way. Tolkien calls Morgoth 'the Diabolus', but he and his successor Sauron operate mainly on the physical plane (though it does seem that Morgoth was responsible for the Fall of Men). In MacDonald, Satan appears as the Shadow in *Lilith*, but he is only a vague and even impotent menace, the real danger lying in Lilith herself. MacDonald clearly believed in his reality (and even in his ultimate repentance) – though a character in *Alec Forbes* wonders whether even Satan's present state might be easier than *that* repentance! – but *Lilith* would not lose much if the Shadow were dropped altogether, and in MacDonald's other fantasies he does not appear. Williams's attitude is more hesitant; he neither affirms nor denies the existence of a devil – either way he is an 'indulgence'; he is not affirmed even in the novels that deal with black magic, and the Satan of *The Rite of the Passion* is not the usual one. The nearest you get is the Emperor of P'o-lu and Mrs Sammile in *Descent into Hell*; but the fact that the former is a person in the poems and for the purpose of the poetry says nothing about the actual facts. Mrs Sammile is a difficult figure in a difficult book. Certainly she tempts people to serve and adore themselves (like Lilith in *Heroes and Kings*); certainly she is not a human being; but she is hardly supernatural either.

To Lewis, though, Satan is definitely a person, and only by accident a personification; indeed, he can hardly be a full personification as well as a person without something close to Manichaeism. (Lewis repudiated dualism, but certainly used 'dualist' language at times.) In the 'Hansom' novels he is, like Tolkien's Morgoth, confined to this planet. But in *The Problem of Pain* it is suggested that 'a mighty created power ...may well have corrupted the animal creation before man appeared', and this no doubt might apply to other planets. We could find out by interstellar travel, which Lewis for one hoped would never become a reality: 'we are not fit yet to visit other worlds' – though it is theoretically conceivable that for some 'Redemption, starting with us, is to work from and through us' (as in Romans 8: 19ff.) 'Only if we had some such function would a contact between us and such unknown races be other than a calamity' (*Fernseeds & Elephants*, pp. 89 ff.). But all this, as he says, is 'trying to cross a bridge, not only before we come to it, but even before we know there is a river'; it is 'in the realm of fantastic speculation' (*Christian Reflections*, p. 176). But even fantastic speculation has its attractions, as the Inklings well knew.

Chapter Eleven

Charles Williams and
C.S. Lewis as Literary Critics

George Sayer

In 1936, a few weeks before the publication of C.S. Lewis's
The Allegory of Love, Sir Humphrey Milford handed
Charles Williams a proof copy and told him to write something about it to help the sales staff when they offered it to
booksellers. He read it with great excitement, astonished to
find that Lewis, of whom he had never heard, shared many
of his ideas about the nature and importance of Romantic
Love. He had thought of writing a book on the subject,
but now Lewis had done it with far greater detail and
learning than he was able to command. Lewis had not many
pupils at that time – few undergraduates at Magdalen read
English – but I think nearly all those fortunate few shared
Williams's enthusiasm. *The Allegory* was not just a literary
work. It recorded one of the few really important changes in
European feeling, one that affected the lives even of undergraduates. To repeat a paragraph that Williams quoted in
He Came Down From Heaven:

> French poets, in the eleventh century, discovered or
> invented, or were the first to express, that romantic
> species of passion which English poets were still writing
> about in the nineteenth century. They effected a change
> which has left no corner of our ethics, our imagination or

our daily life untouched .... Compared with this revolution, the Renaissance is a mere ripple on the surface of
literature.(*AL* 4)

The characteristics of this courtly love were humility,
courtesy, and the religion of love. The lover must have
but one lady, towards whom he should be modest and
humble, claiming little virtue except that which arose from
obedience to her, even to her slightest whim. His behaviour
was controlled by what became an elaborate code of manners,
from which the courtesy shown to ladies by elderly gentlemen
even of our own day is derived. This love had little to do
with marriage, which was a humdrum relationship concerned
with prosaic but necessary matters such as money, land and
the production of children. In it passionate love would have
been thought out of place. In the opinion of some author-
ities even sinful. 'Far from being a natural channel for the
new kind of love, marriage was rather the drab background
against which that love stood out in all the contrast of its
new tenderness and delicacy'. (*AL* 13) At this stage in history courtly love could hardly help being an idealisation of
adultery.

As for the religion of love, it was as if 'here is my heaven'
is expanded into a system with a god, saints, command-
ments, and a lover who prays, sins, repents, and is finally
admitted to bliss.

This intoxicating doctrine was spread by the poets
throughout Western Europe. No doubt it at first influenced only the lives of the literary and fashionable, but
it was never just a literary movement. It is one of the
most striking examples of the influence of literature on
life. Lewis reviews brilliantly its development in France and
England, through Chretien de Troyes, Chaucer and Lydgate
to Spenser. The book ends with a long section on *The Faerie
Queene* in which he shows that Spenser has done something of
great importance. He has effected not just a reconciliation but
a union of the ideals of courtly love with Christian marriage.
To quote Lewis, Spenser is 'the greatest among the founders
of that romantic conception of marriage which is the basis
of all our love literature from Shakespeare to Meredith.'
(*AL* 360) Of course this too was never a literary movement.

The work of the poets, especially Shakespeare, profoundly influenced educated men in this country so that their desire became to marry for love, and if possible to be in love with those whom they had married.

Like Williams, Spenser is an allegorical writer. Lewis's interpretation of his allegorical treatment of the ethics of courtly love almost rivals in subtlety and depth his interpretations of Williams's poetry in the second part of *Arthurian Torso*. Williams is more theological and, though more speculative, more profound. In *He Came Down From Heaven*, he had written magnificently on the spirituality of falling in love. He describes it as 'something like a state of adoration and it has been expressed of course better by the poets than by anyone else'. (Note the 'of course'. Williams never doubted that the poets were wiser than the rest of us.) The experience of the beloved arouses an unanalysed sense of significance. Though it cannot be defined, it is of great importance. The lover becomes aware of the archetypal perfection of the beloved. She is seen as Eve might have been seen before the Fall. She is radiant with a portion of the Divine Light. She has a paradisal comeliness of candour and restraint, seen especially in the eyes and mouth, 'the two places where the beauty of the soul most chiefly appears.' (*HCDFH* 95).

The beloved has the power to renovate nature in those who behold her. She is the helper of the faith. 'She was created not only to make a good thing better, but also to turn a bad thing into good.' (Ib) She produces humility, the self-forgetfulness which alone makes room for adoration. She is the vision of the divine glory and the means of the divine grace.

This will seem to some people as far-fetched as the courtly love of Chretien de Troyes that Lewis describes, but there is no doubt that it was presented by Williams quite seriously as a way of life that some of us may be called to follow. What he calls Hell has made three main attacks on it. The first is by leading us to assume that it should be permanent. This is false and dangerous, though the state of being in love should lead to an exchange of vows and in some cases to marriage. The second is jealousy, a mortal sin. The third is the supposition that this love is the property of the lovers. On the contrary, it possesses them. 'It is their job, their direction, their salvation.'

The subject is treated at greater length in *The Figure of Beatrice*, Williams's book on Dante, and shown in action in *Taliessin Through Logres*, on which Lewis wrote a commentary that clarifies the duties of the lover. What is this thing, he asked, flashing between Bors and Elayne? There is only one way to find out. The two must become the one flesh that alone can utter the secret name of their love. This will take them in two directions. One to 'the smooth plane of the happy flesh'. The other to Christ, so that they become one living symbol of the great 'twy-nature'. Lovers 'have had a vision of reality that would have been common to all men if Man had never fallen' (*TL* 16). A similar experience can come through nature as in Wordsworth's case. It is a call towards a disciplined way of life that strives towards perfection. The attention of the lover must not be diverted away from the beloved's body. He must love her whole person, not just her soul, for the division between soul and body is momentarily resolved by the experience. The 'glory' appears in the flesh. (*TL* 119).

Most of us need a good deal of help in understanding *Taliessin Through Logres*. Lewis gives us just enough. The difficulty of such literary criticism he once wrote 'arises from the fact that the poetic vision has almost too much meaning for prose ...' (*AL* 344) ...'

> The more concrete and vital the poetry is, the more complicated it will become in analysis; but the imagination receives it as simple in both senses of the word. Oddly, as it may sound, I conceive that it is the chief duty of the interpreter to begin analyses and to leave them unfinished. They are not meant as substitutes for the imaginative appreciation of the poem. Their only use is to awaken the reader's conscious elements in him which alone can fully respond to the poem'. (*AL* 345).

Lewis is a great critic because over and over again he succeeds in doing just that. Another subject of Williams's theological criticism and one which also greatly interested Lewis was evil and its nature. Williams was convinced that everything in the world was good. Yet he was at the same time extremely aware of the horrors, of the dark side. How were the two to be reconciled? What was the cause of the contradiction? How did men come to see good as evil?

For clues to the understanding of evil he went again to the poets, for 'they understand everything', as he wrote in the first paragraph of *The Forgiveness of Sins*. He went to Shakespeare and to Milton, the most theological of English poets. In his first critical work, *The English Poetic Mind*, he quoted some of the opening lines of *Paradise Lost*:

> Him the Almighty Power
> Hurl'd headlong flaming from th'etherial sky
> With hideous ruin and combustion, down
> To bottomless perdition, there to dwell
> In adamantine chains and penal fire
> Who durst defy th'Omnipotent to arms.

Different critics have written most various things about this passage. Some have written about the sentence construction or paragraph structure, others on the vocabulary, the meaning of the words in Latin and in the English of Milton's day. Of those concerned with the subject matter one might ask us to note how the tyrannical behaviour of the deity produces in us sympathy for Satan and admiration of his courage, another might wonder if Satan was intended to be the hero, and a third might write about Milton's Judaic or Old Testament conception of God. The questions Williams asks are quite different. They are more important and at once help the reader to grasp the essential meaning of the poem. 'Who was this being who durst defy omnipotence?' What could have been his motive? He must have forgotten his own true nature. He must have come to imagine that he shared the same nature as God, that he was, like him, self-begot, but unfortunately less powerful. Of course the sensible thing and the only way to happiness would have been for Satan to submit. But he cannot bear the idea. He must cling to the false idea he has of himself and of his own importance. So 'Better to reign in Hell than serve in Heaven'.

Williams is concerned to show us that Satan's predicament is relevant to ourselves. The state is well known to modern man. 'The corner of a suburban road, a metropolitan doorway are equally adequate surroundings.' Many men prefer their own myth to obvious reality. To quote from *The English Poetic Mind* 'the only choice that a man can make in such a crisis is between submitting to the good or refusing to submit to it, and if he refuses to submit he does so because so and only so can he hold "divided Empire with Heaven's King." "Every bad baronet in the old stories did the same thing." (*EPM* 123).'

The idea is developed in *Reason and Beauty in the Poetic Mind*, published three years later. Because he has been forced to leave Heaven, Satan has lost his sense of reality, his knowledge of what Heaven is really like. He has come to see good as evil and holds a false idea of what happened there. With the other rebel angels he 'shook God's throne'. This sounds fine and heroic, but a little thought shows us that it could not have been true. Almost more absurd still, he believes that by his mental attitude he can turn Hell into Heaven.

Farthest from him is best
Whom reason hath equalled, force hath made supreme
Above his equals. Farewell, happy fields
Where joy for ever dwells. Hail, horrors, hail
Infernal world, and thou, profoundest Hell,
Receive thy new possessor; one who brings
A mind not to be changed by place or time.
The mind is its own place, and in itself
Can make a heaven of hell, a hell of heaven.

The rhetoric is so splendid that it is easy to be carried away by Satan's heroics, but again a little thought shows us the foolishness of his attitude. Williams points out that Milton makes him supremely absurd as well as sinful. How absurd, how silly to war in heaven against 'Heaven's matchless King'. He continues: 'What is this heaven against which he is rebelling? It is a state where the paradox of human love at its finest is true of the very nature of life itself . . .(*R & B* 111). But to stay in Heaven Satan would have to be grateful.

'Gratitude is the deliverance of the soul, the very way of life and the activity of the creation.' But poor Satan cannot bear to have anything given him. 'It makes him feel subordinated'. Satan has another objection. He hates equality – 'Heaven's free love dealt equally to all'. . . . 'One can't be full of happy gratitude if one is always saying: "Put me first"' (*R & B* 111). In such a situation a man may prefer to be blind to the beauty of love and to 'stand on his rights'. It is a quite impressive phrase. But, as Williams points out, the pronoun cancels the noun. There are none.'

This attitude to Satan will be familiar to the happy few of us who were taught by Lewis in the nineteen-thirties. Does this mean that he took his ideas about Satan from Williams? The answer is 'Certainly not!' He discussed Satan with me in 1935, a year before he had any contact with Williams or had even heard of him. It is my second example of the extraordinary way in which the two men thought on the same lines. It seems from the dedicatory letter to Lewis's *A Preface to Paradise Lost*, which was published in 1942, that Lewis knew first about Williams's ideas through listening to the lectures on Milton that he gave in Oxford.

'To think of my own lecture', he wrote, 'is to think of those other lectures at Oxford in which you partly anticipated, partly confirmed, and most of all clarified and matured, what I had long been thinking about Milton . . . There we elders heard (among other things) what we had long despaired of hearing – a lecture on *Comus* which placed its importance where the poet placed it – and watched "the yonge fresshe folkes, he or she", who filled the benches listening first with incredulity . . . then with toleration, and finally with delight, to something so strange and new in their experience as the praise of chastity . . . It is a reasonable hope that of those who heard you . . . many will understand henceforward that when the old poets made some virtue their theme they were not teaching but adoring'. (*P to PL* v).

The last sentence is really important. 'Not teaching but adoring' virtue. It describes just what the poet who is truly wise does. The function of the literary critic is to revere the virtue thus revealed, and to help us to kneel and revere it with him.

Like Williams, Lewis emphasises the moral relevance of *Paradise Lost*. His tone is urgent and disturbing:

> 'to admire Satan is to give one's vote not only for a world of misery, but also for a world of lies and propaganda, of wishful thinking, of incessant autobiography. Yet the choice is possible. Hardly a day passes without some slight movement towards it in each one of us. This is what makes *Paradise Lost* so serious a poem... We have all skirted the Satanic island closely enough to have motives for wishing to evade the full impact of the poem. For, I repeat, the thing is possible, and, after a certain point, it is prized ... Satan wanted to go on being Satan. That is the real meaning of his choice. 'Better to reign in Hell, than serve in Heaven'. Some, to the very end, will think this is a fine thing to say; others will think that it fails to be roaring farce because it spells agony.' (*P to PL* 100).

In the powerful chapter on Satan's followers, he labours to show that their situation is similar to ours because Milton describes the very situations from which human situations grow. Explanation is necessary because modern readers often do not believe in Hell. 'Each of them is like a man who has just sold his country or his friend, or like a man who by some intolerable action of his own has just quarrelled irrevocably with the woman he loves. For human beings there is often an escape from Hell, but there is never more than one – the way of humiliation, repentance, and (where possible) restitution. But Satan's followers refuse to consider this seriously. The whole debate is an attempt to find some way out other than the only one that exists.' Moloch's way out is that of a rat in a trap, fury, blind hatred – their furious enmity may help them to forget the misery of their situation. Belial's attempt to escape is to be inactive, and above all not to awaken the memories of their appalling loss. Hell may gradually become more bearable. Human analogies might be in the case of the traitor the thought of the time when he first saw the real nature of what he was doing, for the lover memories of the happiness he has destroyed and his last unforgettable conversation with the woman he has cheated. Such memories are agonies that must not be reawakened. Henceforth, keep away from high thoughts, aspirations, emotions that might dispel 'the comfortable glooms of Hell', avoid 'great literature and notable music and the society of uncorrupted men as an invalid avoids draughts' – that must be his policy. As for Mammon, the human analogies with him are the man who can't see the difference between Heaven and Hell. 'What do you mean by saying we have lost love? There is an excellent brothel round the corner. What do you mean by all this talk of dishonour? I am positively plastered with orders and decorations ... Everything can be imitated, and the imitation will do just as well as the real thing.' (*P to PL* 103–4).

All these are examples of classical literary criticism, such as might perhaps gain the approval of Dr Johnson. They depend on a particular view of the value of good literature. Lewis summed up the contents of many books of literary aesthetics by saying that the purpose of literature was to make one 'better, wiser or happier'. This combines the statement of Dr Johnson, in his *Preface to Shakespeare* that 'it is always a writer's duty to make the world better' with that of Sir Philip Sidney in his *Apology for Poetry* that the object is to teach and delight, a view that had been hackneyed since Horace, and was never challenged, until the nineteenth century. Even at that time some of the great romantic poets would have accepted most of Lewis's summary. Wordsworth, who thought good poetry the result of the 'spontaneous overflow of powerful feelings', most certainly had a moral purpose. Good poems were never produced except by those who had thought long and deeply. 'The understanding of the reader must necessarily be in some degree enlightened, and his affections strengthened and purified.' He wants, too, to counteract 'the degrading thirst after outrageous stimulation' which he finds in the England of his day. Shelley in his extraordinarily lofty *Defence of Poetry* almost identified great poetry with wisdom. 'Shakespeare, Dante and Milton are philosophers of the very loftiest power'.

'Poetry makes immortal all that is best and most beautiful in the world ... Poetry redeems from decay the visitation of the divinity in man.'

In one of his last books Lewis produces another explanation of the value of literature. It provides an enlargement of our being. Through reading we enter into other men's beliefs even though we think them untrue, and share their emotions even though we think them depraved. Reading admits us to experiences not our own, experiences which may be beautiful, terrible, awe-inspiring, pathetic, comic or merely piquant.

'Literature gives the entrée to them all. Those of us who have been true readers all our lives seldom realise the enormous extension of our being that we owe to authors. We realise it best when we talk with an unliterary friend. He may be full of goodness and good sense, but he inhabits a tiny world. In it we should be suffocated. The man who is contented to be only himself and therefore less a self, is in prison. My own eyes are not enough for me, I will see through those of others.

'Even the eyes of humanity are not enough. I regret that the brutes cannot write books. Very gladly would I learn what face things present to a mouse or a flea; more gladly still would I perceive the olfactory world charged with all the information and emotion it carries for a dog ... in reading great literature I become a thousand men and yet remain myself. Like the night sky in the Greek poem, I see with a myriad eyes, but it is still I who see. Here, as in worship, in love, in moral action, and in knowing, I transcend myself, and am never more myself than when I do'. (*An Essay on Criticism* 140)

I do not think that this theory should be regarded as an alternative to the classical one. What Lewis is really doing is to describe with wonderful eloquence a way in which reading can make us both wiser and happier. If one accepts this theory, it follows that, as far as the ordinary reader is concerned, the role of the literary critic should be to act firstly as a signpost, to direct us to those authors and books which we are likely to find most enjoyable and profitable, especially to those whom we might otherwise never have come across on our own. Among poets Coventry Patmore, who was much admired by both Lewis and Williams, is an example, and perhaps Elizabeth Gaskell among novelists. His second purpose should be to give us some help in understanding the writers to whom he has directed us.

The best example I know of this traditional literary criticism is Lewis's *English Literature in the Sixteenth Century*. This is the best seller among the Oxford Histories of English Literature. And no wonder. The book opens with an astonishing survey of sixteenth century ideas. Lewis tells us that the Renaissance never existed, or, if it did, it was of no importance. He mounts a powerful attack on the humanists. 'They killed Latin by refusing to let it develop and grow. They were obsessed with the decorum which avoids every contact with the senses and the soil. They could not believe that the poets really cared about shepherds, lovers, warriors, voyages and battles. Medieval readers had been wiser in weeping with the heroines and shuddering at the monsters'. Humanism was a Philistine movement in philosophy. 'The new learning created the new ignorance.'

Most explanations of the new romanticism are wrong. Astronomy is rarely mentioned in literature. The discovery of the New World was a great disappointment because it meant an end to hopes of an easier route to the East. The new Science was something to which the humanists were indifferent or hostile. It was anyway closely allied to the old magic. Platonism was connected in the public mind with a system of demonology. The view many of us have of the Puritans is wrong. The Protestant Doctrine of Salvation by Grace is not gloomy or terrifying. It is joyous. The person who experiences that conversion 'feels like one who has awakened from nightmare into ecstasy'. It was the Puritans who praised the marriage bed. They were accused of being young, lusty and radical. It was the Catholics who exalted virginity. The creed of Calvin was that of progressives, even of revolutionaries. It appealed strongly to those whose tempers would have been Marxist in the nineteen-thirties. 'The fierce young don, the learned lady, the courtier with intellectual leanings were likely to be Cal-vinists. He was a dazzling figure, a man born to be the idol of revolutionary intellectuals'.

All this and much more in the first sixty pages. The dust and the controversy their brilliance provoke has never died down. We know that they delighted Charles Williams. The rest of this great work consists of a concise yet thorough survey of all the principal and many minor writers of the period. During the nine years he had worked on the book he had read every text on which he gave a judgement. He was often bored — those who looked through his books after his death sometimes found at the end a date and, neatly written, the letters 'n.a.'. They stand for 'Never Again'.

No one can read without delight the many pieces of enthusiastic literary criticism. Sometimes they are of new discoveries, such as that of Tyndale as a great prose writer. Let me quote from his comparison of Tyndale and More. This illustrates also Lewis's skilful choice of quotations which makes his book a joyful anthology.

'What we miss in More is the joyous, lyrical quality of Tyndale. The sentences that stick in the mind from Tyndale are half way to poetry:

> Who taught the eagles to spy out of their prey? even so that children of God spy out their father. That they might see love and love again.

> Where the spirit is, there is always summer.

In More we feel all the smoke and stir of London; the very plodding of his sentences is like horse traffic in the streets of London. In Tyndale we breathe mountain air.'

In his splendid chapter on the Scottish Chaucerians, he invites us to share his enthusiasm for Gavin Douglas and Dunbar to whom he gives real greatness. Listen to this on an uncharacteristic poem of Dunbar's: 'It is speech rather than song, but speech of unanswerable and thunderous greatness. From the first line to the last it vibrates with exultant energy. It defies the powers of evil and has the ring of a steel gauntlet flung down.' The longest chapter is on two of his favourites, Sir Philip Sidney and Edmund Spenser. I am speaking for many if I say that I can never dip into that chapter without feeling compelled to go to my bookcase and take down either the *Arcadia* or *The Faerie Queene*. No one has written so well on the lyrics of Edmund Campion, with such under- standing of their metrical subtleties. He was able to do this because he was, like Williams, a fine poet, and unlike Williams, also sensitive to music.

Because he believed John Donne to be over-rated and a lesser poet than Campion, Lewis gave to him just five pages. When I spoke to him about it, he said: 'I have given him space according to his merit, as it seems to me, No more and no less.' This illustrates his independence of fashion and the views of other academics. Like Williams, he trusted his own sensibility and was fearless in attacking idols, cant and trendiness.

There were of course academic tutors and reviewers who disliked the views of Williams and Lewis. Williams could be written off on the grounds that he was no academic, indeed a man who had never undergone a course of study at any uni- versity. It was of course impossible to do this with Lewis. The attacks were nearly always about the introduction of Christian doctrine in his criticism. Professor Garrod of this University wrote in the Oxford magazine that for him the prime hindrance to enjoyment of *A Preface to Paradise Lost* was its 'theological rubbish'. He does not argue against Lewis's point which was of course that it is impos- sible to understand a theological work such as *Paradise Lost* without knowing a little theology. In the same way it is not possible fully to appreciate a painting of an Old Testa- ment theme without knowing the story that it illustrates. Another reviewer, L.C. Knights, describes Lewis's argu- ments as 'abstract, irrelevant and unconvincing.' Even Dame Helen Gardner, who in many ways admired Lewis, wrote of *English Literature in the Sixteenth Century* 'the book is marred throughout by an insistent polemical purpose, expressed in the title of the first chapter "New Learning and New Ignorance". This extraordinary chapter ... is devoted to proving that the Humanists did immense harm. Though the index gives many references to Erasmus ... when one looks up the references one finds that they are nearly all derogatory.' I did look up the references to Erasmus. There were 19 of them, and really I could not find one that was derogatory. But the standards Williams and Lewis followed and the books that they loved are now up against far more serious dangers than those of academic critics. Many people, especially those who are young, have come to look at life and consequently literature in a different way. The result is that they feel that these and many other classics have no message for them. They are irrelevant to the way they think and live. The subject has been examined at length by Professor Allan Bloom in an important book, *The Closing of the American Mind*. I will mention some of the points that he makes. One must bear in mind that he is an American professor and England is fortunately a less advanced country: Truth is relative. So is virtue. Nothing is certainly right or wrong. Tolerance and openness are the most desirable qualities. 'The true believer is the real danger. The study of history and of culture teaches that all the world was mad in the past; men always thought they were right and that led to wars, persecutions, slavery, racism ... The point is not to correct the mistakes and really think you are right; rather it is not to think you are right at all.' (p. 26). Sin, Goodness, Heaven, Hell are medieval conceptions with no meaning for the modern mind. Every one has a right to choose his or her own scheme of values and to adopt his or her own life-style. 'Romantic love is now as alien to us as knight errantry and young men are no more likely to court a woman than to wear a suit of armour, not only because it is not fitting, but because it would be offensive to women. As a student exclaimed to me, with approval of his fellows: "What do you expect me to do? Play a guitar under some girl's window?" Such a thing seemed to him as absurd as swallowing goldfish.' The word love is in fact rarely mentioned. Instead there is talk of a commitment, or a relationship or just of sex.

Because I thought Professor Bloom's views about the collapse of traditional culture might be purely American, I tried them out on my step-daughter and her friends, all young Oxford graduates and none of them fools. The results, much to my surprise, amply confirmed Bloom's criticisms. None of the books and plays we talked about had any relevance to their lives. Some were entertaining and this is why they read them. They were often unaware of the existence of any theme or moral. Obvious moralising was always disliked. They thought Marx, Freud and Darwin had influenced the way in which they lived. So of course had some of the scientists and inventors of technical processes. They doubted if anyone else had. They too believed that almost everything, certainly all morality, was relative and that tolerance towards the life-styles that other people chose for themselves was an essential virtue. This attitude to the past has produced in America and to some extent in England a most unhappy rootlessness. The wisdom of the past is no longer there to console, encourage and confirm. They are worse off than far less well educated people were not very long ago. My grandmother, for instance, had only the ordinary education of a village school, yet she could quote much of the Bible and quite a lot of Shakespeare. She often quoted these books in times of doubt and difficulty. I can hear her reciting: 'Love is not love which alters/When it alteration finds . . . /O no! It is an ever fixed mark/That looks on tempests and is never shaken . . . Love's not time's fool . ./ Love alters not with his brief hours and weeks,/ But bears it out even to the crack of doom.' I have no doubt at all that it helped her very much in a difficult marriage.

I am sure that we can all think of times when we have received support from the wisdom of the poets. C.S. Lewis told me that the memory of the sonnet: 'Th'expense of spirit in a waste of shame' had often preserved him when tempted. 'Grace often comes to us through the poets. And of course they need not be Christian. I owe an immense amount to the Greek poets, and many times I have been helped by a couplet of Yeats.' What a pity it is that the learning of poetry by heart is and has been for twenty or thirty years out of fashion in our schools! Except of course as a part of the task of swotting for exams.

Both Lewis and Williams were quite clear about what literary criticism was for. It was to direct us to the best literature and, if necessary, to help us to understand it. Unfortunately such a simple approach is unlikely to be acceptable in academic circles, which are often influenced by various post-Kantian philosophical ideas. Our view is that literature is not really an imitation of life. The opposite is nearer the truth. The world we think we know we know only through language. Each novelist, each writer constructs his own pattern of words, which need not be related to any other reality. Each piece of writing is thought of primarily as a word structure. Academic criticism is also influenced by linguistic philosophy. It seems that meanings in language arise from differences in a system of signs. We grasp their meaning by thinking about how they are distinguished from or connected with each other. Literature is about making new things out of the available signs, and literary criticism is about how the author has done this. The object of these new ideas is perhaps to cure us of what those who hold them might call 'the realistic fallacy'. Their cause is like that of the art critics who want to cure us of an affection for realistic or representational painting. Fortunately they have little influence except on academics who seem to me self-conscious in their writing and uncertain about how to evaluate the literature of the past. Present day writers are seriously handicapped by moral and religious uncertainty. To quote Iris Murdoch, who is a philosopher as well as a novelist (rare combination!)

> ... literature is about the struggle between good and evil, but this does not appear clearly in modern writing, where there is an atmosphere of moral diffidence and where the characters presented are usually mediocre. The disappearance or weakening of organised religion is perhaps the most important thing that has happened to us in the last hundred years ... Life is soaked in the moral, literature is soaked in the moral. Values are only artificially and with difficulty expelled from language ... the author's moral judgement is the air which the reader breathes. The bad writer ... exalts some characters and demeans others without any concern for truth or justice ... The good writer is the just intelligent judge.' (*Men of Ideas* ed. Magee p. 282).

'The just intelligent judge'. The same phrase fits admirably the good critic, says the C.S. Lewis of *English Literature in the Sixteenth Century*. Yet it seems cool praise for him and still more for Charles Williams who was in his best work an inspired critic if ever there was one. This goes for the

brilliant *He Came Down From Heaven* and also for much
of *The Figure of Beatrice*. This book sees the theme of all
or almost all of Dante's writing as what Williams calls the
Way of Affirmation, one of two ways to sanctity in religious
practice. The other Williams calls the Way of Rejection. It is
the ascetic way, and consists of the renunciation of pleasures
and other inessentials (which Williams calls images) in order
to concentrate on a relationship with the deity. The Way of
Affirmation consists of perceiving and praising the presence
of God (the 'Glory' as Williams often called it) in His
creation. Williams's book and Dante's *Divine Comedy* deal
with this as a method of progress towards the inGodding
of man, but in particular with romantic love as a mode
of the Way. Williams insists that Beatrice is a real woman
or girl, not an allegorical figure. She was seen, body and
soul, in her heavenly perfection. 'Many lovers', he writes,
'have seen ladies as Dante saw Beatrice. Dante's great gift
to us was not the vision, but the ratification by his style
of the validity of the vision'. Why then don't we see it in
everybody? Williams's answer to this question illustrates his
originality.   'It   is   because   of   the   Divine   Mercy.
Yes Mercy. He quotes Dante's *Convivio*. 'The soul is so
intoxicated after gazing it at once goes astray in all its opera-
tions.' If seeing one in this way is enough to send the soul
reelingly astray, what chaos would follow if we saw many
of our fellows in this way, what sin, what despair! This per-
version of the image, this going astray is the subject, really
the only subject of the *Inferno*. The *Purgatorio* is then the
recovery and the *Paradiso* is an image of the whole act of
knowing, ending in a balanced whole. It is an image of the
whole redeemed universe and also an image of a redeemed
love-affair.' It is a book full of good things. Williams's usual
themes are here, often put better than anywhere else. Thus
of the inter-life of souls: 'It is the moral duty of lovers, as
they certainly at moments know, to plunge with love into
each other's life – bringing power; power to resist temptation, to reject, to affirm, to purify, to pray. "I will pray
for you" is a good saying; a better "I will pray in you"'.
And on work: 'Almighty God did not first create Dante
and then find something for him to do ... all the images
were created in order to work. Hell is the cessation of work

and the leaving of the images to be without any function, merely themselves'. And on the last page: 'The Way is not only what the poem is about; it is what Love is about. It is what Love is "up to" and the only question is whether lovers are "up to" Love'.

If we except *He Came Down From Heaven* in so far as that remarkable work is literary criticism, *The Figure of Beatrice* is much the best of Williams's critical books. Its importance to the student of Dante is shown by the fact that it is the only critical work that Dorothy Sayers recommended in her translation of the *Inferno*. She dedicated the book to Charles Williams 'the dead master of the Affirmations'. This indicates its real importance for the rest of us. She accompanies this dedication with a quotation from the *Inferno* which, quoted in full, in her translation reads: 'for I keep with me still, / stamped on my mind, and now stabbing my heart, / The dear, benign, paternal image of you, / You living, you hourly teaching me the art / By which men grow immortal; know this too; / I am so grateful, that while I breathe air, / My tongue shall speak the thanks that are your due.' (*Inf.* xv, 80–86). Books on the Way of Affirmation are very few. *The Figure of Beatrice* is one that can show us the way from the first vision of the Glory to the gates of Paradise.'

Chapter Twelve

Charles Williams and Twentieth Century Verse Drama

Glen Cavaliero

That Charles Williams's plays make good theatre has by now been established in numerous performances, albeit on a small scale (he has yet to undergo the challenge of a major West End production) and in the teeth of the evidence of at least one of the actors in them, Richard Heron Ward (whose *Names and Natures* (1968) gives us a distinctly unfriendly portrait of Williams, both as man and playwright). It would not, I think, be a difficult task to demonstrate the superior vitality of Williams's verse over that of most of his contemporaries, certainly in its rhythmic inventiveness and flexibility and its avoidance of the measured tread of the iambic foot: speed, a speed not unlike his own utterance in life, is a characteristic of his dialogue. In the following paper, however, such considerations will be secondary to an examination of how Williams's dramatic art developed, both in relation to his thought, and, in turn, in relation to the effect of his theological ideas upon his art. The inter-relation between form and content in Williams's work is of a peculiarly fruitful kind.

His early plays, found in *The Myth of Shakespeare* (1928) and *Three Plays* (1931) are wordy and derivative in expression, pseudo-Shakespearean and quite unaffected by the rhythms and syntax of the Modernist movement. Even so, one detects in the Shakespeare play, as in the Masques performed at Amen House, an apprehension of a timeless present that indicates Williams's essentially metaphysical cast of imagination. Dramas in time, the enactment in a linear progress of human actions and their temporal consequences, actually slowed down and thus clogged up the darting force of Williams's perceptions: *The Witch* and *The Chaste Wanton* reflect this in a blank verse that veers between the clotted and the flabby. Ornamental language, swamping metaphors, are essentially materialistic: they draw attention to themselves, not to the reality they are supposed to indicate. So too with archaic diction. All the 'doths' and 'thereofs' and 'wots' and 'sooths' spell out for their readers that this is 'poetry'. It is to Williams's credit that he became aware of what was wrong with his own verse; but the interesting thing about that awareness is that it appears to have come to him less through sensitivity to the literary climate of the time than to the theological problems of Incarnation. How was the knowledge of God to be reconciled with the knowledge of man?

There were to be two paths to a solution. One was the realisation of timelessness, the other the experience of contradiction. The realisation of timelessness is foreshadowed in *The Rite of the Passion*. This might be described as a kind of non-musical oratorio, in which the performers recite their parts and the action is produced through what they say rather than through what they do. Conceived as part of a Three Hour service of Good Friday devotions, it does, in its presentation as well as in its content, suggest the existence of a timeless world of absolute realities to which the characters conform and to which and in which their personalities are relative. This is underlined by the pairing of characters, Peter with Caiphas, James with Pilate, John with Herod, in addition to the more obvious apposition of Gabriel to Satan. But more than apposition is implied: 'contraries are not negations' and clearly we can see the seeds of Williams's later understanding of the mutuality of good and evil in human experience. I stress in 'human experience': that no untimate dualism is implied becomes explicit in Williams's later plays. But the abandonment in this early work of even a relative dualism witnesses to the eschatological nature of Williams's imagination, for which all things are seen in relation to their place in an ultimate pattern which controls, and is exhibited in, the contradictions and diversities of experience as we know it.

In *The Rite of the Passion* the opposing forces exist side by side rather than in strife or, as in the later plays, apparent indissolubility. And this is reflected in the verse, which simply states its propositions limply. When Williams makes Satan proclaim that

> Lord, I am thy shadow, only known as hell
> where any linger from thy sweet accord.

we feel that the dictates of rhyme and the regularity of rhythm alike drain the statement of dramatic force: the idea is debilitated by the feebleness of its expression. Williams's theological insight was to grow in and through his understanding of poetic energy and form.

The exploration of contradiction was to be the moving force in this poetic growth. At the time he wrote *The Chaste Wanton* he was also exploring in his critical writings the problem of divided consciousness, the simultaneous awareness of conflicting qualities in any given experience. In his Introduction to *The Letters of Evelyn Underhill* (1943) he coins the term 'the Impossibility' for this state of knowledge. In her case it involved her dilemma, as a Catholic postulant, when Pius X's Encyclical of 1907, condemning Modernism, contradicted her own intellectual probity. Whether the situation was as acute as Williams makes out is open to question; but in continuing going to Mass while refraining from communion, she lived out a contradiction in terms. Williams comments:

> It is imperative, and in the end possible, to believe that the Impossibility does its own impossible work; to believe so, in whatever form the crisis takes, is of the substance of faith; especially if we add to it Kierkegaard's phrase that, in any resolution of the crisis, so far as the human spirit is concerned, 'before God man is always in the wrong'.

The phrase might serve as an epigraph to Williams's *Collected Plays*.

The Chaste Wanton has the experience of Impossibility for its theme; but in form and language it is simply a rather leaden, though obviously deeply felt, presentation of the crisis in linear terms, resulting in a purely mental resolution: the characters choose the consciousness they will have of their predicament. The sublimation of forbidden sexual impulses (in this case the love of the Duchess for a commoner when she is called to make a state marriage) was a familiar theme of the time, from Housman's *A Shropshire Lad* on; but Williams declines all temptations to romantic nostalgia. The contradictory experience allows for no easy emotional resolution. The Play's failure to convince is in itself a tribute to the author's rigorous imagination. The invitation to write *Thomas Cranmer* must have seemed heaven − as well as ecclesiastically − sent − a rare combination as Williams would have been the first to point out.

Since the production of John Masefield's *The Coming of Christ* in 1928, the Canterbury Festival had been an important occasion for the presentation of verse plays with Christian themes, foreshadowing the post-war renaissance of this kind of drama at the Mercury Theatre and the achievements of Christopher Fry, himself a friend of Williams. The play preceding Cranmer, Eliot's *Murder in the Cathedral* had been an attempt to combine an authentically Christian drama, in a specific time and place, with a sense of contemporary relevance. The problem of relevance in a society of dwindling religious belief is partly a question of language. The capacity of religious language for extending the imagination is pre-empted by pious associations: it has an inbuilt, predetermined resonance. Eliot's achievement in *Murder in the Cathedral* was the presentation of a historic religious conflict in such a way that the issues were seen to be valid for his own time. Becket's martyrdom is interpreted sacramentally: that is to say it both enacts the redemptive passion of Christ and points to that Passion as part of the fundamental pattern which underlies life at every moment of time. Eliot's way of achieving this is through a combination of spiritual analysis with the realistic presentation of the murderers and the rationalisation of their case. Two interpretations of experience are proffered, the knowledge of the world and the life of Christ. This particular action demonstrates the eternal pattern.

The word 'pattern' is central to Williams's thinking, and illuminates his particular contribution to religious drama. Fired by Eliot's example, he writes a play which follows the historic progress of Cranmer's career and at the same time makes it a portrait of humanity's relationship with a Creator who is simultaneously and painfully a Redeemer. This theological point of view in part arises as the solution of a dramatic problem. How to infuse a religious drama with a contemporaneity that would not renege on that drama's initial premises? How to make the past truly present, true both to its own contemporaneity and to ours? Williams's solution is to abolish time, place and external events, so that the play's time and place is shared by the audience and the characters. The action does not take place through a series of set dramatic pieces; rather scenes dissolve into each other cinematically. External events are conveyed through a stylised symbolism (the resemblance to Brecht is apparent here); and the characters are representative less of qualities or humours than of capacities and attitudes. The language too has changed. Instead of regular stresses and elaborate metaphors Williams writes a vigorous rhythmical verse which varies the beat of the decasyllabic line with one strung on five irregularly placed stresses, inlaid with rhymes. He is attempting a marriage between poetic and colloquial idiom. But the experiment is not an entire success. The language is too knotted and succinct; there are insufficient concessions to the naturally sluggish ear.

The key figure is of course the Skeleton, the Figura Rerum or shape of things, the knowledge of God as fallen man experiences it. He derives from Satan in *The Rite of the Passion*, there designated 'dark viceroy of the Holy Ghost'; and his function is to be developed in the succeeding plays. These figures of remedial providence are Williams's unique contribution to twentieth century drama, a remarkable instance of the embodiment in dramatic terms of a complexity of theological associations. They reflect his interest in the writings of Kierkegaard, and are the outcome of his preoccupation with the springs of action and the nature of tragedy, as found in the biographies and the two books on the poetic mind. In these he posits that men and women can only truly act when their fortunes conflict with their natures, so that they are compelled to deny their self-sufficiency. Man exists, as it were, in dialogue with his circumstances. In *Cranmer* the fact of the opposition between fortune and nature, the Impossibility, is personified in the Skeleton, the divine providence that is adverse fate, 'Christ's back': The Skeleton does here for one man what such figures as the Accuser and the Flame do in the later plays for many. This play is, for all its historical trappings, an interior drama, one that takes place within Cranmer's mind: the subordinate characters exist primarily in relation to his state of soul. It is not so much the interaction of personalities that interests Williams as the hounding of a man into salvation. *Thomas Cranmer* is an exhibition of how God takes man at his word.

Cranmer is a man who prides himself upon his integrity, his singleness: the division of his fortune from his nature is the action of the play. The Skeleton (death-in-life?) says:

> ... I must divide
> his life to the last crack and pull his soul
> — if it lives — through the cracks ...

It scourges Cranmer to his heavenly doom with sardonic laughter, in which the rhythms of Eliot's *Sweeney Agonistes* may be detected,

> crying from the tomb of the earth where I died
> the word of the only right Suicide,
> the only word no words can quell,
> the way to heaven and the way to hell.

By outraging the expectations of his audience, and by introducing violently discordant associations into his presentation of the providence of God, Williams involves that audience in the action of his play: in this scene he goes beyond Brecht. We share, take part in, the experience of the play's protagonist from within. Moreover we do so through the verse itself. When the Skeleton answers Cranmer's demand to know 'Have I erred?' with the words:

> In thinking, though it was important for you to be
> right,
> it mattered at all in the end whether you were right

it is the metre which determines the sense of the line: the stress comes on 'you', not 'were'.

Here was a perfect medium for Williams's peculiarly intellectual imagination – one, too, which was at its happiest operating within predetermined limits. Religious drama provided a set framework of images and myths; the conventions of the theatre enabled him to embody abstractions and to clothe his pictorial, associative method of thought in appropriate forms of character and action. And nowhere was he to be so entirely himself as in the Nativity play *Seed of Adam*. It is a spirited attempt to revivify traditional religious imagery. Indeed, such revitalisation was a feature of all Williams's writings, from the early poems on, reaching its logical term with the Arthurian poetry.

The problem facing any specifically Christian dramatist is that, while the play's form must arise from the author's imagination, the form of religious drama is predetermined by the author's beliefs. It is Williams's great strength as a Christian apologist that in him Imagination and belief fully coincided. In *Seed of Adam* we see imagination illuminating belief. The dramatic stroke whereby Mother Myrrh the negress who symbolises Hell acts as midwife at the Incarnation, is a stage in Williams's realisation that Hell is ultimately to be seen as Heaven's complement. It is a state of negation so intense as to beget its opposite. Together, the negress and the Third King turn out to be another manifestation of the Skeleton. The essentially schematic nature of Williams's imagination fuses Nativity and Redemption in a single vivid piece of symbolism. His work as a literary artist always impels him towards the affirmation of a total spiritual world – 'event-landscape-web' over-arching or subsuming or enveloping or inter-penetrating this one.

Seed of Adam goes beyond *Cranmer* in its supra-temporal personifications, and becomes a vehicle of multi-significant references. Thus the first two kings are not merely iconographical representations: they embody the life-experiences involved in the capacities they symbolise. For one, Paradise 'is bought for a penny/and slept off'; for another, 'wise men have recognized/it is only our mothers' forms rationalized.' For both, 'tomorrow everything begins again.' The human setting for the Incarnation is thus not so much the historical moment as the timeless need.

The verse attempts a similar timelessness. The imagery is a blend of Islamic, English and Biblical references. The 'folk' element is pervasive. At his best Williams achieves a marvellous fusion of physical and mental experience, as in Mary's description of the Archangel, in which the angel emerges from the sounds and activities of everyday life at the fair; but at other times his language can be intolerably pretentious:

> Do not with descent, O altitude, even of mercy,
> sweeten the enhanced glance of those still eyes
> which to my lord's house, and to me the least
> illumine earth with heaven, our only mortal
> imagination of eternity,
> and the glory of the protonotary Gabriel.

No one, surely, ever, ever talked like that.

Williams's subsequent plays attempt a more naturalistic treatment: he entrusts his message to his tale. They continue to personify the divided consciousness and to make use of the innovatory breakthrough from the framework of time and space achieved in *Seed of Adam*. But they also lay greater stress on the authentic life of the symbol; they are increasingly naturalistic because more truly sacramental in approach. In the pageant play *Judgement at Chelmsford* Williams was helped by the form of the play itself. The naturalistic detail flourishes in the individual episodes, the mythical timeless element governs their framework: as John Heath-Stubbs observes, the retrospective action, from Hell through Purgatory to Paradise, owes much to Dante. The function of the Skeleton is taken over by the Accuser, designated, by a nice fusion of celestial and demonic associations, 'the dweller on the threshold of love.' His role is to be a devil's advocate within the self, a conception less mythical than existential. This play seems to me to be generally undervalued. It is one of the most immediately accessible of Williams's works, and one of the most satisfactory in its presentation of an over-arching providence.

Its greater naturalness is put to good use in the small plays written for the Oxford branch of the Pilgrim Players, where the sharper personifications, such as that of Grace as a mischievous urchin or Pride as a slithery gushing cheat, amount in their total effect to an imaginative theology. Their verse carries the theological overtones with ease. Here is Man telling Pride about his new friend, Faith:

> She was a friend of Immanuel, the child born
> the night you went ... O well, Pride –
> I beg your pardon; it is old habit in me –
> we need not go into all that now.
> There was a misunderstanding of what he meant
> and a tussle – you, my dear, will understand
> there was something to be said on my side;
> but anyhow – it was all rather unfortunate – he died.

Such verse has a suppleness that retains its lilt while responding to the demands of idiomatic speech. It is more authentically Williams's own than the prose employed in *Terror of Light* (as he recognised when he proposed to turn the latter into verse); here he seems to be aiming for the kind of popularity (but also scandal) enjoyed a year later by Dorothy L. Sayers' broadcast sequence, *The Man Born To Be King*. But this was not his metier. 'Oh Augustitude pray for me', says John to Mary Magdalene. Elsewhere the language is flat and over-definitive: Thomas speaks of being 'put completely into one's own identity'. Williams was always tempted to define what he meant instead of saying what he meant.

But both this play and the radio play *The Three Temptations* afford evidence of how Williams's use of the drama to explore the divided consciousness had resulted in a comprehensiveness of theological statement which sees creation and redemption, joy and pain, as aspects of a single reality, God's way with man. Indeed *The Three*

Temptations, freed from the requirements of stagecraft takes us back to the alignments of *The Rite of the Passion*, Herod, Caiphas and Pilate now being fused with Christ's three temptations in the wilderness. The compression shows how essentially spatial Williams's imagination was: he sees the events of time as so many facets of eternity. The austerity of his moral viewpoint is now absolute. Everything relates to everything else; and men shall have what they have chosen. 'Hell is always there for the craving, and the having is easy.'

I cannot do better than describe *The House of the Octopus* in the words of one contemporary reviewer: 'the play stands to his entire output much as the final note or chord of a piece ... stands to the foregoing musical elements; it designates their relative positions, and reveals their deeper significance.' This play represents the full maturity of Williams's thought on the question of human integrity and its relation to the providence of God, and it throws a searching light on a certain kind of religious temperament. It was evidently too searching for comfort, since it is said that at one performance by the students of a theological college the missionary was praised in the synopsis for his courage and devotion. Williams might, or might not, have appreciated that.

The temptation of this second Anthony is presented with a skill that matches Eliot's in *Murder in the Cathedral*. The Imperial Marshall of P'o-L'u knows what he is about:

Every pious man − and, of course, woman −
has one − just one − surface where religion and he
are so delicately mixed in his soul as to be
indistinguishable; he is never quite sure −
and does not (believe me!) ever want to be sure −
whether his religion or he is being soothed
into a lascivious spiritual delight.

The House of the Octopus, more than any of Williams's plays succeeds in blending the mythical and the naturalistic; and in its use of political issues this drama of redemption through self-knowledge compares favourably with Eliot's more esoteric treatment of the theme in *The Family Reunion*.

The Skeleton's function in this play is filled by the Flame – one of the tongues of Pentecost. One notices how appropriate to each play these embodiments of Divine Providence are – the skeleton for secret guilt, the accuser for public arraignment, the flame for purging. In each case the natural process of things is seen as the manifestation of the divine presence, just as the angel came to Mary through the noises of the fair. It is the peculiar property of Williams's dramatic art that it does succeed in uniting in the action and mode of the play the vision of divine-human co-inherence that is the master-meaning of his work in theology, criticism, poetry and fiction alike. There is no uneasy jerking from one mode of awareness to the other.

I think it would be fair to say that Charles Williams influenced the course of verse drama rather less than the writing of verse drama influenced the course of Charles Williams. Verse drama, despite the post-war popularity of the plays of Eliot and Fry, and the more esoteric appeal of those of Ronald Duncan, has not turned out to be a seminal contribution to late twentieth century theatre. Or not as yet. To say this is to reflect on the contemporary standing and nature of the art of poetry. Contemporary poets tend to be personal, introspective, ironic, reflective, all in the short poem. Verse has become an individualistic form, and the protest poem and the pop-song poem have been written more for a kind of participating audience made up of many individuals welded together by mass emotion than for people existing in a condition of dialogue and exchange.

The failure of Williams's Arthurian poems to attract a large following is bound up with the failure of verse drama to find an audience. We do not, by and large, possess the kind of certitudes which allow for public matters to be spoken of in verse without self-consciousness. By jettisoning ceremony we have, as Williams realised, left self-consciousness exposed and unprotected.

Charles Williams's influence is still potential, in the theatre as elsewhere. It may make itself felt there, I think, through his creation of a drama of metaphysical ideas which, through its imaginative and intellectual energy, can be viewed in existential terms, and experienced by the audience as commonly shared interior reality. It does not chronicle or comment on past events as earlier twentieth century religious dramatists had done: it bears more resemblance to the Mystery Plays. Indeed all Williams's literary output is concerned with exploring the spiritual Mystery of Christendom. He proclaims; he does not seek to argue or persuade. He is an artist in theology, not a mere polemicist. And it was because he used the possibilities inherent in verse drama to further his own theological understanding that he was able to write plays which, for all their testing moral and dramatic qualities, and all the restrictions of form, are arguably among the most enjoyable, because most spiritually liberated, of his works.

Chapter Thirteen

Objections to Charles Williams

Stephen Medcalf

This paper was delivered on the dark and bitterly cold afternoon of 11 February 1978 at All Saints', Margaret Street. I originally intended to revise it, but since it is an exercise in objecting to Williams with which I do not entirely now agree, I think it best now to leave it as it stands. I have, however, added one or two notes at the end.

I suppose that many of us, including myself, find that Charles Williams speaks to their condition, perhaps uniquely: we agree with T.S. Eliot that 'he left behind him a considerable number of books which should endure, because there is nothing else that is like them or could take their place.' Eliot seems to mean primarily that, 'Williams knew and could put into words, states of consciousness of a mystical kind, and the sort of elusive experience which many people have once or twice in a lifetime', and instances *The Place of the Lion*. I would add for myself that *Descent into Hell* is capable of making one feel one has heard the word Ivan Karamazov imagined, that will make it certain that the universe has always been right; and that *The Descent of the Dove* is the only book outside the Bible, and some commentaries on the Bible, that persuades me to see history as the activity of God. But to think as highly of Williams as that raises a problem. For it is plain that the greater part of the world does *not* think so highly of him, and we should ask why, and whether there is any justification for their view. Why do people like or dislike Williams? Even though the answer may not change our estimate of him, it may reveal something about him to us. I shall begin by looking at four hostile critics, and then try to formulate my own difficulties.

Kenneth Allott says of his poetry: 'like other writers (C.S.) Lewis has in my opinion been hypnotised by his memories of the man and by his conviction of the importance and wisdom of the things Williams had to say, into imagining they are said (and happily) in the poems.' Simply stated as a general reason for the appeal of Williams this will not do: it is enough to point out that many people who find Williams speaks, and speaks excitingly, to their condition, have no memories of him other than of his writings. But there is a more subtle version of Allott's remark which I think is true from my own experience. When I first read Williams, from mere curiosity about a writer said to be unlike anything I had read, I found him somewhat impenetrable. When, a year or so later, other paths led me to him which I shall speak of hereafter, I found I grew to like him rather suddenly and to like all of him at once: even books, which I recognise as overall rather poor, I devoured because they were aspects of his personality. Allott is in fact in one way right. Liking Williams can be very much like knowing a person, having memories of a person: and one can believe, rightly or wrongly, that one intuits things said which have importance and wisdom even when one knows that they are apparent only when you know him as a whole person – when some rather sudden and single contract of the imagination has been made. But the contract can be made though the writings. Allott is right in diagnosing the pattern of liking Williams – it is like knowing a person. He is wrong in supposing one could only acquire that pattern by personal acquaintance. This says something about Williams' writings which, again, I shall defer considering.

The second misleading description of the appeal of Charles Williams is that offered by Dr Leavis in *The Common Pursuit*, which can easily be reversed. Dr Leavis makes his own oblique and paranoiac version of Allott's diagnosis, describing Williams' influence as 'a subject worth attention from the inquirer into "sociology of contemporary literature"', and comparing it to that of Robert Bridges. This is Dr Leavis' way of stating that Williams had personal friends in Oxford and London who, merely because of personal acquaintance would use positions of academic power to impose 'his verse-constructions' – Dr Leavis' words – on students. Perhaps too Dr Leavis implies that people like Williams because they are Christians and like overtly Christian literature. It would be easy to reverse this and say that Dr Leavis is suspicious of doctrinally committed Christianity and particularly of the more Catholic kinds, and therefore has an unfair drag of prejudice distorting his reading of Williams. And it does seem likely that Dr Leavis' suspicion of Williams does overlap with his suspicion of Eliot's *Four Quartets* – not perhaps because of what they choose to believe, as Donald Davie wittily comments of other opponents of Eliot so much as because of 'what they choose to disbelieve – the sectarian alternatives to Christianity such as are in our enlightened age so abundantly on offer ... What outrages him is not their credulity but their scepticism'.

However it is again plain enough that this will not do empirically. Good Christians, reading Christians, Catholic Christians do not necessarily have a special liking for Williams: those who like Williams are not at all necessarily Christians. Again something can be salvaged from Dr Leavis' criticism. There is little doubt that no-one is likely to be able to read Williams who has not some kind of religious feeling: not that Williams' writing is religion without literature, but that what he is saying needs some religious capacity to be understood. (The examples I gave of his uniqueness at the beginning, *The Place of the Lion*, *Descent into Hell* and *The Descent of the Dove*, would suggest that.)

Leavis observes that 'Williams' preoccupation with the horror of evil is evidence of an arrest at the schoolboy (and -girl) stage rather than that of spiritual maturity' and that his dealings in 'myth, mystery, the occult and the supernatural belong essentially to the ethos of the thriller. To pass off his writings as spiritually edifying is to promote the opposite of spiritual health'. This is too like Eliot's remark that Williams was concerned not merely with the conflict between good and bad men, but with that between Good and Evil, too close to the kind of religiousness which anyone would find in Williams, to be dismissed out of hand. Had Williams – Eliot goes on – 'himself not always seen Evil, unerringly, as the contrast to Good – had he understood Evil, so far as it can be understood, without knowing the Good – there are passages in (*All Hallows' Eve*), and in other books (notably *Descent into Hell*) which would only be outrageous and foul'. I think Eliot's way of putting it is much better than Leavis', and I think the bulk of Leavis' accusation is due to a lack of moral perception in Leavis: but not all. Perception of evil over and above perception of bad is a dangerous thing, and I think perhaps Williams did quite often cross the borderline into an interest in evil and a reaction which was tainted. You remember that Dante portrays himself as having to be rebuked by Virgil in the lower reaches of Hell for yielding to just that temptation. I doubt if any human being is immune to it, and I think there is at any rate a case for those who say one should not contemplate evil, or if at all, then rarely. One of the soundest proverbs is that you can't touch pitch without being defiled.

This then is another point for later consideration. I will now leave my first two objectors, Allott and Leavis, who concur in finding so little of poetic value in Williams that they believe only personal acquaintance could blind Eliot, Auden, Anne Ridler, C.S. Lewis, etc., etc., to his worthlessness. But I would note that both Allott and Leavis are sensitive listeners to poetry and literature. There is something to be riddled out here: I suspect it is simply that Williams belongs rather emphatically to a class of poets that both of them dislike. In Leavis' case, that should not worry us too much, since the class includes Milton: but we should not ignore it, because it probably does suggest something true about what Williams' work is like. I would next note that in a way Allott and Leavis could not be further from the truth. I think that more harm has been done to Williams' reputation by the advocacy of two of his personal friends than by any attack. I mean here Dorothy Sayers and, alas C.S. Lewis. I spoke earlier of my own first and abortive attempt to read *Taliessin through Logres*. I used Lewis' commentary, and I am sure it did not help. In spite of Lewis' marvellous gift for persuading one to read any poet whom he likes, this is no advantage when he distorts the meaning and tone as much as he does Williams'. It is not only that their minds were unlike, although both enjoyed the same things: it is far worse, that one element of Lewis' capacity — his immense forensic turn, his Irish love of argument, his polemic quality — resembles Williams' commitment and clarity just sufficiently to enable one to confuse the two. And in the confusion, it is the clearer, simpler quality that dominates one's impressions. Some examples. First, one I am conceited about, because later when I knew Williams better I was re-reading Lewis' *That Hideous Strength*: I came on the passage 'something we may call Britain is always haunted by something we may call Logres. Haven't you noticed that we are two countries? After every Arthur, a Mordred; behind every Milton, a Cromwell: a nation of poets, a nation of shopkeepers, the home of Sidney — and of Cecil Rhodes.' It is a passage which formerly I had admired very much: now somewhat purged by Williams, I recognised something wrong, or at any rate something Williams would never have said. Picture my delight, when later again I came across this passage in Williams' *Queen Elizabeth*: 'Money (Elizabeth) treated as a series of events, and no dogma could persuade her to loosen those events. There is in this a peculiar and satisfying likeness between her and that greater spirit, which was to be the chief glory of her reign; nor did the mind of Shakespeare, when it ceased from *Othello*, forget to use reasonable means to recover his proper dues from his debtor at Stratford. The English, a nation of shopkeepers, are a nation of poets, of whom a number of the best come literally out of shops. They, like the angel of the Apocalypse, set one foot on the known and one on the unknown; it is their balance, and Elizabeth and Shakespeare in their different ways are two of those who kept it.' You see the difference: Lewis's genius for clarity, classification, dichotomy, Williams' for complexity, ambiguity, balance. Both in different senses do justice: but Lewis's justice weighs into good and evil, Williams' stands on both sides. If poets and shopkeepers are a pair, Lewis is apt to slide into saying (I do not suppose he would necessarily have thought on reflection) that one is noble, the other base, one bad, one good. Williams, on the contrary, is temperamentally incapable of saying Yes without simultaneously saying No: you remember that his first act in courting his wife was to give her a set of sonnets on Renunciation. Both Lewis and Williams polarise, or at least separate a confused matter into two or more sharply distinguished peaks. (You may again remember how delighted Williams was with the *Report on Doctrine in the Church of England* because it specified three clearly differentiated Eucharistic doctrines, of the Real Presence, Virtualism and Receptionism tenable within the Church.) But Lewis will oppose his peaks simply, Williams will point out how they are interconnected, respond, coinhere. Even when he claims not to, Lewis tends always to make one peak good, the other bad (consider his treatment of what he calls Drab and Golden literature in his *History of Sixteenth Century Literature*). Even, on the other hand, when Williams does say which alternative must in the end be preferred, he does it reluctantly at the end of a striving and with a backward glance (consider him on the relations of scepticism and belief, the coinherence of the two and the final necessity to prefer belief à propos of Montaigne and Pascal in *The Descent of the Dove*).

The same differences appear in Lewis' commentary on the Arthurian poems. Lewis defines Byzantium as 'Order, envisaged not as restraint nor even as a convenience but as a beauty and splendour.' Williams' notes say something more elusive: 'Byzantium is rather the whole concentration of body and mind than any special member. (The Lady Julian I found last night says that the City is built at the meeting place of substance and sensuality.)'

There is nothing actually inconsistent, except that one suspects that Lewis is making Byzantium one side of a division – Order as opposed to what is ordered, or as opposed to disorder – where Williams is certainly insisting on some kind of coinherence. For Williams the City, Byzantium I take it, is built at the meeting-place of substance and sensuality: Lewis seems to be drifting towards identifying Byzantium with substance.

This is clearer when we find Lewis professedly abridging Williams. Lewis had lost Williams' note from which he had abridged and wrote in *Arthurian Torso* that Broceliande is 'a place of making, home of Nimue. From it the huge shapes emerge, the whole *matter* of the *form* at Byzantium –

and all this is felt in the beloved.' Williams' own note read: 'Nimue is almost the same state represented by the Emperor's Court, but more vast, dim and aboriginal. The huge shapes emerge from Broceliande, and the whole matter of the Empire, and all this is felt in the beloved.'

For Lewis, Byzantium is form in the Aristotelian Categories, Broceliande matter. Williams means something definitely, though perhaps subtly different: Nimue and the Emperor's court are almost the same – dare I apply the difference to their countries, Broceliande and Byzantium? – but one is more vast, dim and aboriginal. They balance and interweave: the difference is like that of form and matter, but not I think nearly so opposed, more like conscious and unconscious for a psychologist who finds the one implicit in the other, or like the same person waking and dreaming. How different Williams and Lewis are depends on what Williams meant by matter. I do not think he meant the thing, or aspect of anything which longs to receive form and matter in the Aristotelian senses. Rather, I think he meant in the sense in which we and he talk of the Matter of Britain, the vast mass of story already formed, waiting to receive a special author's sense and direction. Even that is slightly to distort Williams.

My third example is the oddest. Lewis leaves one with the impression that the poem *Taliessin on the death of Virgil* is about 'the problem of the virtuous pagan.' He omits, what Williams' own note to him explicitly said, that the poem is not necessarily about the salvation of pagans, but about anyone's salvation. Is Lewis here simply accommodating Williams to simple orthodoxy? I think rather that he is taking a simple concrete instance of an elusive more general notion. Following his dichotomous instincts, he takes the doctrine of salvation by substitution, and, because the poem takes as an instance the pagan Virgil, assumes it to apply to the conspicuous example of the virtuous pagan, and not the Christian, forgetting Williams' own note.

I may be unfair in citing Dorothy Sayers along with Lewis, but I have in mind her commentary on the *Divine Comedy*, an attempt to systematise the more intuitive commentary of *The Figure of Beatrice*. I have not checked a vague impression supported by the explicit testimony of the scholar and friend of both Williams and Dorothy Sayers, Colin Hardie. The case of Dorothy Sayers and C.S. Lewis is largely a matter of misunderstanding by mistaken systematisation, and it may not be thought relevant as an objection to Williams. I cite it partly because I am interested in all that deters people from reading Williams, and I am sure this mistaken lumping of him with a special and rather polemic group of people, the Inklings, is sometimes such a deterrent. But this has not affected the reputation of other members of the group, Owen Barfield and J.R.R. Tolkien for example, even those who dislike both Lewis and Tolkien have actively tried to make it do so. Nor indeed has it deterred people from enjoying the non-polemic works of Lewis and Sayers themselves. If it has affected Williams, then, for good perhaps as well as for ill, it must be because he is prone to being misconstrued.

Partly this proneness to misconstruction is entailed by the very nature of his virtue − subtlety, balance and complexity are prone to be affected by their very opposite, our urge to make them clear to ourselves, and the answer is to train our perceptions better. But Williams is at times so obscure as to ask for it. And much more importantly, I think there is within his own work an urge, a nisus towards pattern making of whose proper limits I do not think he was himself aware. He was aware of course that that was his failing. Anne Ridler quotes his autocriticism to the effect that if he could give his young self advice he would say: 'Patterns are baleful things . . .'.

And now after Allott and Leavis, I would mention two adverse critics who are very different in that they respond to Williams' genius, and assert it explicitly, but believe that he spoilt it by some such urge to patterning. Those are Robert Conquest and David Jones.

Robert Conquest is a somewhat cranky, extreme liberal who reacts against totalitarianism very violently wherever he suspects it. He regards Williams as a rare, if not unique, case of 'a genuine writer who has fully accepted a closed monopolistic system of ideas and feelings, and what is more, puts it forthrightly with its libidinal component scarcely disguised'. He gives as evidence:

a. the complete acceptance of a closed system of ideas,
b. the manipulation of this system as the only intellectual exercise,
c. the treatment of the outsider with a special sort of irritated contempt which conceals, or sometimes betrays, other emotions,
d. the subordination of all ordinarily autonomous spheres of thought and feeling to the *a priori*: a lack of humility in the presence of the empirical.

Now a lot of Conquest's elaboration of this is exaggerated or even silly. Some of it is due to his treating Williams and Lewis together: although he frequently notes that Lewis is much cruder than Williams, he still takes much too far a Lewis' eye view of Williams, such as I have sketched. At times, Conquest is plain wrong. A man is pretty far gone in opposition to order who finds, as Conquest does, the vision of the policeman as the Emperor of the Trumps totalitarian in the political sense, and who thinks it obvious that his readers will prefer the 'pirate chaos' of *Mount Badon* to Byzantium. But he is wrong, one should note, in the mood that is now dominant: the mood, to take an instance of something now being rebelled against, of the Rousseauist teachers who cause the son of a friend of mine to suffer from tension headaches, because his class is violently competitive and intolerably noisy – direction being abhorrent.

I think in fact criteria (a), (b) and (c) largely wrong of Williams. But I suspect some justice in the accusations of too much pattern: of a libidinal component in the acceptance of that pattern: and of something missing in the relation of *a priori* to empirical.

My fourth and last adverse critic of Williams is also a great admirer of his, and moreover a rather similar poet who has suffered a rather similar neglect, from which however he seems to be emerging much the sooner. This is David Jones. He wonders whether the poetry is not lacking in something difficult to express

something wholly to do with time – with now-ness. Somehow, somewhere, between content and form, concept and image, sign and what is signified, a sense of the contemporary escapes, or rather appears to me to escape. I know it is there in *idea*; I don't doubt but what the characters and situations were linked up in Williams's mind with now: but I do not often feel this now-ness in the words and images, or rather I feel it does not inform and pervade the poems as a whole ... What the artist lifts up must have a kind of transubstantiated actual-ness. Our images, not only our ideas, must be valid *now*: ... of now, yet reaching back to 'the foun-dation of the city' and ... *Therefore* valid for the future.

He gives two examples of now-ness: first the phrase just quoted, the Roman way of reckoning time 'from the foun-dation of the city', 'from then till now'. Better, however, he says, is a sentence which includes also 'how then became now' and 'the change of people on an unchanged site': 'the sentence is James Joyce's "Northmen's thing made southfolk's place." That is, the Georgian assembly rooms in Dublin in Suffolk Place are made where the Norsemen made their assembly, their "thing". Joyce has done two things with Suffolk Place: he has metamorphosed it in sense and appearance, but also he has *found* it. He has married "a concept and universality" to "the actual, the intimate and the now"'.

This of David Jones is tentative, but carefully considered. Since it occurs in a review of *Arthurian Torso*, it may have been put into his mind, at least part of it may have been, by a qualification from C.S. Lewis' part of the book. Charles Williams' poetic world, says Lewis,

'is certainly not a world I feel at home in, any more than I feel at home in the worlds of Dante and Milton. It strikes me as a perilous world full of ecstasies and terrors, full of things that gleam and dart, lacking in quiet, empty spaces. Amid the "surge and thunder" of the *Odyssey* you can get a snug fireside night in Eumaeus's hut. There is no snugness in Williams's Arthuriad, just as there is none in the *Paradiso*. What quiet there is is only specious: the roses are always trembling, Broceliande astir, planets and emperors at work. Can we then condemn it, as Raleigh came near to condemning *Paradise Lost* because it was insufficiently homely? Not, I think, unless we know that comfort and heartsease are characters so deeply rooted in the real universe that any poetic world which omits them is a distortion . . .'

Now, of course, what Lewis is saying is quite distinct from what Jones is saying. Yet, allowing for the fact that 'now-ness' is not something Lewis would be interested in as any kind of privileging the present over other moments of history, may not both comments originate in a similar response? Jones finds that somewhere between content and form, concept and image there is missing 'the actual, the intimate and the "now"'. Lewis does not 'feel at home in the world of *Taliessin*, it has no "quiet, empty spaces"'. Both feel that very subtly some mark has been missed which has to do with what is called 'relevance' – not of concept, Jones insists, but in expression. Lewis associates it with what, apparently, he misses in Dante and Milton. That suggests to me that whatever is missing is precisely what Leavis, who notoriously despises Milton, and perhaps Allott, think is so essential to poetry that they deny that Williams wrote poetry. And Conquest among other things accuses Williams of 'a lack of humility in the presence of the empirical'.

It is noteworthy that among his positive strangenesses, Williams was perfectly at home in the worlds of Dante and Milton. And perhaps Jones would find what he is looking for in Williams' lovely comment on the last lines of *Paradise Lost*:

They hand in hand with wandering step and slow
Through Eden took their solitary way.

There are no linked lovers in our streets who are not more beautiful and more unfortunate because of those last lines; no reunion, of such a kind, which is not more sad and more full of hope. And then it is said that Milton is inhuman.
The whole of our visibility, metaphysical, psychological, actual, has been increased by him.

I love that: yet ... I don't know. Even there, aren't those 'linked lovers' a little high-falutin'? Has Williams perhaps raised them a little too far into a dream language? I ask because the parallel sentence − from an unpublished letter − which I had in mind to illustrate his at-homeness in Dante has the right touch, the touch Jones is looking for, both in concept and expression:

> If it is not true of a sunblistered girl at a Brighton factory dance, it is probably not true of Beatrice.

But it so happens that the 'relevant' phrase about the sunblistered girl is quoted by Williams from a review written by his correspondent, Hugo Dyson. The concept, no doubt, is Williams': the expression still Dyson's.

Chapter Fourteen

Charles Williams and R.H. Benson

Gwen Watkins

This essay will be more in the nature of an entertainment than a scholarly paper as such. I cannot offer you an academic thesis because I have no real evidence – no evidence, I mean, which would be accepted by a scholar – that Charles Williams ever read much of R.H. Benson's work, much less that he was influenced by it. What I am offering, therefore, is merely a hypothesis but one based on a very close study of both Benson's and Williams' work. Those of us who have an affinity with a particular author will agree that there is a perception intuitively arising from reading and re-reading, which, though not based on proof, yet presents itself to us as valid criticism.

We do know, from an entry in Williams' Commonplace Book, now in the Bodleian Library under the title of The Holy Grail, that he had read at least one of Benson's novels – *The Necromancers*. We also know from his review of *The Quest for Corvo*, called Antichrist and the City's Laws, that he must have known about Benson's relationship with the novelist Frederick Rolfe, the self-enobled Baron Corvo. I think it extremely probable that Williams read most, if not all, of Benson's novels, since he was an avid reader, Benson was a best-seller and his books widely advertised and reviewed and published in very cheap editions. Moreover many of them were, singularly for that or any other era, what Benson himself called 'spiritual fiction', and dealt with themes that were closely related to Williams' own interests. I think it unlikely that having read one, he would not have been eager to procure others.

C.S. Lewis, by no means such an omnivorous reader of light fiction as Williams, had certainly read Benson and it is curious that he should have specifically denied, in a letter to an American academic, having been in any way influenced by him. Yet it is plain that the scene in *That Hideous Strength* in which Jane Studdock, visiting Ransome as an eldil is about to appear, feels the whole room tilting as though the centre of balance were outside the known world, repeats almost in exact words a scene from Benson's *None Other Gods*. Here the room of the dying hero, filled with angelic or archangelic presences, is subject to the identical vertiginous slanting or tilting. Some aspects of the Unman in *Perelandra* also probably owe something to Benson's characterisation of the demon in *The Necromancers* especially in the scene where Ransome sees the Unman's shoulders shaking and thinks he is sobbing only to find that he is silently and horribly laughing. It is evident that Lewis had completely forgotten his sources for these details, and the American scholar recognised them.

There is nothing quite as close to Benson as this in Williams' novels. Still, a character in *The Conventionalists* says of another who is rapidly developing spiritual powers: 'It's like finding a lion in your garden' and I have wondered whether this remark led to the appearance of the lion in *The Place of the Lion*.

Robert Hugh Benson was born in 1871, only fifteen years before Charles Williams. No two men could have been born to more widely different circumstances. Benson was the son of a clergyman whose dominating personality raised him from the first Mastership of Wellington College, chosen by Prince Albert himself, through the first Bishopric of Truro to the Archiepiscopal throne of Canterbury itself. His mother too came of a distinguished family; his homes were all rich and romantic – the Master's Lodge at Wellington, where he was born, the medieval Chancellory of Lincoln, the Bishop's Palace of Lis Escop outside Truro, the palaces of Lambeth and Addington, then the country seat of the Archbishops of Canterbury, and his mother's beautiful Jacobean mansion in Ashurst Forest. Hugh was educated at Eton and Trinity College, Cambridge, took Holy Orders in the Anglican Church and converted to the Roman Church in 1903, with, being the son of the former Archbishop of Canterbury, the maximum of publicity. Charles Williams was 17 at the time, and never likely, as he probably thought, to be accorded any kind of publicity. The son of lower middle class parents, having been born in rented rooms and later living in a house attached to the shop his parents ran with very indifferent success, unable because of financial difficulties to take a degree at the University College to which he had won a scholarship, his sight affected by illness, soon to become a mere drudge in a Methodist bookroom, he cannot have looked to his future with much confidence.

Yet with all the differences of birth and environment, there were remarkable similarities between the two men, both in beliefs and personality. Anne Ridler wrote of Williams 'trembling, slight, tense, always in movement but never fidgeting, always smoking ...'. This is an exact description of Hugh Benson. Both had been brought up in Christian families and neither was called on to endure assaults on his faith. Both loved ritual, with its attendant pleasures of dressing up. (Although Hugh Benson's own clothes were deplorable – indeed his sister said his shoes were like something you saw washed up on a beach after a storm – he much enjoyed dressing up in his monsignorial purple when he had been elevated to the rank of papal chamberlain.) Both men had an early interest in the occult. Williams read the works of A.E. Waite and joined the Golden Dawn. Benson, whose mother had from the early days of her marriage used the planchette, tried automatic writing and held seances (embarrassing hobbies for the wife of a bishop and archbishop!) followed her example by experiments in mesmerism at Cambridge and later by attempting magical experiments with Rolfe. Williams and Benson both had their horoscopes drawn, and appeared to take the result with some seriousness.

Both men had strong and extremely charismatic personalities. Both attracted shoals of adherents with emotional and spiritual difficulties, of which a large number were women, and both appear to have dealt with them in ways which showed the extent and the limitations of their powers. Hugh Benson said that he could not 'prop'; that people came to him for advice or support and then passed on. He felt that God had not intended him to form intimacies. Both C.S. Lewis and Alice Mary Hadfield have described Williams' relationship with those who came to him. Hadfield wrote: 'However freely he seemed to give of his energies, he had always a certain inner detachment ... you felt that he depended on no-one ... He did not repel them but he did not need them.' Both Benson and Williams passed through a mid-life crisis, a shock to their moral being: Benson when Rolfe so suddenly and inexplicably turned against him (and made his revulsion public) and Williams in his Celian crisis.

They resembled each other in their writing also. Both started writing at an early age. The whole Benson family indeed appeared to have inherited a form of logorrhea and began to scribble as soon as their infant hands could hold a pencil. Hugh is said to have composed a puppet play while still very young on, curiously enough, the subject of Cranmer. Both had an early interest in drama which later resulted in verse plays, including some 'mystery' plays. Their historical interests centred around the same periods, the sixteenth and seventeenth centuries. But it was in their 'spiritual fiction' that they most resembled each other, and it is in this genre that I shall try to show that Benson did influence Williams to some extent, or at least was a source from which he drew some of his ideas.

Anne Ridler has said of his work: 'The conflict between the powers of good and evil, romantically expressed, was always one of Williams' most intense literary enjoyments, but even more deeply felt was the theme of substitution in love.' Now these were the sole and entire themes of Benson's novels, as well as the themes of the Negative and Affirmative Ways. His work could therefore hardly fail to be of the greatest interest to the young Williams, even though he may have forgotten such early reading.

In Benson's novels the plot concerns itself continually with the choice made by the characters between good and evil, or even with the choice between what appears to be conventionally harmless and the greater good. In *Lone-liness*, *Initiation*, *None Other Gods*, *The Sentimentalists*, *The Conventionalists*, an individual is led by many ways and continual choices to his final good, often a good as harrowing, as apparently destructive as that of Chloë Burnett in *Many Dimensions*. The hero of *Initiation* dies of a brain tumour, the heroine of *Loneliness*, a former celebrated opera singer, loses her voice, her career, her lover and many friends. The hero of *None Other Gods* dies after a brutal attack by the lover of a worthless girl whom he has tried to save. The main characters of *The Coward* and *An Average Man* make the wrong choice. I have wondered whether the character of Quentin in *The Place of the Lion* was not to some extent drawn from the character of Val in *The Coward*. Neither man is a deliberate coward, but seems to have inherited or acquired the affliction through no fault of his own. The choice to be made is to acknowledge it, not to conceal it, and to be as brave or kind as possible within the given limitations.

Lord of the World and *The Dawn of All* are the two of Benson's books which most nearly approach science fiction, since they are tales of the future written, not from opposite points of view, but from opposing premises. In one, the whole civilised world, except for a few atheists, humanists and socialists, has embraced Christianity; in the other, the whole world except for a remnant of the faithful has rejected it. We are reminded of Williams' love of changing sides in the middle of an argument just to see what the other side looks like.

We have in these two novels an almost cosmic opposition of good and evil, but of course this conflict must be the subject of any book dealing with spiritual matters. I am not saying that Williams was influenced by Benson to use this theme, only that books so vividly written dealing with the very themes that so compelled his own imagination cannot have escaped his attention. We must remember too that in the years before the First World War, fiction was given an enormous amount of space, even in the very cheap and popular journals. Although Charles Williams was only twenty-eight when Benson died, the novels were reprinted in very inexpensive editions all through the 1920s.

I have mentioned Benson's vivid writing, and I should here explain, and demonstrate, its peculiar impact. My hypothesis is that, if Williams derived his extraordinarily magniloquent and sometimes grandiose style from anyone at all, it was from the echoes of Benson read in his youth. Although it is possible to see threads of influence in his early poetic style through Abercrombie, Bridges and much less Chesterton than is generally supposed, until he reaches his own unmistakeable poetic voice, it is difficult, if not impossible to see the same threads in his prose style. Obviously at some time the young Williams was immensely struck by Henry James' use of the adverb – 'he charmingly murmured' and the like – but apart from that, there seems no source for his curiously mannered style, unless indeed there is a resemblance to that other outstandingly idiosyncratic prose writer, Benson's friend and enemy, Baron Corvo.

The conversations in Benson's novels are usually more naturalistic than those in Williams', yet there is a startling intensity in his descriptive writing, especially when he is concerned with the inner experiences of his characters, which to my mind is not found in any other writer. The very few quotations for which I have time will serve to illustrate what I mean. The first quotation is simply a description of a headache:

> Then he had got ready for bed; and when all was ready had once more soaked his handkerchief and tied it round his forehead. Then he had got into bed, turned out the light, and pretended that he was going to sleep.
>
> Then the interior drama had begun.
>
> It was first a galloping horse that approached from the immeasurable distance to which the hot water and eau-de-cologne had temporarily banished the agony – that approached to announce to him that they were all coming back as fast as they could.
>
> This horse galloped slowly and rhythmically, at a steady rate of progress: and the beat of his four hoofs all together marked the blows of pain that he experienced. The horse came nearer and nearer, growing,

as was but natural, in weight as he approached; until he was really there, so to speak. He remained there a few seconds – never longer than about a minute, apparently prancing to the same rhythms, in the same place, without otherwise moving at all. Then he began to recede again, intolerably slowly, it is true; but yet it was very nearly pleasure that he should recede at all. It was as this movement began that Neville really resolved to go to sleep before the next. ... But at that moment two horses began to gallop, again in the immeasurable distance; and the worst of it all was that they would not keep in step. These two then punctually pursued the course of their fore-runner; they approached, they arrived; they remained steadily prancing, the four feet of each rising and falling, not quite together; they began to recede.

Then, three horses came; then four; then five; then a regiment. He tried to count them sometimes, in a kind of bitter humour; but they were unreckonable. They kept tolerably in step; that was one comfort; but they took longer to arrive, and remained longer, prancing. It was very nearly interesting, when they all pranced together; they looked almost ludicrous – this long line, from horizon to horizon – (the horizons, of course, were his own temples) – rising and falling together like performers in a circus.

Then even these began to recede – very slowly, it is true – yet they receded, further and further, until the thunder of their hoofs was no more than a murmur ... and at last silence. Neville began to breathe very carefully through his nostrils. He had already arranged his attitude. He turned on his side always, as the troop began to move off; until that he lay on his face with the pillow clasped about his ears: he did so, that is, generally after the group of three began to approach.

He lay then, softly, afraid to stir, lest a horse should gallop up to see what he was doing; and sometimes he managed really to go to sleep. But tonight it was useless. In spite of every conceivable precaution, the single horse begun to suspect something, as he fed there miles away in the prairies, scarcely stirring the ground as he moved.

He began to trot; he began to canter; to gallop ... and the hunt was up.

It was as the clock struck half past one in the hall below that Neville sat up in bed, very nearly delirious with pain. 'This is perfectly ludicrous!' he said aloud to the listening night.

We all remember very well, I am sure, Charles Williams' description of the first perceptions of a soul after death, in the opening pages of *All Hallows' Eve*. Here is an equally remarkable description of the actual process of dying from R.H. Benson's *Initiation*:

Once again at some remote point in time, detached from all experience, he found that his consciousness was still attached to his body; but it was attached in a new kind of way. He was aware that somewhere in the universe, as if at an enormous depth beneath the point where he himself stood poised, great wheels of blue flame were all crashing and whirling together. The clamour of them was incredible, harsh and grinding; but they no longer affected him. There was a loud rasping sound of breathing, too, such as he had heard when his father died. Then, through the crashing and the gasping, he heard the thunder of a voice repeating Latin. He was as a man who, at the edge of a huge dream, himself at ease and in safety, looks down on the tumult below, where great forces strive together.

Dying, then, was still in process somewhere; and he watched with a kind of pity that dreadful conflict that roared below. It was to him, in some sense, that Latin was spoken; and he understood its power... Here and there he could catch a phrase. He was being bidden to 'go forth' in the name of Powers and Principalities ... of all those great Existences which, he knew now, waited invisible in that wide expanse that was all about him, poised here above the struggle that raged beneath ... It was down there, then, that all those whom he loved waited about his struggling body. He knew they were there, as a man who has climbed to a great height knows, as he looks back, that there in the valley are the fields and the house that he knows so well. They were all in the surge and the stress still – there in that plane from which rose up the great words of power that battled with the roar of the pulses in his head, and the blinding shocks of pain, and the fighting for breath – and not with these, only or chiefly, but with the rushing tides of evil and revolt that swayed and tossed – seen by him from up here as a great tumbling torrent or a tossing waste of water looked down upon by a man on a cliff. But he himself was far off and remote. ... Where then, was he? Then, as he considered this, he, too, began to thrill and vibrate. From beneath rose up thin, imperceptible tides; or, rather, he perceived now for the first time that he was in them still; that he was not yet wholly apart as he had thought from all acts and volitions and experiences. But they were thin and subtle, as befitted his new condition; and he saw that he could not yet act ...

Then a great and piercing sorrow surged through him, not indeed at the memory of his sins and rebellions, but at his consciousness of their very essence. It was not that life passed before him as a series or progress of events, but that the quality of it – as he had lived – had a thin and bitter aroma which he had never suspected. And, as there met him from above that piercing breath of the world to which he went – as clean and sharp and radiant as the light reflected from snow – these two tides mingled in him like a chord of sorrow and love and ecstasy ... Every image faded from him; every symbol and memory died; the chasm passed into nothingness; and the Grail was drunk, and colours passed into whiteness; and sounds into the silence of Life; and the initiation was complete.

Finally, there is a very ambitious pieces of writing, such as Williams would have loved: a description of the end of the world. In *Lord of the World*, Felsenburgh (who is finally revealed as Antichrist) has totally destroyed Rome, where most the remaining Christians were gathered, and six of his 'Volors' are now approaching Nazareth, where the Pope and a tiny remnant of the faithful are at Mass:

Yet even at that sound and sight his soul scarcely tightened the languid threads that united it through every fibre of his body with the world of sense. He saw and heard the tumult in the passage, frantic eyes and mouths crying aloud, and, in strange contrast, the pale ecstatic faces of those princes who turned and looked; even within the tranquil presence-chamber of the spirit were two beings, Incarnate God and all but Discarnate Man, where locked in embrace, a certain mental process went on. Yet all was still as apart from him as a lighted stage and its drama from a self-contained spectator. In the material world, now as attenuated as a mirage, events were at hand; but to his soul, balanced now on reality and awake to facts, these things were but a spectacle.

... he turned to the altar again, and there, as he had known it would be, in the midst of clear light, all was at peace: the celebrant, seen as through molten glass, adored as He murmured the mystery of the Word-made-Flesh, and once more passing to the centre, sank upon His Knees.

Again the priest understood; for thought was no longer the process of a mind, rather it was the glance of a spirit. He knew all now; and, by an inevitable impulse, his throat began to sing aloud words that, as he sang, opened for the first time as flowers telling their secret to the sun.

O Salutaris Hostia
Qui coeli pandis ostium ...

They were all singing now; even the Mohammedan cat-echumen who had burst in a moment ago sang with the rest, his lean head thrust out and his arms tight across his breast; the tiny chapel rang with the forty voices, and the vast world thrilled to hear it ...

Still singing, the priest saw the veil laid as by a phantom upon the Pontiff's shoulders; there was a movement, a surge of figures − shadows only in the midst of sub-stance,

... Uni Trinoque Domino ...

− and the Pope stood erect, Himself a pallor in the heart of light, with special folds of silk dripping from His shoulders, His hands swathed in them, and His down-bent head hidden by the silver-rayed monstrance and That which it bore.

... Qui vitam sine termino
Nobis donet in patria... .

... They were moving now, and the world of life swung with them; of so much was he aware. He was out in the passage, amongst the white, frenzied faces that with bared teeth stared up at that sight, silenced at last by the thunder of 'Pange Lingua', and the radiance of those who passed out to eternal life. ... At the corner he turned for an instant to see the six pale flames move along a dozen yards behind, as spear-heads about a King, and in the midst the silver rays and the White Heart of God ... Then he was out, and the battle was in array.

That sky on which he had looked an hour ago had passed from darkness charged with light to light overlaid with darkness – from glimmering night to Wrathful Day – and that light was red. From behind Thabor on the left to Carmel on the far right, above the hills twenty miles away rested an enormous vault of colour; here were no gradations from zenith to horizon; all was the one deep smoulder of crimson as of the glow of iron. It was such a colour as men have seen at sunsets after rain, while the clouds, more transluscent each instant, transmit the glory they cannot contain. Here, too, was the sun, pale as the Host, set like a fragile wafer above the Mount of Transfiguration, and there, far down in the west where men had once cried upon Baal in vain, hung the sickle of the white moon. Yet all was no more than stained light that lies broken across carven work of stone.

... In suprema nocte coena,

sang the myriad voices,

Recumbens cum fratibus
Observata lege plena
Cibis in legalibus

Cibum turbae duodenae
Se dat suis manibus ...

He saw, too, poised as motes in light, that ring of strange
fish-creatures, white as milk, except where the angry glory
turned their backs to flame, white-winged like floating
moths, from the tiny shape far to the south to the monster
at hand scarcely five hundred yards away; and even as
he looked, singing as he looked, he understood that the
circle was nearer, and perceived that these as yet knew
nothing ...

    ... Verbum caro, panem verum
Verbo carnem efficit ...

... They were nearer still, until now even at his feet there
slid along the ground the shadow of a monstrous bird,
pale and undefined, as between the wan sun and himself
moved out the vast shape that a moment ago hung above
the Hill ... Then again it backed across and waited ...

    ... Et si sensus deficit
Ad formandum cor sincerum
Sola fides sufficit ...

... He had halted and turned, going in the midst of his
fellows, hearing, he thought, the thrill of harping and the
throb of heavenly drums; and across the space, moved
now the six flames, steady as if cut of steel in that stu-
pendous poise of heaven and earth; and, in their centre
the silver-rayed glory and the Whiteness of God made
Man ...
    ... Then, with a roar, the thunder again, pealing in
circle beyond circle of those tremendous Presences –
Thrones and Powers – who, themselves to the world as
substance to shadow, are but shadows again beneath apex
and within the ring of Absolute Deity ... The thunder
broke loose, shaking the earth that now cringed on the
quivering edge of dissolution.

Tantum ergo sacramentum

Veneremur Cernui
Et antiquum documentum
Novo Cedat Ritui ...

Ah! yes: it was He for whom God waited now – He who far up beneath that trembling shadow of a dome, itself but the piteous core of unimagined splendour, came in His swift chariot, blind to all save that on which He had fixed His eyes so long, unaware that His world corrupted about Him, His shadow moving like a pale cloud across the ghostly plain where Israel had fought and Sennacherib boasted – that plain lighted now with a yet deeper glow, as heaven, kindling to glory beyond glory of yet fiercer spiritual fame, still restrained the power knit at last to the relief of final revelation, and for the last time the voices sang ...

Praestet Fides supplementum
Sensuum defectui ...

... He was coming now, swifter than ever, the heir of temporal ages and the Exile of eternity, the final piteous Prince of rebels, the creature against God, blinder than the sun which paled and the earth that shook; and, as He came, passing even then through the last material stage to the thinness of a spirit-fabric, the floating circle swirled behind Him, tossing like phantom birds in the wake of a phantom ship ... He was coming, and the earth, rent once again in its allegiance, shrank and reeled in the agony of divided homage ...

... He was coming – and already the shadow swept off the plain and vanished, and the pale netted wings were rising to the check; and the great bell clanged, and the long sweet chord rang out – not more than whispers heard across the pealing storm of everlasting praise ...

... Genitori genitoque
Laus et jubilatio
Salus honor virtus quoque
Sit et benedictio
Procedenti ab utroque

Compar sit laudatio ...

and once more

PROCEDENTI AB UTROQUE
COMPAR SIT LAUDATIO ...

Then this world passed, and glory of it.

Williams may have derived some of the content of his books
from Benson. Benson had been used to meet all the aris-
tocracy of Church and State in his father's palaces, where
his mother also entertained distinguished writers and artists;
Archbishop Benson sat in the House of Lords and was persona grata at Court. When he converted to the Roman
Church, it was with the maximum of publicity, since it
was only the second time in the history of England that a
son of the Archbishop of Canterbury had become a Roman
Catholic; he was naturally well received at the Vatican and
met many eminent clerics. It was therefore natural to him to
fill his novels with the kind of people he had always known,
and the important issues with which his family had always
been concerned. Cabinet Ministers, cardinals, duchesses and
earls appeared in his books because these were the kind of
people he knew. Prime Ministers, dukes and Lord Chief Jus-
tices were not the kind of people Williams had known from
his childhood; but he must have felt that this was the world,
if only he had been born to different parents, in which he
could have made his mark, and in which his powers would
have been recognised. I think Benson's familiarity with this
world, and with national and international affairs, fascinated him, and compelled him to introduce the same sort
of atmosphere into his own novels.

Another kind of figure which he might have first met
in Benson's work was the *Uebermensch*, the would-be
superman. Williams' imagination was always held by power,
and by the acquisition of supernormal powers − it was
almost certainly why he joined the Golden Dawn. I have
often wondered whether the figures of Nigel Considine
and Simon the Clerk owe anything to the character of
Felsenburgh in *Lord of the World*. The plot concerns the

eradication of Christianity over the whole world, and the man who plans and masterminds this gigantic operation is one Julian Felsenburgh. He is a mystery figure, who has perhaps lived much longer than the normal span of life but appears not to age, who is seen in all parts of the world, possibly simultaneously, who has charismatic powers and is able to dominate huge numbers of people, and who is worshipped almost as god. It is easy to see how this character might have seized Williams' imagination, and reappeared in his own books. Interestingly enough, the two supermen appear in Williams' first and last books.

I have wondered too whether he did not first meet the theme of substitution in love, which Anne Ridler called one of his most deeply felt preoccupations, in Benson's novels. I have read fairly widely in Victorian and Edwardian fiction, but have met this theme nowhere else, although the theme of self-sacrifice (which is a different thing altogether) is very common. Both Benson and Williams believed in this practice in life as in literature, and both saw every form of coinherence as possible only because of the Crucifixion, in which Christ bore the weight of all sin. Benson wrote in 1903 to a convert: 'You *can* offer your life for another, as long as you in no sense regard it as apart from Our Lord's One and Only Oblation.' Likewise, one of Williams' recommendations for the Order of Coinherence was 'It [the Order] concludes in the Divine Substitution of Messias all forms of exchange and substitution, and it invokes this Act as the root of all.' Benson, like Williams, actually followed this practice. He once offered to bear the desolation of a convert. 'That sort of thing', he wrote, 'is not at all reserved for the Contemplatives and Religious Orders: people of the most ordinary and sinful sorts do it every day in various forms. It is just the literal acceptance of "Bear ye one another's burdens, and so fulfil the law of Christ."

In *The Conventionalists* there is a sentence which, if Williams read it, may well have suggested to him the idea of substitution in love. The hero is a young man brought up in a conventional upper-class family who go to church on Sundays as a social duty but who would be horrified if religion were to intrude upon daily life. They are therefore outraged when their second son begins to take his religious duties seriously, and disown him when he becomes first a Roman Catholic and then a Carthusian Monk. The sentence which may have struck Williams is spoken by a priest about the young man (who is struggling with his new emotions without much help) 'For example, he asked my opinion about a very odd idea that had come to him — he did not remember ever having read it or heard it mentioned — but it was nothing else than the Law of Mystical Substitution.'

In fact, of Benson's eleven non-historical novels, seven contain the idea of substitution as a main or subsidiary theme. In *Initiation* the hero, at first hating all ideas of pain or self-sacrifice, with almost pagan beliefs in the right to pleasure and happiness, is gradually led to feel that he must take on himself the burden of his father's unexpiated sins, and all the things in which he took so much enjoyment are gradually withdrawn from him. In *Loneliness*, a foolish but loving old maid offers herself as expiation for a mortal sin which the heroine is determined to commit, and her death ensures that the girl shall remain innocent. *A Winnowing* has a neat twist on the idea of substitution; a young wife whose husband has died suddenly makes a vow on his deathbed that she will give herself entirely to God if only He will bring her husband back from the dead. The husband does indeed return to life, but it is he who is now completely possessed by the idea of giving himself to God, while his wife is horrified at the prospect of giving up her luxurious life, and opposes all his attempts to live more religiously. It is only when her constant opposition has worn him down, and he begins to take up all his former habits and interests, that, to her horror, and determined resistance, she finds herself impelled towards doing whatever God wishes for her. In *The Necromancers*, Benson's most famous novel, and one which was made into a film in the thirties, the young hero, after the death of the girl he loves, takes up spiritualism in order to communicate with her. He is at last possessed by an evil demon, and his soul is saved only by a battle waged against Hell on his behalf by his adopted sister.

I have given you these few brief summaries to show you how very powerful are the themes of coinherence and substitution in Benson's novels. Williams acknowledged his debt to Chesterton, but it is not in Chesterton's work that he found these themes. I have not had time to mention Benson's collections of short stories, *The Light Invisible* and *A Mirror of Shalott*, which deal entirely with the occult from a religious standpoint, and which may have given Williams the idea of 'spiritual thrillers'. There is a rivetting story in *A Mirror of Shalott* called 'Monsignor Maxwell's Tale', in which a very devout man, whose love of God is his whole life, actually promises to give up his faith for the salvation of his apostate brother: 'There is only one thing to be done,' says the man. 'I must offer myself for him.' 'I didn't understand him at first', says the priest who is telling the story, 'But we talked a little, and at last I found that the idea of mystical substitution had seized on his mind. He was persuaded that he must make an offering of himself to God, and ask to be allowed to bear the temptation instead of his brother. ... To tell the truth, I had never come across it before in my own experience.' Neither have I come across that phrase in any novelist but Benson.

This very condensed account of R.H. Benson's writing will not of itself have convinced you that my hypothesis is a possible one: but his books are still to be obtained in second-hand bookshops, and I urge you to try to read some of them. You will, I think, admit that there is at least a very real affinity between their themes and beliefs and those of Charles Williams.

I should like to end with a quotation from a biography: 'One cannot take up a pen without remembering him — remembering his patience, his courage, his generosity to his correspondents ... who overwhelmed him with letters; ... remembering the long list of books he has left us, books at which, too often, he toiled with weary brain and wearier fingers ... No living writer has so given of himself in his books, the very depth of his soul, the breadth of his mind, and the heights of his soaring spirit — he has given us all. In the heritage he has left to us, he, being dead, yet speaketh.' That was written of Hugh Benson; this Society will know rightly it might have been written of Charles Williams.

Chapter Fifteen

Charles Williams and Albert Schweitzer

James Brabazon

It came to me that Charles Williams (CW) is one of the people whom I have responded to most passionately as a writer in my life, and the only other person I remember responding to in the same way is Albert Schweitzer (AS). They appear to be such totally different people that I wanted to find out what it can be that makes some kind of common ground in me if nobody else. I thought, therefore, I would work this out in this paper.

I was reading CW and found the phrase 'Greater Joy' in a quotation by him from Dante. The words that CW uses in *The Figure of Beatrice*, quoting his own translation from *The Divine Comedy* are: 'I saw, I believe I saw, because in saying this it feels to me as if I had Greater Joy'. He believes because of his joyful response and that belief makes him see – a rather unconventional, but valid, way of accepting something. The world's full of prophets and sages of all sorts and I have spent much of my life trying to work out which of these sages is right, and why it was that a lot of other people seemed to think that a particular person was on the right lines. It seems to me now that nobody has this kind of monopoly of truth. There can only be the truth for oneself. Not because there is not a truth but because it is far beyond our ability to grasp. CW quotes Kierkegaard as saying: – 'before God man is always in the wrong' – and if he is always in the wrong it does not really matter too much in what way he is in the wrong but he must try to get it as right as he possibly can for himself. So, following CW's recommendation, I trusted the heart rather than the mind, trying to remember that the mind is just as fallible as the heart but the heart has a certain purity and directness of apprehension. Understand as much as you can, but then respond to whatever seems to you worth responding to. And this is where joy came in. My response to both CW and AS was joy. It was a response to the joy which both of them experienced, and responded to, and on which they built their beliefs.

This is not to say that the visions these two men had were comforting, cosy or sentimental in any way. They were very much nicer than the negative visions of Nietzsche or John Osborne or even AS's cousin Jean-Paul Sartre; they were not negative but they were not without their black side. So it is not sentimentality we are talking about. The joy itself is a form of understanding, a sense of recognising right through one's whole being that what is said fits what one is and experiences, and that is at one and the same time belief and joy. It's a point at which truth and beauty touch and one rejoices because the truth is recognised as beauty or beauty as truth. I want to talk about what these two men have meant to me and my response to them.

Let me start with CW – how I got to know him and my response to him as it happened. In the summer of 1940 I was working at the Admiralty; they would not let me fight for my country because of my poor eyesight. I was living in a Toc H hostel in Kennington, and the Toc H padre, a man of great dynamism, invited me to a lecture at a place called St Anne's House in Soho. Dorothy Sayers was giving the talk, so I went. I got very closely involved with the people at St Anne's House and after a while I went to work and live there. One of the clergy who ran it, Patrick McLaughlin, knew and loved CW, who was an associate of the House, coming there when he could. There was a party there once when he was the guest of honour and recited some of his poetry, and that was the first and only time I set eyes on him and heard him speak.

It was an extraordinary experience and I remember feeling surprised at his high-pitched, rather excessive way of reciting poetry; it might easily have been taken to be a bit absurd, but it was not 'ham'. I define 'ham acting' as big, exuberant, large-scale acting which is not filled with sufficient emotional truth to make it work. CW was not 'ham' because whatever stylisation he used, one took it seriously because one knew he had to do it like that and that he meant it; one would only mock if one was deeply insensitive to the whole thing. As a result of that I decided I must get to know more about this extraordinary person, but very soon after that he was dead. But I started to read the novels and poetry and anything else of his I could get hold of. It all seemed very peculiar. It seemed as though he inhabited a world I found very hard to recognise, except in chunks. But when those chunks arrived they seemed to say something which was more important and more interesting than chunks of anybody else. They just did not seem to fit into any kind of coherent world which I could really recognise or understand. But as I proceeded and persevered, I found increasingly that the chunks began to fit together.

Dorothy Sayers, who knew him much better than I did, put it this way: 'To read only one work of CW is to find oneself in the presence of a riddle, a riddle fascinating by its romantic colour, its strangeness, its hints of a rich and intricate unknown world just outside the barriers of consciousness. But to read all is to become a free citizen of that world and to find in it a penetrating and illuminating interpretation of the world we know.' Her whole translation of *The Divine Comedy* was set off by CW's interest and love of Dante, and it was as a response to his book *The Figure of Beatrice* that she started on that enterprise.

That was her response to CW. For me it was a little different for I did not find that the world he inhabited was a totally strange one. It was as though as you got to know it, a whole landscape which did not seem to fit together, slowly swung round until you realised that actually all the roads did lead somewhere, all the pylons which had appeared to be spaced across the landscape were really in a straight line and you were standing at last in the position where CW stood, and you realised that this world he was writing about was not a strange world but our own world seen in a very special light and by a very special person. So I would disagree with Dorothy that one was entering another world – one was entering one's own world but in a very interesting new way. When one reached that point there was a certain special sort of directness about the way he looked at the world which was part of this joy; it was recognising things in the new light and thinking 'that's wonderful!'; in a way it actually makes more sense of the world rather than less and so one responds to it at that kind of level. Part of it was the fact that, in his phrase: 'the images were affirmed', one said 'Yes' to life, one said 'Yes' to the world and to everything that mattered in it. No way did one grumble about the world. One might say: 'Yes part of this world is full of horror', but one did not actually grumble about it; one responded to it in an affirmative way even at that stage, because one accepted his understanding that people who chose horror chose horror willingly and that was their choice; in a sort of way that was what they wanted and what they deserved. This seemed to me an insight of incredible validity because I had often wondered why it was that people do wrong. The obvious answer is that they do not think it is. If they think that doing wrong is what they happen to want at that moment, then they have chosen it and the results of it they have also chosen, because they probably know what the results are. I am not talking about people who are deranged, obviously, and there are certain exceptions to this, and there are philo-sophical problems here. There is a Greek saying, something like 'nobody ever sins' – meaning if you really think it is a sin you do not do it – at that particular moment you think that doing that is better than not doing it, and that's why you do it, under whatever pressure you may be. Later on you may think 'I wish I hadn't done it', but you do not do the wrong thing at any given moment knowing that it is wrong. I believe that psychologically that is very true. I think that CW would have said that people who were in a state of ungrace willed that and willed the consequences of it. He would rejoice that the pattern made that happen. The strange, high-pitched, sort of hysterical way in which he wrote, which some people find very off-putting, seems to me the outward and visible sign of that penetrating light that he cast on the world, which is also reflected in that high-pitched excessive way of speaking.

My next experience of anything to do with CW was when I was a member of the cast of a production of *The House of the Octopus*. Perhaps it is worth recording my response to that. I was in the process of learning about CW. I reacted to it in two ways. Personally I found it extraordinarily fascinating, and as I got to know the play and understand it, very valuable and valid, and the lines meant a great deal. But I could never bring myself to believe that anyone who just turned up one evening and sat down and listened to it would have gone away with anything like the same kind of apprehension that I had got. I do not think that CW is a good playwright in that sense. I think that to expect anybody to get more than a very remote glimmering of what the play was about would have been asking too much — unless of course if they knew the play or were familiar with CW's form of thought. So as an actor I felt very much torn between these two feelings about it.

That is how I came to know CW. Now what has this almost ethereal character, radiant being, as he emerges from his writing and as I understand he was in person, got in common with the very burly, peasant-like pastor who built a small hospital in the middle of Africa, cutting down the trees and building with his own bare hands? A very different sort of person you may think. Let me sketch out how I got to know about AS before I talk about the ways it seems to me these two people come together.

I was wondering what to do next in my life when I was asked to write a book about AS. I had no idea why I should be asked but felt it would be very interesting. It turned out that it all stemmed back to St Anne's House, like CW. I had written a piece about Dorothy Sayers when she died, and someone who had read this realised that I knew a little about theology and could write a bit, so he introduced me to the person willing to commission the book, so I was starting entirely from scratch. Really all I knew about AS was what people would know who pick up a very old copy of 'Everybody's Weekly' in the dentist's and read the page-and-a-half and the picture of AS and a black baby. It could either be an article saying he was the most extraordinarily

wonderful creature that ever lived, or it could be saying he
was a bogus character who had to disappear to the jungle in
order to have a nasty psychological time with a lot of lady
disciples, and nobody quite knew what went on in the hospital anyway. Those were the two views of him and I had
to find out which one was true. Obviously neither, but one
had to prove it.

He was born in 1875, the son of a pastor in Alsace.
Alsace had ceased to be French four years before, following the Franco-Prussian war, and was now German.
Schweitzer made the best of such uncertainties saying that
as an Alsatian you eat as much as a German and as well as
the French, but it could be an uncomfortable situation. He
was brought up in the Alsatian hills. He loved them dearly.
He was an incredibly bad scholar for the first ten years, so
much so that his father doubted that he would even make
a good postman. On the other hand he did have very vivid
apprehensions of the value of life and the misery of other
people, and particularly other creatures, birds that got shot
by boys with catapults, dogs that got beaten. There was an
old Jew who used to be mocked by the kids. His response
to these was deeply sensitive and deeply upset.

Later on, having left there and gone on to a larger school
further away, he realised that learning was actually valuable,
and he started to learn so fast that he left everyone else
behind. It was not that he was stupid, only that in his
early years he could not be bothered to learn. Now he
set himself to do so. He argued with everyone all through
his teens, so vehemently that he became a thorough nuisance – and finally settled down to become a pastor himself
in Strasburg.

There he started to study the question of the historical
Jesus – who was this fellow that he had been told about,
why were there so many contradictions in the Bible – and
he set about trying to demolish a whole century's-worth
of German theology and German quest for the historical
Jesus. He came up with his own particular solution which
I find very satisfying, but will not go in to now. He published books about this, about Kant, about Bach – a huge
2 volume job – well before he was 30. He had a wonderful
time, enjoying every minute of it. He slept about 4 hours a

night because he was enjoying life so much he could not be bothered to sleep any longer. Everybody says that he was a dynamo. But he records that on his 21st birthday he woke up and thought − 'I'm having a marvellous time, I'm playing the organ, I'm studying, but there are all these creatures and people who are not enjoying themselves, and I see absolutely no reason why I should be allowed to do so while they are not; it doesn't seem fair.' − It is a very simple reaction and I think that was all it was. He thought that he could not continue to allow this to happen because his apprehension of people's suffering was such that it got in the way of his enjoyment. He decided that he would continue to enjoy himself until he was 30, and then he would find some way of dedicating himself to the betterment of mankind. He had no idea what he was going to do, but he would do it when he was 30. I think most of us have had this kind of impulse to do good to the world, especially around the age of 21, but I am sorry to say most of us forget all about it. But on his 30th birthday Schweitzer sat down and thought about what he should do.

He tried to become a missionary, but the missionaries would not have him because his theology was not sufficiently orthodox. So he decided to become a doctor. He had an extraordinarily sensible idea about missionaries, which was not the common one: that the job of a missionary was not to tell black people what to think but to do them a bit of good because of the number of so-called Christians who had done them harm. That needed putting right, and that is what he intended to do.

He spent 7 years training to become a doctor, and went out to Africa. No-one would support him financially so he raised all the money he needed and he built his hospital and the rest you know. So I responded to him in the end as a totally valid person. I spent 2 years checking out all the criticisms of him, and I found that the people who criticised him had very good reasons for criticising him, but the reason was in the critic not in AS. They were people who would get a lot of money from a magazine if they could do the ultimate bad- taste job and demolish this saintly figure. So I made this search for the flaw in AS − did not find it − and started writing the book.

The most extraordinary thing about him was that he was all of one piece. Most people have contradictions; Dorothy Sayers certainly did. I do not know enough about CW to say, but AS did not appear to have any contradictions in him at all, his inconsistencies were all on the surface. He knew all about them and they were not deep-seated psychological contradictions at all. The worst thing you could say about him was that he was authoritarian and he used to say it all the time. He used to say that if you are running a hospital 200 miles up a river and there is no way of getting a second opinion, then you actually have to tell people what to do. It seems very practical.

So what are the apparent differences between these two men to start off with? First of all AS appears to be a man of action, as against the academic and literary CW. But in fact when you look at AS's character he was a dreamer. Those first 10 years at school were spent in sitting and thinking and dreaming and experiencing, and that is why he was not working. The images that he carried with him of Alsace all through his life were his refreshment and his memory. When he started preaching sermons and when he wrote, his image-making was wonderful. He always saw things in very concrete terms, in paint rather than poetry, in the terms of an artist. As an example, once he talked for 4 hours when he had only been asked to talk for one, and when this was pointed out he said: 'There's a bird in Africa which, when it opens its mouth, it shuts its eyes, and I'm very sorry to say I'm a bit like that.' It was this kind of beautiful, humorous vision of life and his apprehension of images that made him a kind of poet and a beautiful user of words. And of course there is no real difference between CW and AS as academics because AS was an excellent academic – he just wanted to do something different afterwards. In fact one of the famous stories about him is that he was lugging some timber one day in his hospital and there was a black gentleman who was very nicely dressed sitting watching him; AS asked him to help and he replied: 'I'm awfully sorry I can't, I'm an intellectual.' AS said he too had tried to be one of those but it did not quite work.

So he was an academic and he would have understood CW in that sort of way. They would have had a great deal to talk about had they ever met. The word that AS used when talking of his thought is 'denken'. It took me some time to understand this word, it did not seem to be adequately translated by the word 'thought'. AS was always talking about thought as something which enabled him to penetrate very deeply into his own consciousness, whereas we tend to think of thought as something which enables us to follow a logical sequence. In fact 'denken' means precisely that penetration into oneself: you apprehend something with your whole being. D.H. Lawrence had a poem about it which finishes: 'Thought is the whole man, wholly attending.' That is what 'denken' means and it seems to me that that is a very good description of how CW thought too. His thought is something that penetrates and pierces and quite clearly has gone deep into his own consciousness in order to find what is there − an immediate and vivid apprehension of reality. In the same way, AS looked at reality and searched within himself for a response which was not in any way a contradiction to logical thought, it just did not end there. If there was a logical reason why what he experienced was wrong, then it was wrong; the logic must not be denied in any way. There was no silly mysticism which denied logic or truthful response to fact, but it penetrated beyond that.

There is a very good remark of Anne Ridler's about CW, that 'he argued not to vanquish but to discover', and it seems to me there again the argument is not the argument of an academic to defend a position, but to find out and to reject anything which does not seem valid, and to go further and deeper.

Now there is another difference between the two men: quite clearly their religious backgrounds. CW had an Anglo-Catholic background, he obviously based his thought very much on the Catholic tradition. AS was a Lutheran. They are very different ways of looking at things and there is no way those two can be reconciled at that level. But both of them pinned their final apprehension of religion on the figure of Jesus. And although I suspect CW would be forced to say that AS was a heretic, one of the things that I like about CW is the fact that he regards heretics as great if they were great heretics. They are not dismissed because they are heretics but he regards them as being very valid contributors to the truth; that the Almighty has perhaps elicited more out of a great heretic than out of a minor Orthodox, and he would respect them immensely for that very reason. That kind of respect he would probably have offered to AS, and I am absolutely sure that AS would have offered it to CW.

But having got past those two dissimilarities that are perhaps more apparent than real, the similarities are the ones that seem to be the most striking. First of all, it seems obvious that both men were geniuses, in the sense that they had an absolutely personal and totally direct apprehension of the way they saw the world. They both had the kind of energy that genius requires, a passionate energy, a passionate response, though the energy was exhibited in different ways. Neither of them would have accepted the second-hand or the sentimental because their own blinding apprehension would wash that away.

Both were ecstatics and both were deeply practical. The vision of CW was of a very real world seen in a very special way, and I think that is also true of AS. His world was less odd at first sight, but at the same time it was an immensely practical world and yet seen in a very special way. His special way was what he called 'reverence for life'. In Africa he was constantly aware of the amount of death and destruction, pain and suffering; much more of course than he had first experienced in Alsace. In Africa, the diseases were abominable. People came into his hospital complaining of one and probably had three more. Incidentally, he was not just a leper doctor — that is a strange misapprehension — he was a doctor for anyone who came in, he had to treat what was there. The First World War was going on in his own home country and people were being killed in France just up the hill from where he had lived. He was desperately concerned to find the basic ethic — he was more interested in ethics than CW I am sure — he wanted to find some true north that mankind could steer by and he could not find it in any of the philosophers or in any of the theologians or anywhere. In Africa he found it in the phrase 'reverence for life', starting with the proposition that the only thing we have which we are absolutely sure of, in common with everybody else and all creatures, is life. Life is the thing that we actually need and preserve most, therefore that is what you start with. That is what we reverence in other human beings. You do not reverence their intellect, their colour, their race, their ideas or anything else. If you start with the proposition 'I think, therefore I am' you are already on a very over-intellectualised path. What matters is not that you think, but that you live. I live and you live, therefore I respect your right to live and you respect mine and that is all you have to start with.

And that seems to me to be exactly the same sense that I got from CW when I first came across his conception of coinherence, his conception of the city, of all life, all humanity, knitted together by this immense web of common experience, common responsibility, so that there is no way you can make any move — the spider's web, wherever it is touched, will respond all the way round, not only in space but in time for ever and ever. Everything matters. Now that is also, it seems to me, a way of saying that you have 'reverence for life'. AS used another phrase 'the solidarity of life', and that seems to me to be coinherence. It is the 'courtesy' that CW used to talk about so much as the true response that everyone should have for everyone else. You respect them, you are courteous to them, because they are, because they exist, and every single thing that you feel, say and do has an effect because of this coinherence, this inseparability of ourselves from every other creature, past, present, future and everywhere in the world.

Chapter Sixteen

'James I'. The Art of Historical Biography

Donald Nicholson

The re-issue of Charles Williams' *James I* in 1951 was
accompanied by a valuable introduction from the pen of
the late Dorothy L. Sayers; she gives a fine explanation of
the author's understanding of history; '. . . the least known
the least considered part of Williams' output: the purely historical works. He had an acute sense of the living movement
of history and never forgot that every age is modern to itself
and that this fact, or illusion, links it with our own. Thus
to all men in all ages he has the same direct approach; the
same readiness to accept their behaviour as human . . . the
same charity'.[1] He himself wrote of the moralising approach
to history in almost scornful terms: 'the great Lord Acton
once complained that Bishop Creighton treated morals far
too lightly in his historical works. No doubt, fundamentally, Lord Acton was right. But it is a question of energy:
to exhaust oneself in disapproval wastes so much, and –
since all those strange figures are dead – does no good.
No living person is likely to be improved by denuncia-
tions of phantoms, and as for the phantoms themselves,
what purpose does condemnation serve? "Shrilling on the
wind" they go by; there is something a little comic in trying
to rebuke them. Besides, it encourages us to think that we
are better than they.'[2] His understanding of each character
in his biographical studies must always be seen in relation
to that positive tolerance.

246

Before we embark on an exemplary examination of one of his biographies – the only one familiar to myself – it would be interesting to ask what circumstances of time and place and what trick of temperament dictated his choice of subjects. It may be that his correspondence in the '30s (1933–37) might illuminate us here: I have no access to it, so I am left with speculation; a speculation, however, not unaided by the detection of a certain unity of type in the four chief studies and I am sure that it is a phrase of Dorothy Sayers which provides the key: James I as 'an enigmatic personality whom there have been, generally speaking, "none to praise, and very few to love"'.[3] That last phrase, certainly, does not do justice to the myth of Gloriana, the first Elizabeth ... but that she was (and intended to be) an enigmatic personality none can deny. The same is true of her successor James I, of his Attorney-General and Lord Chancellor, Francis Bacon and it is pre-eminently true of the first Tudor sovereign Henry VII whom few indeed praised and fewer loved. It is not without interest that the first 'official' life of the King was in fact written by Francis Bacon: the learned and subtle scientist and lawyer, that most secret man, tried to smooth out the folded pleats of a personality even more convoluted than his own.

Bacon had written: 'He was of high mind, and loved his own will and his own way, as one that revered himself and reign indeed. Had he been a private man he would have been termed proud. But in a wise prince it was but keeping of distance – which indeed he did towards all, not admitting any near or full approach either to his power or to his secrets, for he was governed by none. His queen, notwithstanding she had presented him with divers children, and with a crown also (though he would not acknowledge it), could do nothing with him. His mother he reverenced much, heard little. To his confederates abroad he was constant and just, but not open. But rather such was his inquiry, and such his closeness, as they stood in the light towards him and he stood in the dark to them.' 'He was a prince, sad (grave) serious and full of thoughts and secret observations . . .' 'He was a comely personage, a little above just (average) stature, well and straight limbed, but slender. His countenance was reverend and a little like a churchman, and as it was not strange or dark, so neither was it winning or pleasing, but as the face of one well disposed. But it was to the disadvantage of the painter, for it was best when he spake'.[4] This perhaps tells us most of all: humour in the eye, perhaps? affection in the smile? An enigmatic personality, indeed, whom CW brought to life – to the slightly condescending surprise of Alice Mary Hadfield, who can say: 'No individual even Henry VII is uninteresting, when known through the medium of CW's observations'[5] *Even* Henry VII, indeed!

Mrs Hadfield comments on Queen Elizabeth that the author's 'presentation of a real woman of past time is as good as in some of the novels his presentation of an imaginary woman is stilted and awkward' and goes on to say that 'The study of Bacon goes beyond imagination almost to the point of an exchanged life ... there was a moment in Bacon's life to which CW was peculiarly sensitive by reason of the movement of his own ...'[6]

Henry, Elizabeth, Bacon and James: enigmatic personalities. It would be relevant – and wholly profitless, of course – to make a list of historical personages of roughly the same period whom CW did *not* choose to immortalize: Henry VIII, Thomas Wentworth, William Laud, Charles I. Why not? Because, I would maintain, each presented a character of such directness and simplicity – particularly in the case of the two non-royals – that they failed to fascinate. Henry VIII was transparent even in his worst duplicities; his blustering lies had almost an air of innocence about them. The very consistency of Laud and Strafford was their undoing. Charles, again, though devious, was un-subtle and saw his rank, his state, his kingship with a single eye. 'There is no evidence that he considered that there could be another loyalty than that which bound men to the anointed King'. Mathew goes on to describe 'the perfection of his manner: the quiet gait; the entrances which held so much of majesty; that grace so restrained and yet so sumptuous, the angle at which he held his silver cane. He had that taste for ornament which Vandyck valued, the occasional diamond and the Mechlin lace. In general, his taste was sure but too impeccable.'[7]

The father, James I, presented a very different picture: affable without charm, erudite but obstinate, without personal pride and totally lacking in aristocratic tastes and manners. 'His tastes were not aristocratic. He was the King.[8] He was so convinced of James as the King that he could afford to be careless of James as James. His son, compared to him, took his royal office solemnly, even to himself. But James took it so simply that he did not need to be solemn'.[9] James was not proud. He was aware of his mysterious divinity, but he was not proud of it; indeed it would have shocked him to think that he was proud of the miraculous grace of God. He was not even proud of his learning, his theology, his Latin accent. But he was conceited. He liked to talk of them; he plumed himself on them with a simple, obvious, tiresome and sometimes silly persistence. To the reserved dignity of Sully, the industrious Hugenot minister of Henry of France, he seemed 'the "wisest fool" in Christendom'.[10]

The 'wisest fool's' enigmatic personality, its unfolding and its secrecy form the theme of CW's greatest biography. David Mathew, no mean authority, declares it to be 'the finest book ever written on the subject'.[11] To it we now turn for more detailed consideration; whether we are considering James Stuart or Charles Williams himself may be open to question ...

Charles James Stuart was born on June 19th, 1566, as the only child of Mary, Queen of Scots and Henry Darnley her consort. Within the year, his mother had abdicated and he had been crowned. CW gives him three 'birthdays': his natural birthday, his supernatural birthday or baptism and his babyhood's coronation and anointing. 'He was man, and Christian, and King. What those three things meant to him is his biography; what they meant to others is history'.[12] The regency was in the hands of the Earl of Moray, 'having reached that position by a series of inspired absences from any spot where a murder happened to be taking place. In the history of the world no one else can have been away at the right moment quite so often as the Earl of Moray';[13] and tormented years ensued, years of plots and education, of a hero-worshipping love-affair with his father's cousin, Esme Stuart, Earl and then Duke of Lennox; his discovery of poetry. That was in 1582. In 1585 he published *The Essayes of a Prentise in the Divine Art of Poesie* together with *The Reules and Cautchis to be observit and eschewit in Scottis Poesie.* 'The monarchs who have written on prosody have been few'[14] says CW and as a poet himself he is concerned to examine, not without sympathy yet not blinded by royalty's dazzle, the young King's theories.

Lennox was exiled to France, but from France came 'that wonderfully beautiful young man, Patrick, Master of Gray. The Master of Gray kneeling for the first time to James VI is a figure worthy of the wildest melodramatic novel. But it is a mere fact of history'.[15] It is not without significance, however, that CW lingers lovingly on this fact. Why? C.S. Lewis was to write of him — 'Firstly he was a man fitted by temperament to live in an age of more elaborate courtesy than our own. He was nothing if not a ritualist. Had modern society permitted it he would equally have enjoyed kneeling and being knelt to, kissing hands and extending hands to be kissed. Burke's "unbought grace of life" was in him. But secondly, even while enjoying such high pomps, he would have been aware of them as a game; not a silly game to be laid aside in private, but a glorious game well worth the playing.'[16] In another place and of another incident CW says 'like the Stuart that he was, he was always adequate — after his own grotesque manner — to the dramatic condition'.[17] Again the gay diplomatic traitor, the Earl of Gray, is by him and young King's hand fondlingly rests on the Master's shoulder or is 'flung round his neck for affection, for support, for the indulgence of an aesthetic delight in beauty, for the enjoyment of cerebralized sensual emotion'.[17]

So! The time has come to look at the King's sexuality, charmingly described in Jane Austen's *History of England by a partial prejudiced and ignorant Historian* (Aged 15) — 'His Majesty was of that amiable disposition which inclines to Friendships'. He married in 1589 and fathered 7 children upon his queen, Anne of Denmark, and wrote verses about her when she died. 'But, much as he sipped the wines, he never drank deep and was never drunk, and it is not impossible that, much as he sipped at this other deep strength of emotion, he never cared to get drunk on that either.'[18]

Contemporaries were not inclined to believe this and could express themselves with considerable force.

There were perhaps 'strong candidates for the role of royal favourite. It was not, however, until 1607 that there appeared upon the scene a figure whose influence was in any way comparable to that which had been exerted by Lennox in Scotland in the early 1580s, although by now James' affections were taking a far grosser and less restrained form.'[19] CW describes the arrival of the new friend —

In 1607, an unpurposed incident at one of the jousts had awakened emotion in the King. The great affection and violent passion of love which was in him (so they said — but he tasted it with his head rather than his heart; he took delight in the apprehension of devotion) had had for long no intense and permanent centre. The Lord Hay, the Lord Montgomery, pleased him, but in his suburbs; and Hay at least knew it. He was as wise as he was magnificent; he was 'known to be a cunning observer,' and to 'comply with all Favourites'. He had now a great opportunity. One of his squires, at that joust, fell from his horse, and sustained a broken leg. James, looking from his seat, was touched by the accident and smitten by the young man's good looks. He caused him to be removed and attended; he made inquiries about him. It was Robert Kerr, or Carr, cadet of a Scottish house, whose father had been devoted to Mary Stuart. The King showed an increased sympathy, called on the invalid, talked with him, found him less learned than he might be, and proceeded to enjoy himself in one of the pleasantest ways that can be — by instructing a young, docile and handsome inferior. He began to teach him Latin; the Court, openly polite but privately sneering, said that there was need his Majesty should teach him English too, 'for he is a Scotch lad, and hath much need of a better language.' The King and Carr did not think so; the Scots served them for their growing affection even better than the less intimate and familiar English. James felt that here at last was a harbour 'for his most retir'd thoughts' — thoughts which for long he had not shared with any, high thoughts of politics and persons; here was a subject friend.[20]

The appalling scandal which ensued – not a homosexual scandal but one of divorce and re-marriage and conspiracy and murder – need not detain us. The Scottish favourite fell but even before the end the Court was seeking to supplant him in the King's affections by another male beauty, George Villiers ... The Archbishop of Canterbury himself did not scruple to promote his cause. The Queen was persuaded to request for Villiers the appointment as Gentleman of the Bedchamber. The King's Majesty was to be approached through the Queen's. 'There was a ritual in such things, and James delighted in it'.[21]

Mathew, writing forty years after his first studies of the King, has this late judgement to make. In 1938 he had written of 'the impression that paternalism was the essential quality in King James' attitude towards his last and greatest favourite. He had then grown elderly, fatherly in his love and in the wise counsel he bestowed'.[22] In 1967 he examines their relationship a little more closely: – 'It has always seemed to me that King James' relations with his last favourite were technically innocent. He was certainly the type which attracted the king; but the latter was now in weakening health. There are certain converging arguments ... Archbishop Abbot was not likely to try to supply the king with another lover. He had always been a Puritan and rather stern. Again there was the case of the favourite's mother. Lady Buckingham was an unpleasant woman with a sense of worldly values and in the charge of Jesuit confessors; it does not seem to me that she could have managed the cosy relationship which she worked up with the king if he had seduced her favourite son. But the third instance has much more weight with me. The Prince of Wales had a hard cold purity which verged on prudishness. He was linked with Buckingham by the strongest friendship of his whole life. Surely this development would have been impossible if the favourite had been his father's *mignon*?'[23]

CW had already come to the same conclusion. He, the King, sipped at his wine but was never drunk; and whatever passion he felt for George Villiers, Duke of Buckingham – as he had certainly felt passion for Robert Kerr, Earl of Somerset – was never consummated, and Williams already has taken up Mathew's last point: 'the extreme friendship which grew up between the last and greatest of the Favourites – George Villiers – and the highly moral Prince Charles. It is difficult to believe that Charles would have accepted Villiers so profoundly and intimately if he had supposed that he was serving, or had served, the King so. But it is more difficult to suppose that, had it been so, some enemy of Villiers would not have seen to it that the Prince was told. Villiers might have explained that it was all over. But ... and so the argument can go on. In effect, we must admit an unusual delight in masculine beauty accompanied by loose behaviour and wanton speech. Beyond that James locks up his coffer. It is one of the most annoying things about James that in everything it is the very last secret which he hid so carefully and so finally away'.[24]

The King's marriage introduced (or emphasized) another element into his life. He had enjoyed his long visit to Denmark, drinking, enjoying the intellectual conversation of a renaissance Court, and even visiting an astronomer, Tycho Brahe. 'Sonnets by Kings to astronomers are rare',[25] but James perpetuates one on the high authority of the planets:

Then great is Ticho who, by this his books
Commandment doth o'er these commanders brooke.[26]

In May the Queen arrived in Scotland and there was trouble about her Coronation.

The King fixed it for a Sunday; the ministers objected. He demanded that the Queen should be anointed; they objected. The King overruled them and threatened to import one of his bishops into the ceremony. The ministers grudgingly gave way. Oil was less papistical than episcopacy. The Jews had oil, but not bishops, being in this respect closer to the pure Church of Christ than Catholics. The harlequinade swept up to the altar of marriage and majesty – 'the Countess of Mar, having taken the Queen's right arm, and opened the craigs of her gown, Mr Robert Bruce immediately poured forth upon those parts of her breast and arm of quhilk the clothes were removed, a bonny quantity of oil'. It is necessary to remember that Mr Robert Bruce, a great man of God, must have loathed doing it.[27]

The 'hot and holy matter' of his marriage, as the English agent called it, having been safely established, James turned his attention, while yet his country was in moderate peace, to those who had sought to stay her journeys. For his safe return with her had been a spiritual triumph as well as an earthly, and now there were to be proper reprisals upon the King's enemies. The pardon which James was often willing to extend to the leaders of earthly treason must not reach to the leaders of those who had denied their God. In this he need not fear the hostility of the Kirk; long before he had laid any but a baby's hand on sword and sceptre, the witch hunt had been raised in Scotland. Now in his years of discretion, the King headed it. Witchcraft was an abominable sin. 'I have been occupied', he said in the June of the next year, 'these three quarters of a year for the sifting out of them that are guilty herein'. His activity had been quickened by the activities of the sorcerers against him and his bride at sea. By December certain of them – one warlock and three witches – had been sought out and set in ward. John Fian was a schoolmaster, and it was he who was first brought to trial.[28] The King, sitting there with the lords of the Council about him, looked on the wretch and knew what had happened; in that supernatural absence he had met again the supernatural Prince of the abyss and made new covenants. The supernatural evil that James feared and defied lifted itself in that moment in his own soul; vividly it lived in the chamber, no more about John Fian, broken schoolmaster, but in the hearts and faces of his judges, achieving its end (as the habit of supernatural things, good or evil, is) by the apparent rejection of itself.[29]

All this was something very close to James' interests and it must be remarked that it was also close to those of CW himself. *Witchcraft* appeared in 1941 and reveals a relish, a curious penchant towards the darkness. Donald MacKinnon is reputed to have said – 'Oh, Charles Williams, a strange

man; a strange man with a dark side to him'. ('CW knew
something of darkness and knew it intimately'.)[30]

Williams mentions in *James I* that the account he gives
of Scottish covens was published in 1591 as *Newes from
Scotland* and he asks: did Shakespeare read it? I would dif-
fidently suggest that the witchcraft scenes and description in
Macbeth almost presuppose that he did.

In 1603 James VI became also James I of England. 'The
covens of witchcraft had faded; their nearest image in
England was the House of Commons'!![31] and he must
first enter upon a new experience, the Church of England
and her bishops. Mathew is authoritative on this.

> Everywhere the Anglican episcopate was accepted as an
> influential, political and social factor. As a body the
> bishops had achieved a wide measure of respect due to
> their administrative competence, their sedate accessibility
> and their grave proclamation of those maxims in State
> and Church which in the seventeenth century met with
> such wide acceptance. They had a profound feeling for
> their own dignity. William Laud was 'ever conscious of
> his state of prelacy'.[32] It was a sphere governed by a
> code of integrity and courtesy ... The Bishops had the
> power to unite extreme loyalism with an accommodating
> temper ... there seems no reason to doubt that their reli-
> gious reverence for the Crown was as sincere as it was
> surely fortified by all their learning. Easy manners marked
> the approach of the Jacobean prelates to their equals
> and they showed a generous hospitality in their dealings
> with all persons of low condition ... The portraits in
> the college halls of their universities give an admirable
> impression of these churchmen, with the shrewd inquiring
> eyes and the pursed lips and the hands folded in their great
> lawn sleeves.[33]

'James in his Scottish years had had experience of the Pres-
byterian, the Roman, and the necromantic Churches; he
had now one other to find. The Roman he still had, and
the Puritans instead of the Presbyterians, much the same
thing as they were, in spite of the difference in ecclesiastical organisation. The Presbyterians in Scotland were

a Kirk of their own; the Puritans in England were but a part of a greater Church. He was free now from any need of conciliating, and he hoped he was free from any difficulty in controlling, those mutual enemies. Politically, he was more firmly seated than ever before, and theologically· he had found a new thing, he had discovered the Church of England.[34]

The Church of England had nourished and inspired many poets, saints, and martyrs. It has, however, had few royal children who have taken so intelligent an interest in it as James Stuart. At first that interest was largely self-preservative and tutorial. He delighted to take refuge with his new Bishops under the pretext of allowing them to take refuge under him. Of all classes of men the Bishops of the Church of England were least likely to form conspiracies against his person, as Jesuits and Presbyterians had done. He was in good hope they would not even preach at him, or seize him by the arm and call him "God's silly vassal", or attach their titular signatures to blanks meant for the King of Spain. Yet they were at once Bishops of as true a faith as those of Rome and of as pure a religion as super-intendents in Fifeshire. He and they mirrored themselves in each other. He was disposed to benevolence as they to obedience. The general episcopal mind was as loyal as he was royal. The doctrine of the two kingdoms began to disappear and leave the much pleasanter landscape of the one kingdom of God, the King and the Bishops, dispensing a single supernatural authority. It was therefore not surprising that he relaxed happily into the cushioned throne which the Church of England appeared to provide'[35] . . . and so the probing search for finality and actuality, historical and psychological, continues in the hand of a masterly surgeon-historian. He bears comparison with the great: Powicke and Maitland, at least (I could claim) in his view of history and research – not into dead folk but into living characters who matter and who have their rights.

Powicke wrote:

The search after truth plays strange tricks with an historian. He sets out to tell a plain straight-forward story, and he finds himself running about in all sorts of places.

Insensibly the interest of his story is merged in the excitement of the chase. He cannot bring himself to believe that his readers will not be as interested as he has been in seeing how one point leads to another, how this fact throws light on that, why one clue has to be discarded, and another pursued to the end. As Maitland once wrote – 'Out of the thicket may fly a bird worth powder and shot'; but the thicket must be a clue, not any thicket, and bird must be worth powder and shot, not any bird. If this condition is observed, the story becomes more than a story; it breathes a troubled life of its own as part of a living past. The things which first stirred interest, the picturesque, the amusing, the dramatic, are still there, but are no longer the essential things. Sometimes, as I work at a series of patent and close rolls, I have a queer sensation; the dead entries begin to be alive ... These are real people, this casual official letter is telling something that really happened, it was written on the impulse of a real emotion. To be sure that this William is William son of Geoffrey and not William son of Jordan becomes as important as any problem of identity can be in a court of law today. It is necessary to take great care, no longer in the interests of learning, but for their sakes. I fear that the historian is quite incorrigible, when he has once had this experience. He becomes indifferent to insinuations of pedantry; for pedantry is a kind of darkness, and he is trying to let in the light.[36]

'Letting in the light', this is precisely what this man 'with a penchant for the dark' has been doing all along.

The reign goes on and the King grows old. He contemplated a Spanish marriage for Prince Henry, then for Prince Charles. He sees himself as the slandered child of barbaric Stirling becoming the beloved father of Europe's oldest kings. However 'no grandchild of James Stuart would ever carry in his veins the mingled Scottish and Spanish blood'.[37] Nevertheless, and not through Henry or Charles but through his daughter, Elizabeth, Queen of Bohemia, he is today the ancestor of the sovereign princes of Belgium,

Denmark, Great Britain, Holland, Lichtenstein, Luxem-
bourg, Norway, Sweden *and of Spain itself!* — both King
and Queen alike.

In 1625 he died; absolved, receiving viaticum, conscious,
'Veni, Domine Jesu' he murmured — and all was over.

Mrs Hadfield, in speaking of CW's poetry, lays great
stress on his appreciation of human form, of the human
body and its members, especially of the arm and hand. 'The
hand and arm were ever his favourite contemplation'[38] and
so it is not surprising that he ends his story of the King with
the upward spiralling of John Donne's voice evoking the
royal hand signing patents and pardons, touching for the
Evil, balancing his three kingdoms, locking up and letting
out armies — that hand lying dead. 'It was not so hard a
hand when we touched it last nor so cold a hand when we
kissed it last . . .'[39]

So we leave this enigmatic man secure in his kingship, made
more secure (one might almost say) by the intense internal
understanding of Charles Williams, an understanding of a
King and of a Kingdom, finite, actual.

> Its finity, its actuality, were his strength. The purposes
> of the lords might vary from day to day; they sought their
> own profit, and their profit was often changeable. His
> never was. Had the chance of history ever brought James
> face to face with any of the great Popes, he might well
> have gone down. But he hardly met, hardly even saw —
> save as a child of ten months — another sovereign. His
> amities and his hostilities with the other members of that
> unique guild of crowns were — save for a brief knowledge
> of the King of Denmark — always conducted by corre-
> spondence. They were therefore purely mental. He never
> received the shock of the physical presence of equal or
> superior royalty. That physical disturbance which is our
> only salvation from our own dreams and our own inter-
> pretations in this respect never touched him. He never
> beheld the mitred forehead of the Pope, or the vivid eyes
> of Elizabeth, or the callous smile of the French Valois.
>
> Only at long last there arose from near his Throne the
> obstinate gravity of his son, and pressed him from his
> seat.[40]

References

1. D. L. Sayers – Introduction to *James I* – 1951, XIII.
2. C. Williams – *James I* – 1934, 1951 ed. 62–3.
3. D. L. Sayers, XII.
4. F. Bacon – *The Reign of Henry VII* – 1622 – Fol. Soc. ed. 1977, 230 – 5.
5. A. M. Hadfield – *An Introduction to Charles Williams* – 1959, 93.
6. Ibid, 91–2.
7. D. Mathew – *The Age of Charles I* – 1951, 31–2.
8. C. Williams, 51.
9. Ibid, 85.
10. Ibid, 200.
11. A. M. Hadfield, 91.
12. C. Williams, 10.
13. Ibid, 20.
14. Ibid, 60.
15. Ibid, 62–3.
16. C. S. Lewis in *Essays Presented to Charles Williams* – 1947, IX, X.
17. C. Williams, 73.
18. Ibid, 105.
19. R. Ashton – *James I by his Contemporaries* – 1967, 108.
20. C. Williams, 205.
21. Ibid, 217.
22. D. Mathew – *The Jacobean Age* – 1938, 24.
23. D. Mathew – *James I* – 1967, 292.
24. C. Williams, 105.
25. Ibid, 102.
26. Ibid, 103.
27. Ibid, 103.
28. Ibid, 106.
29. Ibid, 110.
30. A. M. Hadfield, 177.
31. C. Williams, 185.
32. D. Mathew – *The Age of Charles I*, 105.
33. D. Mathew – *The Jacobean Age*, 9–10.
34. C. Williams, 185.
35. Ibid, 185–6.
36. M. Powicke – *Ways of Medieval Life and Thought* – 1949, 67–8.
37. C. Williams, 289.
38. A. M. Hadfield, 85.
39. C. Williams, 300.
40. Ibid, 87.

Chapter Seventeen

Taliessin in Byzantium

George Every

I think I may be able to say something useful about the role of the Byzantine empire in the later poems of Charles Williams. I took Byzantine special and optional subjects for an external degree of the University of London in 1928–9, while I was a student at the University College of the South-West of England, now the University of Exeter. There, and in these subjects, I had the advantage of supervision from Christopher Dawson, who had just finished *Progress and Religion* and was at work on *The Making of Europe*. Ten years later, in 1938, as a lay brother of the 'Anglican Society of the Sacred Mission at Kelham, I was introduced to Charles Williams, who gave me *Taliessin Through Logres* and his anthology on *The Passion of Christ*. The poems I found difficult, as T.S. Eliot did until he read *The Descent of the Dove*, but they were in my mind when I wrote in 1943–4 the first chapter on Byzantine civilisation in *The Byzantine Patriarchate, 451–1204*. This was not published until 1947, but by 1944 I had cited from 'The Vision of the Empire':

The logothetes run down the porphyry stair bearing the missives through the area of empire.

in an account of liturgies performed by Byzantine functionaries, not only the clergy and 'clerks of audience' in the emperor's sacred palace, the Whitehall of Constantinople, but peasant farmers in regulated communes, who sowed seed, built houses and dug wells according to rules prescribed by liturgical tradition, believed to be in harmony with the movement of God the creator through the universe, and with angels and archangels, apostles and prophets, martyrs, virgins and other saints portrayed in their churches, where Christ the Pantokrator reigned over all, with the Mother of God by his side, but in obedience to the Father.

I might have begun my quotation earlier:

The organic body sang together;
dialects of the world sprang in Byzantium;
back they ran to sing in Byzantium;
the streets repeat the sound of the Throne.

To Charles Williams the Roman empire was the seedbed of the Christian Church in and after the age of persecutions. The empire was the same empire with the same name from the rise of Rome to the fall of the new Rome at Constantinople. The Muslims, Arabs and Turks, called it Roum or Roumelia, the Franks, including the English, Romania or Roumania. The Greeks still call their spoken language Romaic. The Byzantine name was given to the empire by French scholars who wished to distinguish it clearly from the Holy Roman Empire which by the seventeenth century had become one of the appertenances of the house of Austria. Some of them were Gallicans who would not wish to identify the Eastern Roman Empire with the Holy See. Charles Williams, as an Anglican, may have felt a like embarrassment, as I did when at Damascus I had to enquire for the patriarchate Rum-Orthodox, Rum meaning Greek. But he knew that in the period envisaged in his Arthurian poems there was no alternative centre of civilisation. The old city of Rome was in ruins, and in his mind civilisation meant cities. The West did not begin to have a culture of its own until Paris had a university in the twelfth century, and after that fresh waves of Eastern influence continued after the Crusades, the fall of Constantinople, and in his own day the Russian emigration.

C.S. Lewis was no doubt right in saying that his first acquaintance with Byzantium was in Gibbon, as was mine, but neither of us could share Gibbon's perspective in *The Decline and Fall of the Roman Empire*. *The Descent of the Dove* shows the depth of his positive interest in the formation of Christendom, to Gibbon the great disaster. This he shared with T.S. Eliot and Christopher Dawson. His interest in slavegirls points to his enthusiasm for the typists and shop-assistants who came to his extension lectures. These seemed to him more intelligent than undergraduates, at any rate until he met their like at Oxford during the war.

No doubt there were slaves in Byzantium. The word slave in German and English is taken from the Schlavs or Slavs of Eastern Europe. This usage first appears in the ninth century, in German and only later in Latin and Greek. But I am not sure that all the servant-girls listed by Brenda Boughton in her essay earlier in this volume are slaves. They rather stand for the working classes in an urban civilisation, accomplished in arts and crafts. The serving-maid in 'The Star of Percevale' speaks in familiar terms to the Archbishop, and he to her. The girl in the stocks in 'The Ascent of the Spear' endures jeers from 'the stable-slaves' for her part in a brawl, but Taliessin calls her 'Ah lady'.

> Under the Direction she denied pride;
> her heart flowed to the crowd.

Later 'She said "I was wrong from beginning ...". In 'The Sister of Percevale' a back 'scarred from whip or sword' bent to draw water from a well. 'The scar lightened over a curved horizon', but

> A round plane of water rose shining in the sun;
> she steadied the handle, the strain ceased;
> her arm balanced the line.

Taliessin saw this mathematically and turned it into poetry. This reminds me of *Byzantine Aesthetics* by Father Gervase Mathew, who told C.S. Lewis that Charles Williams understood Byzantine history better than Gibbon.[1] The Athenian slave-girl in 'The Departure of Dindrane' rode in the retinue of Taliessin. In this she chose to remain. The Caucasian, liberated to be 'The Queen's Servant', is stripped naked and clothed with the body of her resurrection.

> The wool rose gently on no wind,
> and was flung to her shoulders; behind her, woven of
>   itself,
> it fell in full folds to a golden-creamed cloak;
> hued almost as the soft redeemed flesh
> hiding the flush of the rich redeemed blood
> in the land of the Trinity, where the Holy Ghost
>   works
> creation and sanctifications of flesh and blood.

This is an image of redemption, of liberation from slavery in the resurrection of the body, but without bondage there is no salvation.

In *The Descent of the Dove* the abolition of the slave-trade and then of slavery is a belated victory for Evangelical Christianity, but 'never before the nineteenth century had there been so much property to be owned or (proportionally) so few allowed to own it. Millions instead of thousands were dispossessed, and wholly dispossessed ... Mere hunger pre-occupied the lowest classes, and insecurity crept more and more into the lives of the middle-classes.'[2] This led inevitably to revolution, to a command economy and a new and terrible slavery. But the expectation of the Second Coming, lost in the schism at the beginning of the second millennium, was renewed in exchanges between East and West, between Catholic and Protestant, in and out of the Church of England, while the poems in *The Region of the Summer Stars* were being written in the perspective defined in the preface to them. To Malory and his sources the Matter of Britain was the legacy of an heroic age, as Homer was to the Greek tragedians. They saw there the foundation of medieval (modern) kingdoms in conflict with the Holy Roman Empire. To Charles Williams Byzantium was still there, and the Byzantine expectation broke through again in Russia before and after the revolution. His view of Byzantium as the centre of history owes something to J.B.

Bury's notes on Gibbon and his books on the Later Roman Empire, something perhaps to Robert Byron's *Byzantine Achievement*, published in 1929 with a different reading of Byzantium in relation to Rome, much to friends in the emigration. Since his time the Roman Catholic Church has been partially Byzantinised, sufficiently to take me out of the Anglican communion into it. This may go further with more revolutions in Russia, where the Third Rome has survived the Third International. In this context Byzantium in the poetry of Charles Williams may make sense.

Notes

1.   In *Arthurian Torso* p. 206
2.   p. 224.

Chapter Eighteen

Charles Williams
and the Occult

Huw Mordecai

Many people who enjoy Charles Williams's writings would
be made uneasy by this subject. There is an instinctive feeling
that, with so many positive ideas and concepts readily to
hand within the corpus, there are many more profitable
concepts to which critical energy should be devoted. This is
undoubtedly true, and yet I feel that the area of the occult,
and Williams's relationship to it, is one that deserves examination. His novels contain clear esoteric elements, and such
symbolism lies close to the surface in many of his poems.
These elements have been enough to repel many would-be
readers, who have summarily judged Williams to be the literary equivalent of the Hammer Horror films. F.R. Leavis
did not speak for himself alone when he said:

> Charles Williams is ostensibly inspired by Christian doc-
> trine, but if you approach as a literary critic, unstiffened
> by the determination to 'discriminate Christianly', or if
> you approach merely with order, sensitiveness and good
> sense, you can hardly fail to see that Williams's preoc-
> cupation with 'the horror of evil' is evidence of an arrest
> at the schoolboy (and -girl) stage rather than of spiritual
> maturity, and that his dealings in 'myth', mystery, the
> occult, and the supernatural belong essentially to the ethos
> of the thriller. To pass off his writings as spiritually edi-
> fying is to promote the opposite of spiritual health.[1]

The immediate context of his remarks was a dismissal of Williams's understanding of Milton, but the comments imply a criticism of Williams's entire corpus. They suggest that we are dealing with an author who, while explicitly claiming to be extolling the virtues of the light, is fascinated· by the terrors of the darkness. This is a serious charge, and one that deserves to be addressed directly.

In order to tackle this issue, I propose to try to establish some biographical information, and then to see how Williams used these personal experiences in his creative work. There is no doubt that he was involved, for a time, with a society that could be loosely described as occult. In the 1983 edition of her invaluable biography, Hadfield stated:

> Charles' contact with A.E. Waite had led to their meeting and thus to an invitation for Charles to join his [Waite's] Order of the Golden Dawn ... On 6 September 1917 Waite wrote to Charles arranging for his reception into the neophyte (lowest) grade of the Society at the autumnal equinox (17 September) ... His active membership was probably no more than four or five years ... In the end, what did Waite's Golden Dawn mean to him? Surely his outlook and philosophy were not generated or much affected by it. He was thirty-one when he joined and his mind was already well-based, developed and directed.[2]

However, this was a side of his life which Williams did not often discuss, and some corrections need to be made. Even though he talked of having belonged to the Order of the Golden Dawn,[3] Williams had actually been a member of the Fellowship of the Rosy Cross, which had been founded and was led by Waite after a split within the Golden Dawn. More significant is the length of time he spent within the Fellowship. The Minutes of the society record that Williams was 'received into the Portal Grade of the Rosy Cross under the Sacramental Name of Qui Sitit Veniat' on 21 September 1917. After that he attended the ritual regularly, and progressed through the Fellowship. According to the Minutes, his final participation was in a ritual to lead him into a higher and more secret order, The Hidden Life of the Rosy Cross, on 29 June 1927 – which means he was an active member for almost ten years, instead of 'four or five'.[4] Why Williams left at this point is unclear, and has been the subject of much speculation.

Hadfield's question – 'In the end, what did Waite's Golden Dawn (F:R:C) mean to him?' – is, therefore, crucial, and cannot be answered easily. Part of the problem lies in understanding Waite's thought in general, and his vision for the Fellowship in particular, Waite's own biographer has summarised the situation in this way:

> The Independent and Rectified Rite of the Golden Dawn had been instituted for the benefit of those who saw the Order as 'capable of a mystical instead of an occult construction', and in similar manner the Fellowship of the Rosy Cross was mystical, but unlike its predecessor in that it was *wholly* mystical; and although based upon the Kabbalah, it was also wholly Christian, as laid down in the constitution: 'The mode of interpretation in respect of Kabbalistic Tradition is a Christian Mode'.[5]

However, this begs the question of what meaning should be attached to the term 'Christian' in this context. Another clause of the Constitution says:

> The Fellowship is open to all who desire the knowledge of Divine Things and union with GOD in Christ, and its path of symbolism is a true light of understanding on the Path of Union.

This goal echoes biblical phraseology,[6] and the thinking of the Saints such as John of the Cross and Catherine of Siena.[7] But earlier it was stated that:

> The tradition and symbolism of the Fellowship are a derivation from the Secret doctrine of Israel, known as Kabbalah and embodied in the SEPHER HA ZOHAR.'

For the Fellowship to derive its 'tradition and symbolism' from secret knowledge, however interpreted, sound suspicious. Indeed the very concept of a society sworn to secrecy about its beliefs and practices has a distinctly gnostic feel to it, and is likely to be sub-Christian at best, even if not anti-thetical to Christianity. One writer, talking about the effects of gnosticism, describes the danger of:

> the church [being] replaced by a club of illuminati possessing secrets hidden from the unsalvable multitude, and even from the uninitiated who claimed the same Redeemer.[8]

Such a two-tier system is roundly rejected by many of the New Testament writers, Paul in particular.[9] The stress laid upon hidden knowledge, and the need for secrecy imposed on the members, means that the Fellowship of the Rosy Cross echoes what little we know of early gnostic groups – its members shared an understanding that set them apart from the rest of the world. Waite himself, as the founder, was clearly a remarkable figure, who had experienced an overwhelming personal revelation, which he wished to pass on to others. But such an experience alone does not make someone a saint, and most churches would want to use 'Christian' in a qualified sense to describe someone in his position.

What, then, do we make of Williams? Was he, too, essentially a gnostic, interpreting aspects of Christianity in an esoteric manner in a way denied to the majority? Not only was he a member of the Fellowship, he knew Waite's works in detail, quoted from them and encouraged others to read them.[10] Moreover, the central symbols of several of his novels were also the subject matter for Waite's schol-arship – the Holy Grail (or Graal, as both authors referred to it), a mysterious Stone inscribed with the Divine Name, and the Tarot pack – while elsewhere in the novels and the poems there are echoes of Waite's thought. Indeed Francis King has stated:

> that the Golden Dawn system – or to be correct Waite's heterodox version of that system – is the key without which the deepest and inmost meaningfulness of Williams can never be unlocked.[11]

However, such a conclusion needs to be treated with caution. If we look at the way in which Williams handled these symbols, it seems that he takes great care not to attach too much importance to them in and of themselves. For example, *War in Heaven* revolves around the discovery of the Graal, and the attempts to acquire it made by black magicians who want to use and finally destroy the power it contains. For the magicians the cup itself is important – even their attempts to unmake it testify to their belief in its value. Mornington and the Duke also share this view so that they are in deep distress when the chalice is lost. But their companion, the Archdeacon, although initially agreeing, later comes implicitly to rebuke such an attitude. When an argument breaks out between Mornington and the Duke as to whom the Graal belongs, and old denominational disputes threaten to draw close, the Archdeacon resolves the matter by pointing out its absurdity, and concluding:

> But, on the other hand, I will promise not to hurt anyone's feelings by using it prematurely for schismatic Mysteries. A liqueur glass would do as well.[12]

For the celebration of the Eucharist a liqueur glass is quite permissible, but the Archdeacon seems to be implying that, in the divine scheme of things, the Graal is no more, and no less, important than any domestic cup. Indeed when he hands it over, he apologises:

> For myself, I would not have delayed so long. I would give up any relic, however wonderful, to save anyone an hour's neuralgia – man depends too much on these things.[13]

He is actually giving it up to restore a woman who has been driven mad. But his lack of concern over an item that others perceive to be of great worth because of its sanctity, his readiness to abandon it in order that an immediate need should be met, has parallels with the life and teaching of Jesus. Christ's attitude to the Sabbath, his implied rebuke to the scruples of the priests and Levites,[14] is echoed by the actions of this elderly cleric. To a thorough-going occultist, an object such as the Graal would be a source of power, to be clung to and used – an attitude exemplified repeatedly by the evil or misguided characters in Williams's novels. Why, then, can the author be so relaxed in his attitude to this relic?

One common theological objection to an occult view of the world, is that it presupposes dualism – two equal and opposite cosmic forces in an eternal struggle, in which human decisions for good or evil can sway the balance. The Archdeacon's perspective, which is ultimately vindicated, is a deep trust in the omnipotence and benevolence of God. When the Duke is incensed because of a blasphemy, an insult to God:

> 'How can you insult God?' the Archdeacon asked. 'About as much as you can pull His nose. For Kenneth to have knocked Mr Persimmons down for calling him dishonest would have been natural – a venial sin, at most; for him to have done it in order to avenge God would have been silly . . .'[15]

Admittedly, his companions do not share this faith – and if they did, there would be little action in the novel – but it grows stronger and deeper in the priest, until even when he is being offered as a sacrifice, even when he feels abandoned by God, he can still say: 'I have come because God willed it'.[16] And out of that desolation he knows salvation. This trust is expressed in his constant quoting of Psalm 136, with its refrain: 'For His mercy endureth for ever', and is the same as Williams's own. When talking of the nineteenth century, he could say:

> The great scientific discoveries of that age (or that then purported to be scientific discoveries) threw both Christendom and non-Christendom very much out of control. The pious feared they might, and the impious thought they undoubtedly had, upset Christendom. This was excusable in the impious, but inexcusable in the pious.[17]

It is the same voice speaking directly in the historical comment, indirectly through the persona of the Archdeacon – the voice of a tried and settled faith. Against such a faith the details of elaborate and malevolent magic rituals seem empty and puerile.

The same picture is clear in *The Greater Trumps*. Here the Tarot pack is more prominent even than the Graal was in the earlier novel, with imagery from the cards rising up in many different situations. Again there are links back to Waite, who produced his own version of the pack (which is still widely used) and wrote a book explaining his interpretation of the symbols. Williams's understanding owes a clear debt to Waite, particularly in his interpretation of the Fool, whom both men understand as sublime, rather than ridiculous.[18] But Williams describes enough of these cards to make it clear that he is not thinking of the Waite pack. No-one has yet discovered a Tarot that matches these descriptions, and it may be that Williams had designed and was using his own cards, which were never available commercially. If so, it underlines the fact that he was immersed in esoteric lore, using sources so widespread that they are hard to identify.

Yet, for all the learning and devotion which had gone into this Tarot, the author refuses to overestimate its importance. The novel describes the discovery of the original pack, from which all other cards have been derived. Possession of them brings power; reuniting them with the golden images which are their counterparts reveals 'the measure of the everlasting dance'. But, from the beginning, this revelation is shown to come as much from the insight of romantic love as from the piercing of arcane veils – a theme that recurs throughout Williams's work. When Nancy is first shown the cards by her lover Henry, who is one of the gipsy guardians of this mystery, she asks what he means by 'the everlasting dance'. He replies by pointing to the seventh card – the Lovers.[19]

As the novel develops Henry and his grandfather, Aaron Lee, are identified as the protectors of the images, the repositories of hidden knowledge – they are the adepts, who might be expected to enlighten the other characters. But not only are they jealously possessive of what they do know, it emerges that, despite their learning, they do not understand the arcana they have hoarded. Having studied the letter, they have missed the spirit, so that Christ's words to the Jews apply to them also:

Ye search the scriptures; for in them ye think ye have eternal life: and they are they which testify of me. And ye will not come to me, that ye might have life.[20]

The gipsies have searched the Tarot pack, and yet have not found life. In understanding 'the measure of the everlasting dance' they are soon shown to be immoral novices. The true adepts are Nancy's aunt, Sybil (who alone can see the Fool moving, the mystery which the gypsies have puzzled over for centuries), and Nancy herself who, under Sybil's guidance, increasingly gives herself to be a channel for Love. This self-giving leads her to be reconciled to Henry when he has tried to kill her father, and to love a mad woman who is tearing her hands – acts of sacrifice parallel to the Archdeacon's. And, as in the earlier novel, this giving to the point of despair becomes the pivot out from which restoration and healing proceed.

The Biblical imagery that lies behind these acts scarcely needs drawing out. The picture of suffering willingly endured so that others may benefit can be found in *Second Isaiah's* Suffering Servant, is deeply rooted in *St John's Gospel* in particular, and in the rest of the New Testament also.[21] Christ's was the ultimate act of self-giving, but it is an act which every Christian is called upon to repeat and so share in [22] – every Christian, not only those who have received illumination.

Williams is careful to underline the universality of this demand by making an explicit connection between even those themes which at first sight seem most esoteric and the traditional Anglicanism of the period (himself a lifelong member of the Church of England), in a key episode that occurs almost exactly half-way through the novel. Nancy is deeply confused by events, and so she goes to church on Christmas morning because the service will be uneventful, even dull, and so give her a respite:

A door opened; the congregation stirred; a voice from the vestry said: 'Hymn 61. "Christians, awake," Hymn 61.' Everyone awoke, found the place, and stood up. The choir started at once on the hymn and the procession. Nancy docilely sent her voice along with them.

Christians, awake, salute the happy morn,
Whereon the Saviour of the world was born;
Rise to a-

Her voice ceased; the words stared up at her. The choir
and the congregation finished the line —

adore the mystery of love.

'The mystery of love.' But what else was in her heart?
The Christmas associations of the verse had fallen away;
there was the direct detached cry, bidding her to do precisely and only what she was burning to do. 'Rise and
adore the mystery of love.' What on earth were they
doing, singing about the mystery of love in church? They
couldn't possibly be meaning it. Or were they meaning it
and had she misunderstood the whole thing?[23]

To me this passage captures some of the best points of
Williams's prose. The gently ironic humour — 'Everyone
awoke' — establishes a mundane backcloth against which
Nancy's discovery can shine. For it is important that
this understanding, this challenge, does not come from
any hidden wisdom or secret tradition, but from something so well known that it has become almost stale —
'a very commonplace hymn, a very poor copy of verses',
as the passage continues. The confusion Nancy feels is
reflected by antitheses — 'They couldn't possibly be meaning
it/were they meaning it?', 'defence/attack' — the urgency
by restrained alliteration — 'bidding her to do ... what
she was burning to do.' The prose is simple and direct,
and therefore successful. The point is made. Williams was
not promoting an esoteric sect, rather he was linking the
wonders he describes with the conventional — humdrum,
even — details that make up so large a part of the life of
a Christian of any tradition. When he established the Companions of the Co-inherence in 1939, he did not turn back to
the detailed covertness of the Fellowship of the Rosy Cross.
Instead of pledges of secrecy, there is an openness about all
the arrangements. The sentences Williams drew up to guide
the Companions begin:

The Order has no constitution except in its members,

that is, there were to be no conditions of membership, unless a concern for others be reckoned such. The mysteries he commends do not come from the Kabbalah, or any Secret Doctrine. Rather, they are the study:

> of the Co-inherence of the Holy and Blessed Trinity, of the Union of the Two Natures in One Person, of the relation of the God-bearer and Flesh-taker, of the exchange of the offerings of the Eucharist, and of the whole Catholic Church.

He was not bringing a new revelation, but showing the glory there is in what we already know but have overlooked. All the fantastic imagery of *The Greater Trumps* surrounds this single point – 'the mystery of love'.

This openness is what, more than anything else, distinguishes Charles Williams from Waite, and other similar figures. Waite's biographer concluded that, although in his novels Williams used:

> concepts that [he] could, and probably did, find in A. E. Waite's Fellowship of the Rosy Cross, the elegant structure of his work and the peculiar orthodoxy of his theology are Williams' own.[24]

And it is that 'peculiar orthodoxy' which, despite Leavis, continues to promote 'spiritual health'.

Notes

1. F R Leavis *The Common Pursuit*, Pelican Books 1978, p. 253, reprinted from *Scrutiny*, vol. 16, no 4 (Winter 1949) pp. 339–44, 'The Logic of Christian Discrimination'.
2. A M Hadfield *Charles Williams: an Exploration of his Life and Work*, OUP, 1983, pps 29–30. In her previous biography *An Introduction to Charles Williams*, OUP, 1959, Waite was not mentioned.
3. A Ridler, introduction to *The Image of the City*, OUP, 1958, p. xxiv.
4. I am grateful to R A Gilbert for showing me the Minutes of the Fellowship of the Rosy Cross, which are in his possession. See

also his *A E Waite: Magician of Many Parts*, Crucible, 1987, pp. 148–150.

5. *Magician of Many Parts*, p. 142. For the entire Constitution of The Fellowship of the Rosy Cross, ibid, pp. 183–5.

6. Among others, *St John 17.3, The Second Epistle to the Corinthians 5.19*.

7. St John of the Cross, 'Et una Noche Escura' Stanza 1; St Catherine of Siena, *Dialogo*, cap. 1.

8. A F Walis, 'Gnosticism' in *The New Bible Dictionary*, IVP, 1965, p. 473.

9. Among others, *The Epistle to the Ephesians 3. 8–10, The Epistle to the Colossians 1.26*, both of which talk about the 'mystery', hidden for ages, having been fully revealed in the apostolic preaching and the life of the Church.

10. Williams quotes from Waite's *The Hidden Church of the Holy Grail* in *Arthurian Torso* p. 262 of the One Volume Edition of *Taliessin through Logres, The Region of the Summer Stars* and *Arthurian Torso*, Eerdmans 1976. Ridler records him encouraging her to read Waite's *The Secret Doctrine in Israel*, in the introduction to *The Image of the City*, p. xxv.

11. Francis King *Ritual Magic in England: 1887 to the Present Day*, Neville Spearman, 1970, p. 112.

12. *War in Heaven*. First published Gollancz 1930, reprinted Eerdmans 1982, p. 138. All future references are to the Eerdmans edition.

13. Ibid., p. 184.

14. e.g. the discussion of the Sabbath in *St Luke 6. 1–11*, and the Parable of the Good Samaritan *St Luke 10. 25–37*.

15. *War in Heaven*, p. 135.

16. Ibid., p. 240.

17. *The Descent of the Dove*, Longmans, 1939, p. 219.

18. A E Waite, *The Pictorial Key to the Tarot*. Originally published 1911, reprinted by University Books 1959, pp. 152–5.

19. *The Greater Trumps*. First published Gollancz 1932, reprinted Eerdmans 1978, p. 22. All future references are to the Eerdmans edition.

20. *St John 5, 39, 40*.

21. *Isaiah 52. 13–53. 12, St John 10. 18, 16.20–22, 19. 32–34, The Epistle to the Ephesians 2. 13–16, The First Epistle of Peter 2. 21–24*.

22. *St John 13. 14. 15, The Epistle to the Colossians 1. 24, 25, The First Epistle of John 3.16*.

23. *The Greater Trumps* pp. 107–8.

24. R A Gilbert *The Golden Dawn: Twilight of the Magicians*, Aquarian Press, 1983, p. 87.

Charles Williams: In Anamnesis

'That which was once Taliessin
rides to the barrows of Wales'

This is a likeliness but it does not speak.
   The words are echoes, the image looks from the wall
Of many minds, kindling in each the spark
   Of passionate joy, yet silent in them all.
Pupils grow older, but a long-dead master
   Stands where they parted, ageless on his hill.
The child grows to be father of his father.
   Yet keeps relation, kneels in homage still.

What is the speech of the dead? Words on a page
   Where Taliessin launched his lines of glory
   Capture for him a poet's immortality
As every reader wakes them. So the image
   Speaks through a living mind, as he in life
   Would use from each the little that each could give.

© Anne Ridler
(from 'Collected Poems' published by *Carcanet Press*)

Index